the making of the UK

for common entrance and key stage 3

Colin Shephard   Martin Collier   Rosemary Rees

HODDER
EDUCATION
AN HACHETTE UK COMPANY

Also available: *Medieval Realms for Common Entrance* ISBN 978 0 340 89984 7

The authors and publisher would like to thank Bob Pace of Belmont School, Mill Hill, and Niall Murphy of Radley College, Abingdon, for their valuable feedback.

Note: The wording and structure of some written sources have been adapted and simplified to make them accessible to all pupils, while faithfully preserving the sense of the original.

Words printed in SMALL CAPITALS (first mention only) are defined in the Glossary on page 202.

Although every effort has been made to ensure that website addresses are correct at time of going to press, Hodder Education cannot be held responsible for the content of any website mentioned in this book.

Hachette's policy is to use papers that are natural, renewable and recyclable products and made from wood grown in sustainable forests. The logging and manufacturing processes are expected to conform to the environmental regulations of the country of origin.

Orders: please contact Bookpoint Ltd, 130 Milton Park, Abingdon, Oxon OX14 4SB. Telephone: +44 (0)1235 827720. Fax: +44 (0)1235 400454. Lines are open 9.00a.m.–5.00p.m., Monday to Saturday, with a 24-hour message answering service. Visit our website at www.hoddereducation.co.uk

© Martin Collier, Rosemary Rees and Colin Shephard 2008
First published in 2008
by Hodder Education,
an Hachette UK Company
338 Euston Road
London NW1 3BH

Impression number   6
Year   2013

Artwork by Jon Davis/Linden Artists, Steve Smith, Janek Matysiak, Tony Jones/Art Construction, Peter Bull, Tony Randell, Oxford Designers and Illustrators, Barking Dog Art
Typeset in 12pt ITC Officina Book
Layouts by Fiona Webb
Printed in Dubai

A catalogue record for this title is available from the British Library

ISBN 978 0340 89983 0

CONTENTS

The Making of the UK: an overview

This book has three sections. They follow a roughly chronological order, although some themes and issues spread backwards and forwards from the main events.

SECTION 1   THE TUDORS: POWER AND RELIGION

SECTION 2   THE STUARTS: CIVIL WAR AND COMMONWEALTH

SECTION 3   RESTORATION AND REVOLUTION

The chart opposite will help you to get an overview of the whole period. You can also make your own copy of the chart (you can download a free Word version from www.hoddersamplepages.co.uk). Then you can add your own notes and information to it to help you revise.

We also have a couple more tips to help you to make sense of the period.

1 Living graphs: start with some variable, for example, length of reign, and draw a graph to show this. More complicated, but very useful, is to make a judgement as to how powerful each monarch was, or how successful on a scale of 1–10. Draw a graph to show this.

2 Drawings: there is a picture of every monarch (bar two) in this book. As you work through the book, add your own cartoon or stick drawings to your chart, showing the monarch holding or doing something that reminds you of him or her.

Monarch	Notable events	Dates of reign	Age at death	Cause of death	Pages
Tudor					
Henry VII	Establishing the Tudor dynasty	1485–1509	52	Natural causes (broken heart)	8–21
Henry VIII	Dissolution of the monasteries	1509–47	45	Ill health (gout/syphilis)	22–45
Edward VI	Changes to churches	1547–53	15	Tuberculosis	46–61
Lady Jane Grey	*The nine-day queen*	*10–19 July 1553*	*16*	*Executed*	*62–63*
Mary	Burning of Protestants	1553–58	42	Ill health, possibly cancer	62–70
Elizabeth I	Defeat of the Armada	1558–1603	69	Natural causes	71–101
Stuart					
James I		1603–25	58	Stroke, general ill health (gout, arthritis)	111–115
Charles I	The English Civil Wars	1625–49	48	Executed	116–143
Interregnum	*Oliver Cromwell (Lord Protector)*	*1653–58*	*59*	*Malaria*	*144–153*
	Richard Cromwell	*1658–59*	*85*	*Natural causes*	
Stuart (restored)					
Charles II	The Great Plague and the Great Fire of London	1660–85	54	Apoplectic fit	156–166
James II		1685–88	67	Brain haemorrhage	167–172
William III and Mary II	The Glorious Revolution	1689–1702	Mary – 32, William – 51	Mary – smallpox William – fall while riding	170–172
Anne	Act of Union between England and Scotland	1702–14	49	Ill health (erysipelas)	177
Hanover					
George I	The first Jacobite rebellion 1715	1714–27	67	Stroke	
George II	The second Jacobite rebellion 1745	1727–60	76	Aortic dissection	

Introduction: what was England like in 1500?

You have probably already studied the medieval period. You will have spent some time studying medieval villages and towns. Just because we are now in a new period don't forget that. That is still the background. Things will change, and you will read about the changes in this book, but in 1500 England was still very like the country it had been 100 years earlier in the Middle Ages.

Parts of England were still untouched by humans. There were large areas of forest inhabited by wild animals including wild boar and wolves. They were dangerous places for the unwary. Much of the country was wasteland, covered in scrub and thickets.

There were some small towns and a handful of larger ones. London, with a population of 100,000 was considered to be absolutely huge. The next largest towns were Norwich, the centre of the cloth industry; Bristol, an important port; and York, the main trading and administrative centre in the north of England. In the towns, streets were narrow and houses crammed together. There was little or no sanitation and disease was rife.

Women's lives remained much as they had been in the Middle Ages. Women combined childcare and housework with work in the family's fields, in the family business or with extra paid work of their own. Some brewed beer at home. Some spun and weaved at home – in fact, many more women did this now, as the wool industry was growing. Some women did other jobs at home, such as making hats, sewing gloves or making lace. The number of middle-class families was growing, but even in these richer families, women's lives were still dominated by having and rearing children and by household duties.

Apart from farming, **cloth making** was England's most important industry. Nearly every town had a group of spinners, weavers, fullers, tuckers and dyers.

Only a relatively small part of the land was farmed and a lot of this was used for grazing **sheep**. It has been calculated that in England in about 1500 there were around 8 million sheep and 2.7 million people! The sheep were kept mostly to supply wool for England's cloth industry.

Most people lived in villages and worked the land. Generally they produced enough to live on; any surplus was taken to the nearest market and sold. To make a little extra money women spun wool and men wove cloth. But many villagers worked hard from sunrise to sunset simply to produce enough just to keep themselves and their families alive. A bad winter, mildewed crops or sheep scab could lead to starvation.

Source ❶

What... ?

SPINNER
Someone who draws out and twists wool or cotton into threads.

WEAVER
Someone who makes cloth from thread.

FULLER
Someone who cleans and thickens cloth.

TUCKER
Someone who pounds cloth to make it thicker.

DYER
Someone who adds colour to cloth.

Did you know?

In 1500, about a quarter of children in England died before their tenth birthday. For those that survived, childhood was short. Very few children went to school. Children as young as five years old were expected to work – helping their parents with farming, housework or any other tasks.

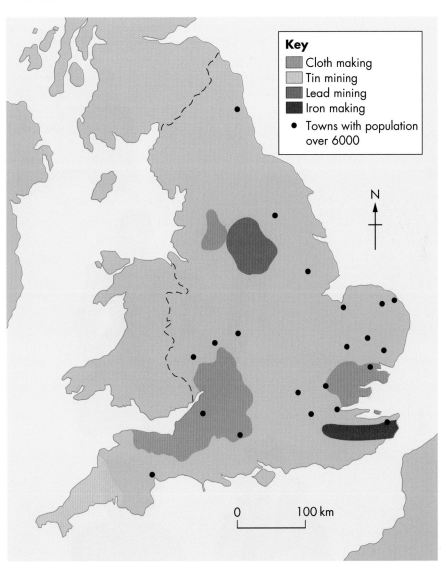

Key
- Cloth making
- Tin mining
- Lead mining
- Iron making
- • Towns with population over 6000

N

England in 1500. ❓ *Use an atlas or Google maps to see if you can identify the towns shown as black dots.*

Task

1 From the information on pages 4–6 make a list of differences between England in the 1500s and England today. Use these headings for your list:

- population
- jobs
- towns
- countryside

Keep your lists. You will need them when you get to the end of this book.

2 If you went back to live in the 1500s what would you miss the most? What would you like the most?

Social groups

A sixteenth-century writer said: 'We in England divide our people into four groups: gentlemen, citizens, yeomen and labourers.' What your life was like and how long you lived depended on which group you belonged to.

Source ❷

Hierarchy of social groups in England in 1500

Dukes and earls

We help the king run the country. We are rich. We own a lot of land. We live in grand houses.

Gentry

We own land, but not usually as much as the dukes and earls. Many of us are justices of the peace. We make people in our villages obey the law.

Yeomen

We rent land from the gentlemen and farm it to produce the food that people need. We have a comfortable life.

Citizens

We live in towns. We make money by buying and selling goods or by making things.

Labourers

We work hard on the farms for low wages. Some of us are very poor indeed.

SECTION 1

The Tudors: Power and religion

If you were asked to choose one image to sum up the Tudors this would probably be a strong contender: proud, pot-bellied Henry VIII, already on his nth wife.

Henry casts a long shadow over the sixteenth century but there is more to the Tudors than Henry and his six wives. In this section we aim to give you a fuller picture of the five Tudor monarchs: their successes and failures; the challenges they faced; and the ways they responded to them.

There is one unit for each monarch but look out for some common themes through the five units: Power (why they wanted it, how they got it and what they did with it) and Religion (why they tried to change the English Church, and what impact this had).

Your final task will be to make a Tudor Gallery summarising and comparing their achievements.

UNIT 1 Henry VII: how secure was he?

What is this all about?

In August 1485, Henry Tudor defeated King Richard III at the Battle of Bosworth. Parliament recognised that Henry was the rightful king of England, and that his heirs would hold the throne forever. He was crowned King Henry VII at a splendid coronation in London in October 1485 and, the following January, he married Elizabeth of York. She was the niece of his enemy, the dead King Richard III. Everything might seem to be set fair for a long and trouble-free reign. So why did Henry keep looking over his shoulder?

The basic problem was that Henry VII was a usurper. He had overthrown a reigning king and, if he could do that to Richard III, someone else could do the same to him. How many people were thinking that, if a small-scale battle in which a king was killed could win a throne and a kingdom, they would have a go, too? Henry was afraid that his throne could be threatened by anyone powerful enough to challenge him.

In part 1 of this unit you will examine how Henry dealt with these challengers who wanted to take over his throne. In part 2 you will examine other aspects of Henry's reign. A successful king needed to work with his nobles, keep law and order in the country, use money wisely, and ensure he had a son to succeed him. How did Henry do in these areas? At the end you will be able to judge how secure he really was.

Task

1 What words would you use to describe Henry as represented in Source 1? Sad? Worried? Thoughtful? Scared?

2 Based on this portrait alone, write a few sentences to describe what kind of person you think Henry was.

Source ❶

This is a portrait of Henry VII. We don't know who painted it, but it's a sixteenth-century copy of a lost original. The original was probably painted from life, soon after Henry took the throne in 1485.

Source ❷

Elizabeth of York, who married Henry in 1486. She is holding the white rose, symbol of the House of York.

1.1 Who challenged Henry VII's position as King of England?

Henry's position in 1485 was in many ways quite strong.

- Richard III had been killed and his naked body slung across the back of a horse for everyone on the battlefield to see. There could be no doubt that the former king was dead.
- Richard III had no living son who could lay claim to the throne on Richard's death.
- Richard's reputation was low. In particular, most people who mattered – and many who didn't – believed that Richard III had killed his nephews, the boy-king Edward V and his brother Richard of York, in order to become king. In the fifteenth century, as now, people viewed this as a terrible crime. Richard's support had melted away.
- Henry didn't owe his throne to the manoeuvring of some powerful noble, who might now decide to bid for the throne himself.
- Henry did have some of the right sort of royal blood in his veins. His mother was the great-great-granddaughter of King Edward III.

But Henry was still fearful. So where was his position weak?

- People saw him as a foreigner. As a boy and young man he had spent many years in Brittany and probably spoke French better than he did English.
- He had taken the throne violently, with French help.
- Few of the great nobles backed Henry, even though he had won the Battle of Bosworth. Plenty of great men thought he was not the rightful king.

Task

At the end of this unit you will be writing an essay about the factors that made Henry secure or insecure. To help you do this, as you read through the unit make two lists like this.

Made him secure
Richard III left no sons who could claim the throne.

Made him insecure
Henry was not accepted as king by some nobles.

Remember, at this time there were four main rules about who would inherit the throne when a monarch died:

1 *The eldest son inherits the throne from his father. That part is simple!*

2 *If the eldest son dies before his father, the throne passes not to the next-eldest son but to the eldest son's son. So the throne can skip a whole generation.*

3 *Males are preferred over females, although there was no outright ban on women becoming monarchs. The last reigning queen, however, had been Matilda and her reign had led to anarchy and civil war so many people believed a woman could not rule effectively.*

4 *If a monarch marries more than once, the sons and grandsons of the first marriage are preferred over sons and grandsons from later marriages.*

NB This is how it worked with sons. If there were no sons at all, the throne would not necessarily go to a daughter: some other male relative would be preferred.

Who might challenge Henry VII?

In order to understand where the challenges to Henry might come from, it's important to look at the family tree of the kings of England from Edward III (who died in 1377) onwards.

Source ❸

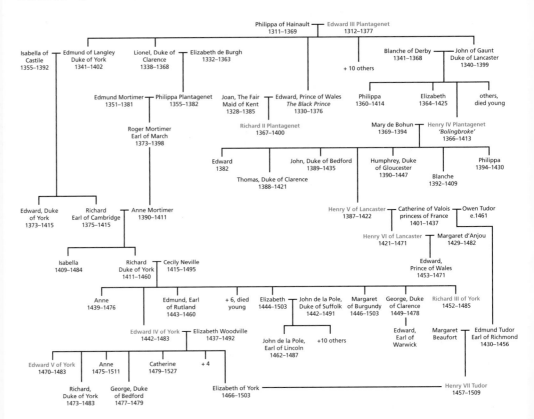

Family tree from Edward III to Henry VII. Note that, sometimes, siblings are not arranged in order of birth. This is to allow the family connections to be shown clearly.

Apart from the missing princes Edward and Richard, the person with the next best claim to the throne of England was Edward, Earl of Warwick. Find him on the family tree. He was the son of George, Duke of Clarence. A few weeks after Bosworth, Henry VII had imprisoned him in the Tower of London.

Then there were the sons of Elizabeth, the sister of Edward IV and Richard III. She married John de la Pole, the Duke of Suffolk. Find them on the family tree. Elizabeth's eldest son, also called John, had been Richard III's official heir. He was an able young man in his twenties with a better claim to the throne than Henry.

Who... ?

KNOW YOUR EDWARDS
From here on things may get a bit confusing because there are two Edwards: the missing-presumed-dead boy-king Edward V; and the imprisoned-in-the-Tower Edward, Earl of Warwick.

With these possible claimants, was it any wonder that Henry VII was nervous?

But the real problem was that no one knew for sure whether or not Edward V and his brother were dead. True, no one had seen them since 1483, but no one had confessed to their murder and no bodies had been found. This was a great opportunity for anyone who wanted to make a bid for the throne. They could pretend to be one of the lost princes, or even the Earl of Warwick, who also hadn't been seen for ages. But who would believe them? Would they be able to rally enough support to overthrow Henry VII?

Task

Look at the family tree. All the people who became monarchs are written in bold letters. Using the four rules, see if you can work out the answers to these questions:

1 Why did none of Edward III's sons become king after him?
2 Which kings were descended from Lionel, Duke of Clarence?
3 Which kings were the result of John of Gaunt's first marriage?
4 Who was Henry VII's royal ancestor?
5 Why was Henry's marriage to Elizabeth of York a good idea?
6 Make a list of the people who were still alive in August 1485. Which of them had a better claim, through blood, to the throne than Henry VII? Why?

What... ?

PRETENDER
A person who pretends to be someone else, not just for fun, but as part of an elaborate scam to claim a throne, land or money.

How serious were the threats made by Pretenders?

The Wars of the Roses between Yorkists and Lancastrians were over. The last Yorkist kings, Edward IV and Richard III were dead and the Lancastrian Henry VII was king. By marrying Elizabeth of York, Henry hoped he had united Yorkists and Lancastrians. But had he? There were still Yorkists who harboured grudges and who might be persuaded, if the risk was not too great, to join a plot against Henry.

What... ?

THE WARS OF THE ROSES (1455–85)
A series of civil wars in England, during which the Crown changed hands six times. The wars were caused by feuds amongst the nobles. They backed either the Lancastrians, led by Margaret of Anjou and the Beaufort family, or the Yorkists, led by Richard of York.

Threat 1: Lambert Simnel (1486–87)

As with all good plots, no one really knows who started this one off. But the best guess of modern historians and, at the time, of Henry VII, was that John de la Pole, the Earl of Lincoln, was its mastermind and arch-planner. Find him on the family tree. John de la Pole was the leader of the Yorkist party, the nephew of two Yorkist kings and the chosen successor of Richard III. He had fought against Henry at Bosworth and, although the two men made peace with each other afterwards, John soon began to plot against Henry.

The story really begins in Oxford early in 1486. A priest called Richard Symonds had amongst his pupils a likely lad called Lambert Simnel. The boy was bright, learned quickly, and had good manners. Even more importantly, he was about the same age, height and colouring as the missing prince, Richard of York. Could he pretend to be the lost prince? At some point it was decided that it would be best if Lambert Simnel pretended to be Edward, Earl of Warwick, who hadn't been seen for over a year. This was a bad idea, as you'll see later, but the plotters had made their plan and they stuck to it. Richard Symonds probably told his bishop, Bishop Stillington of Bath and Wells, who lived in Oxford and who was a Yorkist sympathiser, about the boy and his uncanny resemblance to the royal children. Bishop Stillington told John de la Pole, and things began to move quickly.

Margaret of Burgundy

The most important, influential and rich supporter of the plot was Margaret of Burgundy. If you look back to the family tree on page 10, you'll see that she was the sister of the Yorkist kings Edward IV and Richard III and the aunt of the missing princes. On a personal level she had much to be angry about. She was furious because Henry VII had taken away many of the extremely profitable trading rights granted to her by her brother Edward IV. So when John de la Pole and Lord Lovell arrived at her court in Burgundy she had no problem in agreeing with them that they would try to overthrow Henry VII of England. First, she announced that Lambert Simnel really was her missing nephew, Edward, Earl of Warwick. Then she used her money and her connections to raise an army of 2,000 mercenaries who would try to remove Henry and install her nephew as King of England. In April 1487 this army set sail for Ireland.

The Irish connection

Why Ireland? In the 1450s, Richard, Duke of York, had been Lord Lieutenant of Ireland. He had been extremely popular and was well liked by the Irish nobility. Ever since then, they had supported the Yorkist cause. In January 1487, Lambert Simnel, Richard Symonds and some of John de la Pole's men landed in Dublin. Ireland's most powerful nobleman, Gerald Fitzgerald, the Earl of Kildare, welcomed them and accepted Lambert Simnel as Edward, Earl of Warwick. On 24 May 1487, Lambert Simnel was crowned in Dublin cathedral as King Edward VI. Ten days later, the soldiers of 'Edward VI' landed in Lancashire and began marching inland.

What was Henry to do?

Henry was facing his first challenge. Would he be overthrown, just as he had overthrown Richard III? What was he to do?

- The first, and most obvious thing to do was to produce the real Earl of Warwick. Henry had the Earl brought out of the Tower of London and

Task

1 Why do you think people supported Lambert Simnel?

2 How serious a threat do you think Lambert Simnel posed to Henry's throne? Give him a seriousness score out of 5.

3 Most leaders of rebellions are executed when they are caught. How sensible was it of Henry to give Lambert Simnel a job in the royal kitchens instead?

paraded through the streets for all to see. But people's doubts about Henry were so great that many of them thought that the real earl was a fake!

● Henry then offered all the rebels a pardon, if only they'd go away. This didn't work either.

● So Henry gathered an army together and prepared to defend his crown.

The Battle of Stoke, June 1487

The rebels found less support in the north of England than they had hoped for. Some say that they marched too quickly and didn't give people enough time to make up their minds whether to join them or not. Others say that people were put off joining the rebels because of the large number of ill-disciplined Irish soldiers marching with the rebels. Whatever the reason, on 16 June 1487, the rebel army of 8,000 men faced Henry's army of 12,000. For Henry, this must have been a horrible reminder of the Battle of Bosworth, fought almost two years earlier. Then, his had been the smaller rebel army confronting the much larger army of Richard III. Then, the rebel army had won. Would history repeat itself? Was he doomed to lose, as Richard had done, and would a Yorkist be crowned king of England? Henry need not have worried. His forces were far superior, and won the day. But although 4,000 rebel troops were killed, so were 3,000 of Henry's men.

The victory gave Henry much to think about:

● Two wings of his army didn't begin fighting until they saw that the rebels were going to lose. Why?

● Henry had specifically ordered that John de la Pole, Earl of Lincoln, was to be captured alive because he wanted to find out just who else was conspiring against him. But de la Pole was killed. Was this accidental, or deliberate? Perhaps he was killed so that there was no danger of his secret backers being found out by Henry. One of these secret backers was rumoured to be Henry's own mother-in-law, Elizabeth Woodville.

What happened after Stoke?

● Lambert Simnel was captured alive. Realising that he had been a more or less innocent boy used by powerful men and women to further their own ambitions, Henry spared his life. He was set to work as a turnspit in the royal kitchens and eventually became the king's falconer.

● Twenty-eight of the nobles and gentry who fought against Henry at the Battle of Stoke had their lands confiscated and given as a reward to Henry's supporters.

● Henry spent some months in the areas of the country that had supported Lambert Simnel. He received oaths of loyalty and punished Simnel's supporters by fining them.

What... ?

TURNSPIT

One of the lowliest jobs in a large kitchen. The turnspit's job was to sit by the fire and turn the spit on which an animal was being roasted, making sure it was cooked evenly.

What... ?

FALCONER

The person who looked after the falcons (hunting birds) of a lord or king. Falconers had to keep the birds fit and healthy, were responsible for breeding falcons and rearing the young birds, and for training them to hunt and to fly back to the wrist of the person handling them.

Source ❹

Threat 2: Perkin Warbeck (1491–99)

This picture of Perkin Warbeck was drawn about 50 years after his death and was probably a copy of an original that was made while he was still alive. The resemblance to King Edward IV was so striking that many people thought he could have been an illegitimate son of Edward, conceived while Edward was in exile in Flanders (area of northern France, now part of Belgium) 1470–71.

This is how Perkin Warbeck described how he got involved in a plot to overthrow Henry VII:

> I was working for a Breton merchant called Pregent Meno, who took me to Ireland with him. When we arrived in the town of Cork, I was wearing some silk clothes belonging to my master. The townspeople came to me and said that I must be the Duke of Clarence's son, whom they had seen years before in Dublin. I stoutly denied this. But then they advised me not to be afraid, and that I should make a bold pretence. If I would agree to do so, they and others in Ireland would help me with all their power against the King of England. And so against my will they made me learn English, and taught me what I should do and say. And after this they called me the Duke of York, the second son of King Edward IV.

Do you believe him? Was it really as straightforward as that?

Margaret of Burgundy again

Perkin Warbeck came originally from Tournai, in Flanders. It is highly likely that he was 'discovered' by one of Margaret of Burgundy's agents, who spotted Perkin's likeness to the English royal children. It is likely, too, that it was Margaret who, in 1491, decided to send Perkin to Ireland, the centre of Yorkist plots against Henry VII, probably just to try him out amongst Yorkist supporters. What would they make of him? Would they accept him as a pretender who could, again, threaten Henry's throne? Many people clearly began to believe that Perkin really was Richard, the younger of Edward IV's two sons – one of the missing princes. Even Polydore Vergil, who wrote his *History of England* in 1513 and who was a strong supporter of Henry VII, wrote about the year 1492:

> It began to be rumoured that Richard, King Edward's son, was alive and living in Flanders, where he was known as Perkin. Conspiracies immediately began to multiply. Some, believing Perkin truly to be Edward's son Richard, supported the claim of the Yorkist party.

Many important people in England began to wonder if this boy could be the lost prince. Even the King's step-uncle, Sir William Stanley, advised that contact should be made with Perkin's team, just in case. The nobility began to be uneasy. Were they, after all, supporting a usurper when the real heir to Edward was still alive? Was this young man their rightful King Richard IV? Here was trouble indeed for Henry.

Task

Study Source 4. Do you think this was made by a supporter of Perkin Warbeck or an opponent? Give evidence from the portrait to back up your opinion.

Task

Draw a simple outline map of Europe. On your map:

a) Chart Perkin Warbeck's travels around Europe.

b) Add notes to summarise what support he received from the different countries.

Perkin travels and Henry reacts

Perkin Warbeck was never able to gather the support that had been given to Lambert Simnel. But he managed to make a great nuisance of himself and caught Henry out several times, forcing him into actions he might not otherwise have taken. Here are the main events:

1491 Perkin was in Ireland, where the support he got wasn't enough for him to make a secure base there. Henry sent a small army to chase him out.

1492 Warbeck travelled to France, where King Charles VIII, who was at war with England, welcomed him as a prince. However, Henry made a peace treaty (the Treaty of Etaples) with Charles by which Charles promised not to help Henry's enemies. Perkin had to move on.

1493 Perkin arrived in Flanders, where he was welcomed by his 'aunt', Margaret of Burgundy. Henry put a ban on trade with Flanders, even though this threatened England's wool trade.

1494 Henry's spies discovered that William Stanley, the Chamberlain of the Royal Household, whose decision to side with Henry at the Battle of Bosworth in 1485 had led to Henry's victory over Richard III, was secretly plotting with Perkin Warbeck. Stanley was arrested and executed. Treachery was coming very close to Henry.

1495 Perkin found a powerful backer in Maximilian, the Holy Roman Emperor, who said Perkin was King Richard IV of England and promised to help him regain his throne. In July, Perkin's troops landed at Deal, in Kent. Perkin wisely stayed on board ship. Henry's forces won easily and Perkin sailed to Ireland. Henry's army chased after him and forced Perkin to flee to Scotland.

1496 James IV, the Scottish king, welcomed Perkin. He gave him a pension and Perkin married James' cousin, Katherine Gordon. James funded an invasion of England, which got as far as the River Tweed before the Scots decided to retreat when faced with a strong English force. James and Henry signed a peace treaty (the Truce of Ayton) and Perkin had to move on.

1497 Perkin was again in Ireland, planning an invasion of England through Cornwall, hoping to capitalise on the Cornish Tax Rebellion of 1497. He landed successfully with a small force, but not enough Cornish people supported him to make the invasion successful. Perkin tried to lay siege to Exeter, but fled when he heard that Henry's men were marching towards him.

The end game

This time, Perkin didn't flee to Ireland. He escaped with a few companions to Beaulieu Abbey, near Southampton, where he claimed sanctuary. It didn't take long before Perkin was persuaded to give himself up to the King's men and make a full CONFESSION. In return, Henry treated Perkin well and he was allowed to remain at court, along with his wife. But this was a sort of house arrest, and in 1498, Perkin tried to escape. This was not a clever move. He was captured and this time Henry wasn't so merciful. Perkin was thrown into the Tower of London. Once there, he didn't give up. He made contact with the imprisoned Earl of Warwick and it is said that the two young men plotted their escape together. If true, this was simply stupid and played straight into Henry's hands. Indeed, it was so obviously to Henry's advantage to have this latest 'plot' discovered, that some historians believe Henry set the whole thing up.

In 1499 Perkin Warbeck was accused of trying to escape, found guilty and hanged. A few days later, after a quick trial, the Earl of Warwick was found guilty of treason and executed. At a stroke, Henry had got rid of a Pretender and the last person who had a better claim to the throne than he had.

Task

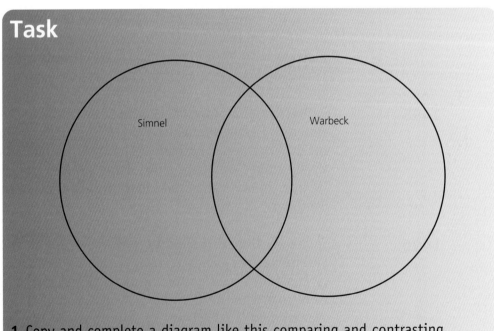

1 Copy and complete a diagram like this comparing and contrasting Lambert Simnel and Perkin Warbeck and the challenges they made to Henry's throne.
2 Which Pretender, Lambert Simnel or Perkin Warbeck, do you think posed the greater threat to Henry VII's throne? Explain your answer carefully.

1.2 How did Henry VII rule England?

What kind of impression have you got of Henry VII so far? He clearly faced challengers but he had dealt with the two Pretenders pretty effectively. He was ruthless when he needed to be but also acted quite generously. Now you are going to look at other aspects of his reign – how he dealt with:

- the nobles
- law and order
- money
- his succession.

As you read, continue to add notes to your chart to show factors that made him secure or insecure.

1 The nobles

One of the worst effects of the Wars of the Roses had been to erode the authority of the King. The powerful nobles had private armies which they used to get their own way or settle disputes with other nobles. So if Henry was to run England he had to control the power of these nobles.

How did Henry govern?

English monarchs had to be obeyed – but they were also expected to listen to the advice of their nobles and gentry. Henry governed with a Council of about twenty men. They didn't meet together very often, as Henry preferred to consult them individually or in small groups. However, when there were important matters to discuss, the King, his Council and the Lords met as a *Magnum Concilium* (Great Council) to decide on the way forward. Sometimes, Henry summoned the Commons – usually when he wanted new taxes to be agreed. The Commons, who were made up of two knights from every county and two representatives from every borough, would meet to pass new laws and to agree to grant the King more money – or not, as the case may be!

How did Henry control his nobles?

Nobles, although they were supposed to work with the monarch to govern the country well, could be troublesome. During the Wars of the Roses (1455–85) they had swapped sides, supporting first one claimant and then the other. Some had grown very powerful indeed. Henry wanted to curb their power so that they could not threaten him. On the other hand, he needed their support in running the kingdom. What was he to do? He used a combination of rewards and punishments, as you will see from the tables on pages 18–19.

What... ?

BOROUGH
A town that had been granted a charter, allowing it to govern itself.

Task

Look through the tables on pages 18–19. If you were Henry VII, what rewards or punishments might you use in the following cases:

a) a noble who had fought for King Richard?

b) a noble who had shown loyalty to Henry all the time?

c) a noble who said he would be loyal to whoever was on the throne?

Rewards

What?	How did it work?	Example
Patronage	Patronage meant being given land and a title by the King. Medieval kings traditionally used patronage as a way of *buying* loyalty. Henry used patronage as a way of *rewarding* loyalty.	Jasper Tudor, Henry's uncle, had given him loyal support before and after Bosworth. He became Duke of Bedford, and was given back his Welsh estates and extra land, too.
Order of the Garter	An important honour, reserved for the King's closest servants. It gave them prestige but not land or power.	Henry created 37 Knights of the Garter, amongst whom was Sir Reginald Bray, Henry's chief financial and property administrator.
King's Councillor	The most trusted lords were made King's Councillors. This was a great honour, and gave them influence over the King but no land.	Henry's five key councillors had all been loyal to him since before Bosworth: Reginald Bray, Giles Daubeney, Richard Guildford, Thomas Lovell and John Riselly.
Great Council	The King appointed other powerful lords to the Great Council. This made them part of the decision making process so they could not reasonably then criticise the King for making that decision.	As well as his own supporters, Henry included those who had fought for the Yorkists, such as the Earl of Surrey.

Punishments

What?	How did it work?	Example
Acts of Attainder	An Act of Attainder led to a family losing its land and any right to inherit land. These Acts were reversible and so Henry passed them to punish or reversed them to reward. He would give the land he confiscated to loyal nobles.	Henry passed 138 Acts of Attainder and reversed 46 of them. Thomas Tyrell paid £1,738 for the reversal of his and his father's attainders.
Bonds and recognisances	Henry could force a noble to sign a bond or recognisance. The noble promised to do something for the King and agreed to pay money if he didn't.	Thomas Grey had never been trusted by Henry because he had supported Richard III. In 1492 he had to give his lands to trustees and make recognisances of over £10,000. However, he helped put down the Cornish Rebellion in 1497 so these recognisances were cancelled. He had proved his loyalty.
Feudal dues	Henry still held feudal rights – just like a medieval king. For example nobles could not marry without a licence from the King. He could fine people who stepped out of line.	Katherine, the Dowager Duchess of Buckingham, was fined £7,000 in 1496 for marrying without the King's licence.

Other measures

What?	How did it work?	Example
Controls on retaining	Nobles had the right to recruit (retain) administrators or soldiers from the gentry. Henry did not want nobles to raise a force that could be used against him. So nobles had to obtain special licences from Henry if they wanted to retain.	In 1506 Lord Burgavenny was fined £70,550 for retaining without a licence.
Crown lands	Much land belonging to the King (Crown lands) had been granted to nobles during the Wars of the Roses. In 1486 the Act of Resumption restored to Henry all Crown lands taken since 1455.	Henry rewarded loyal nobles with land taken from other nobles by Acts of Attainder but he never gave away Crown lands.

Did you know?

The Cornish Rebellion 1497 was a rebellion against the raising of taxes to fund Henry's Scottish Wars that was led by a Bodmin lawyer called Thomas Flamank. Thousands of Cornishmen marched eastwards to London and were defeated at Blackheath in June by forces led by Giles Daubeney. A few months later, Perkin Warbeck unsuccessfully attempted to rouse the Cornish rebels again (see page 15).

Discuss
Do you think Henry's measures to keep the nobles loyal were fair and sensible?

2 Law and order

The Wars of the Roses had damaged law and order in England. The powerful families had sometimes been more interested in fighting one another than in keeping the peace in their area. Henry needed a new system.

How were the laws enforced?

- The Star Chamber was the highest court. This had existed before and Henry brought it back. It was supposed to cut through bureaucracy and reach quick decisions when wealthy and powerful people were quarrelling with each other. It could also hold investigations into suspicious matters, and Henry quite often asked it to investigate plots against him.
- Not many cases got to the Star Chamber in London. Henry appointed travelling judges who moved between the main towns, trying serious cases, and giving out punishments.
- Justices of the Peace (JPs) dealt with less important cases. JPs were unpaid officials who lived locally and knew everything there was to know about a particular area. As well as trying minor offenders, they saw to local legal matters like fixing wage rates and licensing beer houses.

3 Money

To be successful a king had to raise taxes fairly and spend the money wisely.

Source ❺

Testing weights and measures. Setting standards for length, volume and weight was important in order to maintain commercial confidence in trade. Penalties for selling short measures were severe. ❓ *What do you think each of the people in the picture is doing?*

Was Henry good with money?

The short answer is 'Yes'. Henry left England's finances in a far better state than they were in when he became king. How did he do this?

● He put all his royal revenue into a department called the Chamber, rather than the old-fashioned Exchequer, and kept a careful eye on the accounts.

● A parliamentary grant paid him about £39,000 a year. Customs duties – especially on wool – and fees paid to him on the death of a lord or the marriage of a lord's children more than doubled this. Additionally, Henry 'persuaded' his richer subjects to lend him money (forced loans), or even give it to him (benevolences) because – or so Henry said – they loved him so much!

● Henry was a good businessman, who hired his ships to merchants and loaned money at high interest rates.

● Henry wanted England to be a rich country and he signed trade treaties with foreign countries. The *Magnum Intercursus*, for example, set up good terms for the English wool trade with the Netherlands. Navigation laws laid down that certain goods could only be carried in English ships and this boosted the English ship-building industry.

● He avoided war. Although he had won the crown by battle he avoided conflicts with other countries. He was not interested in trying to regain England's lands in France and he tried to keep England peaceful.

● Taxes – lots of them. These were efficiently gathered by his trusted Chancellor, Archbishop Thomas Morton.

Source ⑥

The Tudor Rose (detail from The Pelican Portrait of Elizabeth I). This was like a logo for the Tudor dynasty. It combined the symbols of the Yorkists and the Lancastrians. ❓ You can still see this symbol used on one of the British coins today. Do you know which value of coin?

4 A son and heir

Henry desperately wanted to found a new dynasty – the Tudors. The way to do this was to have lots of children – preferably sons – and so make sure there was a Tudor to inherit the throne when he died.

Henry married Elizabeth of York on 18 January 1486. In doing this, he wanted to please and make peace with the Yorkists, but he also wanted to found a dynasty. They had seven children:

- Arthur, born in 1486
- Margaret, born in 1488
- Henry, born in 1491
- Elizabeth, born in 1492 and died in 1495
- Mary, born in 1496
- Edmund, born in 1499 and died in 1500
- Katherine, born and died in 1503

So only four of Henry's children lived to be adults. Margaret and Mary were married to powerful people to strengthen Henry's position. Margaret was married to James IV of Scotland and Mary married first Louis XII of France, and then Charles Brandon, Duke of Suffolk.

Henry had two sons – Arthur and Henry – so he had an heir and a spare. In 1502, Prince Arthur married Catherine of Aragon which strengthened the alliance between England and Spain. All was going well.

However only a few weeks after his wedding, while still on honeymoon at Ludlow Castle, Arthur died unexpectedly of a fever aged only sixteen. So, suddenly Henry was left with only one son – the ten-year-old Prince Henry, who was now the only direct male heir to the throne of England. Henry needed more sons to be secure but in 1503 his wife Elizabeth, desperately trying to add to the diminishing stock of Tudor children, died in childbirth, along with her baby. This was his second bereavement in a year.

So when Henry died in 1509 he left just a single son – now aged seventeen. What kind of a king would the son turn out to be? Would the nobles accept him at all? Would they obey such a young king? Or would the old wounds of civil war be reopened?

Summary task

Look back to the task on page 9 and to the lists you have been making.

Using this information, write an essay to answer the question 'How secure was Henry VII?' You will need to think about:

- the challenges facing him at the start of his reign
- how he dealt with rivals to the throne

- how the way he governed made him more secure, e.g. consulting advisers, or money
- whether there were any ways that he was still insecure, e.g. could he be sure that he had a son to succeed him?
- your overall assessment of how secure his rule was when he died. Give Henry a 'security score' out of 10 and then explain your score.

Use these five bullet points as your essay plan. Write a paragraph for each.

UNIT 2 What really mattered to Henry VIII?

> **What is this all about?**
>
> When Henry VIII became king it was the first peaceful transfer of power in England for 87 years. Henry VIII started his reign in a blaze of glory. He was young and handsome. He was a talented musician and poet, and he loved jousting and tennis. He spent money lavishly and his court was a place of fun and richness, music, sport and learning. He could have had a very comfortable life living off the wealth his father had created.
>
> However, Henry chose a different way. Everyone knows that he got through six wives – executing two of them – but that was not all. He executed his most trusted advisers. He persecuted his religious opponents. He challenged the power of the Pope and ended forever the power of the Roman Catholic Church in England. He destroyed hundreds of monasteries and convents and took their wealth for himself. The question is: why? What really mattered to him: women, sons, money, prestige, power, religion? All are possible. In this unit you will examine selected aspects of his long reign in detail to see what you think really mattered to him.
>
> - Part 1 investigates the reasons for and results of his 'divorce' from Catherine of Aragon – sometimes called 'The King's Great Matter'.
> - Part 2 examines what is known as the 'Henrician Reformation' – when he made himself head of the English Church.
> - Part 3 is a brief conclusion looking at one of the most spectacular events of his reign – the Field of the Cloth of Gold.

2.1 The King's Great Matter: why did Henry VIII want a divorce?

Before the new reign could get under way, a line had to be drawn under the old one. The dead King Henry VII was given a magnificent funeral. Five black horses, draped in black, pulled his hearse. Archbishops, bishops, lords and barons walked beside and behind it. Henry's armour, his helmet with its gold crown, his battleaxe and sword (sheathed in black velvet) were carried in the funeral procession that wound its way slowly and solemnly to Westminster Abbey. There, on 10 May 1509, Henry the usurper, the victor of Bosworth, was buried.

The old king's death had been kept secret for two days while the most powerful nobles in the land argued about who was to exercise influence over the young king and the ways in which they wanted the new reign to go. Eventually they decided that they wanted the seventeen-year-old

Henry to be 'brought up in all pleasure, for otherwise he should grow too hard amongst his subjects as the king his father did.' In other words, they wanted the new reign to be very different from the old one. Indeed it was, but not, perhaps, in the way they had hoped.

Source ❶

This portrait of the young Henry VIII was painted around 1510 when Henry was about eighteen years old.

Task

1 What words would you use to describe Henry VIII as painted in Source 1? Wise? Proud? Rich? Clever? Stupid?
2 Write a few sentences saying what, just by looking at the portrait, you think Henry's character was.
3 Now look back at what you wrote about Henry VII when you were asked the same question about his portrait on page 8. Write a paragraph about the similarities and differences – using only their portraits.

Beginnings

On 11 June 1509, Henry VIII and Catherine of Aragon were quietly married in Greenwich Palace by the Archbishop of Canterbury. Why quietly? This was the proclaimed King of England and his bride. You would expect a grand marriage. The reason was that Catherine had previously been married to Prince Arthur, who was Henry's elder brother. Arthur died unexpectedly in 1502 after just four weeks of marriage. It was against Church law for a man to marry his brother's widow, so Pope Julius II had to give Henry special permission to do so.

The wedding may have been quiet, but the coronation was quite the opposite. Henry and Catherine were crowned on Midsummer's Day, 24 June, in a splendid ceremony in Westminster Abbey. The streets were packed with well-wishers, celebrating the royal couple. Buildings were hung with tapestries, and streets strewn with flowers. Wine flowed freely. There was dancing and drinking, music and games. There was a grand banquet in Westminster Hall afterwards, with celebrations continuing for days.

The couple seemed genuinely to love each other. They had many interests in common: hunting, music, poetry, politics and theology. Henry wrote to Catherine's father 'If I were still free, I would choose her for wife before all others.' He gave his mother's prayer book to Catherine and wrote in it 'I am yours, Henry R, for ever.' Some days after their marriage, Catherine's confessor described her as being 'in the greatest happiness and contentment that ever there was.' Catherine referred to Henry as 'my Henry' and made it clear that her greatest wish was to please him.

What... ?

CONFESSOR
A priest to whom a Catholic could confess his or her sins.

23

Source ❷

Seven pregnancies, one daughter

This portrait of Catherine of Aragon was painted in 1503/4 when she was about 18 years old. ❓ *Religion was very important to her. How has the artist shown this?*

As the King's CONSORT Catherine was expected to busy herself with charitable works, to support the King in everything he did and to provide a civilising influence at his court. She did all these, but Catherine's main duty was to produce sons. This was more of a problem. It started well. Their first child, a son, was born on 1 January 1511 and christened Henry five days later. Sadly he lived for only two months.

Several pregnancies followed but they mostly ended in miscarriages, stillbirths or the babies only lived for a few hours. Only one child survived and this baby was a girl – the Princess Mary – born in 1516.

Henry was worried. He wanted a son to succeed him as King of England. Henry knew he could father a healthy boy. His mistress, Bessie Blount, gave him a fine son in 1519. Henry proudly acknowledged this child as his own. He made his chief minister, Thomas Wolsey, the godfather and gave the child the title Duke of Richmond in 1525. There were strong rumours that Henry intended making this child his heir. This would have been a risky business since an illegitimate child, even a boy, would not be accepted by Parliament and the people if there was a legitimate, healthy heir living. And the Princess Mary, three years older than her illegitimate half-brother, was healthy and very much alive.

Source ❸

Henry VIII jousting in front of Queen Catherine to celebrate the birth of a son in 1511. The painting was made after the baby had died. ❓ *What does it tell you about Henry's desire for a son that he a) held this tournament, b) had this painting made?*

Did you know?

If you find it hard to remember Henry's six wives and what happened to them, try this acronym CAJACC and this simple rhyme.

Catherine of Aragon   Divorced
Anne Boleyn   Beheaded
Jane Seymour   Died
Anne of Cleves   Divorced
Catherine Howard   Beheaded
Catherine Parr   Survived

And to get the Catherines and Annes in order remember their second names conveniently come in alphabetical order.

A doomed marriage?

By 1527, Henry had been married to Catherine for eighteen years. She was 42 and was unlikely to get pregnant again. Henry now set his sights on a younger woman – Anne Boleyn, one of Queen Catherine's ladies-in-waiting.

At this moment (cynics might say 'conveniently'), Henry began to wonder if his marriage was cursed by God. In the Christian Bible it stated 'If a man shall take his brother's wife it is an unclean thing. They shall be childless.' Henry suggested God might be punishing him because he had married his brother's wife.

Henry publicly stated his doubts about the marriage and asked the Church to consider whether his marriage to Catherine was wrong. Pope Julius had given him permission to marry his brother's widow but maybe even the Pope did not have the right to set aside the law of God. Thomas Wolsey was ordered to persuade the new Pope to ANNUL the royal marriage.

This was quite a challenge. Thomas had often boasted of the influence he had with the Pope, and Henry was clearly expecting him to persuade the new pope, Clement VII, to declare that his predecessor had made a mistake and that the marriage to Catherine was not lawful.

However popes were not well known for changing their mind. And to make Wolsey's job even harder Pope Clement was actually the prisoner of the Holy Roman Emperor Charles V – who just happened to be Queen Catherine's nephew. Charles viewed the whole 'divorce' issue as a plot against his family. Catherine would certainly resist it.

Who... ?

THOMAS WOLSEY (1471–1530)

Wolsey was the son of an Ipswich butcher yet rose to be the most powerful man in Henry's kingdom. He was clever, intelligent and hardworking, and Henry VIII trusted him. But he was also vain, proud, selfish and greedy.

Henry made Wolsey Lord Chancellor. He improved the legal system and handled wars with Scotland and France capably. But he disliked Parliament and didn't manage it well at all. MPs would not grant Henry all the money he wanted, so Wolsey used threats and promises to force rich nobles to lend Henry money. This didn't make him very popular!

Wolsey was also a high ranking person in the Catholic Church. He was a cardinal and a PAPAL LEGATE. He held many other posts in the Church, all of which brought him in an income. He became very rich, dressing in the finest silk clothes and eating the best food. At one point, he had over 500 servants. He entertained his guests with magnificent banquets and had a wonderful palace built for himself – Hampton Court. Many people were horrified that a man of God should be so full of pride and seemed to have so little of what was holy about him.

He fancied himself as the manager of European affairs, but this didn't work out well because he supported the Pope so many European rulers tended to ignore him.

Enter Cardinal Campeggio

Still, Wolsey did what Henry asked. Pope Clement VII, having heard Wolsey's argument, decided to play for time. He sent his agent, Cardinal Campeggio, to England. Campeggio was to listen to both sides. He was to reach a decision and make a recommendation to the Pope. What a job!

Campeggio prepares

Put yourself in Cardinal Campeggio's shoes. It is not simply a case of making a decision.

● Your decision has to be supported by the Bible, but the Bible does not have one clear viewpoint. Henry has quoted from the book of Leviticus to argue that the marriage was wrong from the start. But you know that Catherine will, in her turn, quote from the book of Deuteronomy: 'When brothers live together and one of them dies without children, the wife of the dead brother shall not marry another, but his brother shall take her and raise up seed for his brother.'

● Your decision has to please your master, Pope Clement. Popes should not contradict their predecessors, but on the other hand Pope Clement might like to get his own back on Charles V who had been keeping him prisoner.

Task

You are due to meet the King of England at the end of the week. Here are four possible recommendations:

1 You will ask the Pope to annul the marriage.
2 You will recommend Catherine go into a convent. If so the marriage would be declared void as nuns cannot be married.
3 You will stick by the previous judgement and tell Henry he must stay married to Catherine.
4 You will play for time and find an excuse for not reaching any decision at all.

For each of these four possible courses of action write down the possible good outcomes, and the possible bad ones – find at least one point in each category. Then choose one that you think will produce the best outcome for your boss, the Pope.

Campeggio meets Henry

You meet Henry and hear his argument – his marriage to Catherine was invalid because she was his brother's wife and as the rule was made by God the Pope had no right to set it aside when he allowed Catherine and Henry to marry.

But you don't want to agree that popes make mistakes. So you suggest option 2 – that Catherine becomes a nun.

Henry agrees. If she will do this, and not cause trouble, Henry will give her whatever she wants. She will live well and keep her ladies-in-waiting and servants. She will have enough money for her needs. She will keep her jewels; and he will name their daughter Mary as his heir if he doesn't have any sons by his next wife.

So far, so good.

Campeggio meets Catherine

Catherine surprises you by immediately accusing you of coming to persuade her to enter a religious house. You realise that this lady isn't going to go quietly.

Still you try to persuade her that it would be in her, and her daughter's, best interests if she accepts what Henry is offering. Catherine will have none of it. She is his wife and his Queen before God and in English law, and she intends to stay that way. She is in no mood for compromise.

You retire to consider your next move.

News from Rome

News arrives that Pope Clement is once again prisoner of Catherine's nephew Charles V. Charles won't allow Henry to humiliate his aunt.

Decision time?

June 1529: you assemble your court at Blackfriars to reach a final decision. Henry, Catherine and Wolsey are there too. Catherine kneels at Henry's feet and pleads:

Sir, I beseech you for all the love that has been between us, and for the love of God, let me have justice and right, take pity and sympathy on me. I am a poor woman and a stranger born outside your lands. I have here no firm friend. I have been your wife for twenty years or more, and by you have had many children, although it has pleased God to call them out of this world, which has been because of no fault in me.

Catherine then tells the court that she never had sexual intercourse with Arthur. She argues that because her first marriage was 'incomplete' before God that she was never his wife, so Henry's argument is wrong. She demands justice and, cheered by her ladies-in-waiting, sweeps out of the court, never to return.

And there we leave it...and we leave the shoes of Cardinal Campeggio.

Source ❹

This painting of Catherine of Aragon and the Cardinals *was painted in 1866.*
❓ *Which moment in the story does it show?*

Exit Campeggio

If, like Henry, you were expecting a resolution then you will be disappointed. Campeggio left for Rome without telling them what he had decided, and he never came back. And if, like Henry, that leaves you in limbo and confusion, then welcome to Henry's world. All that effort and argument, the comings and goings, and you have not got what you want. In fact you have got nothing! Things are much as they were one year earlier.

Exit Thomas Wolsey

Henry was furious. His chief and most trusted minister, Cardinal Thomas Wolsey, had failed to deliver the one thing the King wanted most: an annulment of his marriage to Catherine. He turned against him. Wolsey had earned many enemies. Now they were gathered to help bring Wolsey down.

> **What... ?**
>
> PAPAL BULL
> An order that comes directly from the Pope.

- Wolsey was accused of breaking the law of *Praemunire*. This was an old law that forbade priests to undermine the King's authority, for example, by bringing papal bulls into England. This was unreasonable because, as papal legate, Wolsey had to bring papal bulls into England. He'd done it often and Henry had never bothered before.
- Wolsey was dismissed from most of his jobs but he was allowed to carry on as Archbishop of York.

> **Did you know?**
>
> Thomas Wolsey's last words were 'If I had served my God half as well as I had served my king, he would not have given me over in my grey hairs.'

It is just possible that Wolsey could have carried on quietly living out his days as Archbishop of York. But he then did something really stupid. He wrote to the Pope urging him to persuade Henry not to marry Anne Boleyn. When Henry got to hear of this, it was the final straw. He ordered Wolsey to be arrested and thrown into the Tower of London. But Wolsey was already desperately ill and on the journey south he broke his journey at Leicester Abbey. Sensing the end, the disgraced cardinal said to the abbot 'I have come to lay my bones amongst you'. Two days later, he was dead.

Task

When important people die, someone writes an obituary. What it says and how it says it depends on the views of the writer. Write an obituary for Wolsey from the viewpoint of either:

a) a supporter of Wolsey (but who doesn't want to get into trouble with the King), or
b) a critic of Wolsey who wants to find favour with the King.

See page 193 for a practice source exercise on the King's Great Matter.

2.2 How and why did Henry change the English Church?

Thomas Cranmer.

Enter Thomas Cranmer

Henry was growing infatuated with Anne Boleyn. His marriage with Catherine was, in Henry's eyes if not in hers, over. He wanted to get on with his life. He wanted a son. After five years of holding him at arm's length, Anne finally gave in to Henry. Before long, she was pregnant. Both Henry and Anne were convinced that the baby would be a boy. The situation was desperate. The child had to be legitimate when it was born and so in February 1533, Henry and Anne were secretly married. But in the eyes of the Church, Henry was still married to Catherine. The whole messy situation had to get sorted out and Henry turned to a new Thomas for help: Thomas Cranmer.

Thomas Cranmer was a priest and a scholar. He first came to Henry's notice when, at the beginning of the King's 'Great Matter', he had suggested that the universities should be asked their opinion as to whether Henry's marriage to Catherine was lawful. Henry liked the idea and made Cranmer a royal CHAPLAIN, attached to the household of Anne Boleyn's father. Henry sent Cranmer abroad to test out opinion about his marriage but Cranmer didn't seem to achieve much except to fall in love and marry. He must have been surprised when, on his return, Henry made him Archbishop of Canterbury. But this was to prove to be an appointment that was to be extremely useful to Henry.

In April 1533, two months after Henry and Anne's secret marriage, Thomas Cranmer held a special court at Dunstable. He calmly declared that, in the eyes of the Church, Henry and Catherine had never been lawfully married. Henry and Catherine had been living in a sinful relationship. Their one living child, Mary, was declared a bastard. This, of course, meant that she couldn't inherit the throne, and the Tudor dynasty would be continued by the son Henry and Anne were sure she was expecting.

Did you know?

Catherine and her daughter, Mary, were separated and Catherine was forced to leave court. She died in Kimbolton Castle in 1536 and was buried in Peterborough Abbey.

Task

1 Henry had organised a grand tournament to celebrate what he thought was going to be his son's birth. When he heard he had a daughter, he cancelled the tournament. How do you think Anne would have felt about this?

2 What do you think is motivating Henry? It is too early to judge for sure but at this stage, based on what you know, which of these statements best fits Henry's actions? Say why you chose it.
- He only wanted a son and heir. Once he had that he would be satisfied.
- Henry only wanted money. Being a king is an expensive business.
- Henry wanted power for its own sake. He wanted to be in charge – full stop!

Source 6

This portrait of Thomas Cromwell was painted by one of the most famous character painters of the time, Holbein.
? *Compare this style of portrait with the royal portraits such as those on page 8, 23 or 24. How is the style different? Which do you prefer? Why?*

In June 1533 Anne, six months pregnant, was crowned Queen of England in Westminster Abbey. Many people simply couldn't believe what was happening. Queen Catherine had been very popular and suddenly she was gone from the scene. An eyewitness said, 'All the world was astonished, not knowing whether to laugh or cry.'

Queen Anne's pregnancy ran its course and on 7 September she gave birth – to a girl, whom they called Elizabeth.

Enter Thomas Cromwell

Thomas Cranmer had sorted out Henry's marriage problems for him. Now Henry appointed yet another Thomas – Thomas Cromwell – as his chief minister. Cromwell was a clever lawyer and a ruthless politician. He set about replacing the power of the Pope in England with the power of the King.

Who... ?

THOMAS CROMWELL (1485–1540)
Like Wolsey, Cromwell came from a poor family. When he was a young man he had an adventurous time as a soldier and worked for a merchant in Italy. In 1514 he began working for Wolsey and, after Wolsey's death, for the King.

In 1529 he called a parliament which became know as the Reformation Parliament. Unlike Thomas Wolsey, Cromwell was very skilled in dealing with Parliament. And he managed to get this Parliament to agree to a series of laws that entirely changed the relationship between the King and the Church.

- The Act of Annates 1532 ended the payment of taxes to the Pope. In future, all such taxes would be paid to Henry.
- The Act of Supremacy 1534 decreed the King was 'Supreme Head of the Church of England'.
- By the Act of Succession 1534 anyone who denied the right of Anne Boleyn to be queen, or the right of her heirs to inherit the throne, was committing treason and would be punished by death.

Who disagreed?

It was unsafe to disagree with Henry and Cromwell. Cromwell made it clear that their oath of loyalty to the Pope could make them guilty of *Praemunire* (denying the ecclesiastical supremacy of the monarch). This was a major offence. Source 7 shows you what happened to monks of the Carthusian Order who refused to accept Henry's claim to be the Head of the Church of England. To refuse was treason, and they received a terrible punishment.

Source ❼

These Carthusian monks were dragged through the streets of London. Then their hearts were ripped out and put 'hot and steaming' into their mouths. Finally, they were beheaded and their heads put on spikes on London Bridge. Why do you think such a terrible punishment was carried out in public? Why do you think the King ordered these prints to be made and distributed?

Bishop Fisher, who had supported Catherine's cause, was executed. So was Thomas More, a man of great learning who was admired throughout Europe and who had been Henry's Chancellor. More had said he did not believe that Parliament had the right to make the King Supreme Head of the Church of England. These executions horrified many influential people in Europe. But in these circumstances the clergy formally 'apologised' to Henry. They got away with a fine of £118,000.

It seemed that Henry VIII now had got what he wanted. He had a young wife who could give him sons; a Parliament that had made him Supreme Head of the Church of England; and everyone in England swearing loyalty to the Crown above anyone or anything else. Henry was supreme ruler in his own land.

These changes are usually called the Henrician Reformation. This is because Henry VIII, Cranmer and Cromwell had reformed the relationship between the Crown and the Pope.

Task

Here are those sentences again. Which one fits best now? Choose one and give reasons.
- He only wanted a son and heir. Once he had that he would be satisfied.
- Henry only wanted money. Being a king is an expensive business.
- Henry wanted power for its own sake. He wanted to be in charge – full stop!

Did you know?

In 1535 Henry formally annexed Wales. This made English laws apply in Wales for the first time and made English the legal language for all official business in Wales. He also had himself crowned King of Ireland in 1541 although the English actually controlled very little of it.

The dissolution of the monasteries

There were about 800 monasteries and nunneries dotted throughout England and Wales. Some did good work amongst the poor, feeding and clothing them and looking after the sick; some were centres of learning, preserving ancient manuscripts, writing down what was happening in the country and teaching reading and writing. Others operated like big companies, making profits from the rental of their land and from the wool trade. Some were reportedly little more than dens of vice. Henry was not too bothered about all of this. However he was very interested in the fact that together the monasteries owned about a quarter of the land in England and Wales and had an income greater than that of the king. He wanted to get his hands on their wealth. Henry had spent freely on extravagant displays of splendour as well as foreign wars, and the solid financial base he had inherited from his father was, by 1535, badly dented. At the back of Henry's mind there was, too, the niggling worry that he might have to fight another foreign war – against Charles V, Catherine of Aragon's nephew, who was still seriously angry with Henry for putting his aunt aside. There might be rebellions in England, too. Lots of people were deeply angry about Henry making himself Supreme Head of the Church in England.

Thomas Cromwell's cunning plan

Henry wanted the monasteries' wealth but even a powerful Tudor king couldn't just decide to close down the monasteries and grab their wealth. He had to have a good reason for so doing. And he had to get Parliament to support him. Henry gave Thomas Cromwell the title 'Vicar General' and put him in charge of Church matters. Cromwell was determined to find the evidence Henry wanted – evidence that would convince Parliament that the monasteries had to be closed down.

Cromwell put together a team of inspectors whose job was to find the evidence he and Henry wanted. The inspectors were lawyers who were hand-picked because of their opinions about monasteries: they scoffed at the relics and treasures and mocked the rituals. In 1535, Cromwell sent them out with instructions to visit all the monasteries and nunneries and send him reports on:

- the monks who were breaking monastic rules, particularly with regard to sex
- the names of monks and nuns who wanted to leave their monasteries and nunneries
- whether there were any rituals going on that involved relics
- the income of every monastery and whether there were any debts.

What did the inspectors find?

The inspectors didn't visit all the monasteries, although they were supposed to. Sometimes they just talked to people who lived nearby;

sometimes they made up their reports. And sometimes they made a really thorough investigation. Cromwell had made it clear to them that if the reports they sent back to him weren't critical enough, they would have to be re-written!

Here are some extracts from the inspectors' reports:

1
The Crossed Friar's monastery, London
I found the prior in bed with a naked woman at 11 o'clock in the morning.

2
Woolsthorpe in Lincolnshire
The abbot is well beloved, having eight religious persons, being priests of right good conversation and living religiously, having such qualities of virtue as we have not found before in any place.

3
Fountains Abbey in Yorkshire
The Abbot of Fountains had greatly ruined his abbey, wasting his woodland and keeping six mistresses. Six days before our arrival he committed theft. At midnight he went with a local goldsmith and removed a great emerald and ruby from a gold cross. The goldsmith bought the emerald and ruby and some silver. The abbot is truly a fool.

4
St Edmund's monastery in Suffolk
The Abbot delighted much in playing at dice and in that spent much money. For his own pleasure he has had lots of beautiful buildings built. There was here much frequence of women coming to the monastery.

5
St Edmund's convent
I could not find out anything bad about the convent, no matter how hard I tried. I believe I couldn't find anything because everybody had got together and agreed to keep the convent's secrets. Among the relics we found were the coals that St Lawrence was burnt upon, the clippings of St Edmund's nails, St Thomas of Canterbury's penknife and his boots, and enough pieces of the Holy Cross to build a whole one.

Task

1 Which of these reports would Thomas Cromwell have been pleased with? Why?
2 Which reports would he have sent back for a re-write? Why?
3 Explain whether or not you think these reports would have given a true picture of life in monasteries and nunneries.
4 If some reports didn't give an accurate picture of the state of monasteries and nunneries, does this mean that a historian can't use them?

Cromwell had the 'evidence' he needed. A shocked Parliament passed an Act in 1536, closing all the small monasteries. Later, the larger monasteries were closed down. By 1540 there wasn't one functioning monastery left in England or Wales. All the monks and nuns had been thrown out of their communities. Most accepted the inevitable and went without protest. All their treasure was taken to London for the King. Their precious manuscripts were thrown out and burned. Many of the

Task

1 Here are those sentences one last time. Which one fits best now? Choose one and give reasons. Or write your own which sums up what you think really mattered to Henry VIII.

- He only wanted a son and heir. Once he had that he would be satisfied.
- Henry only wanted money. Being a king is an expensive business.
- Henry wanted power for its own sake. He wanted to be in charge – full stop!

monasteries were ancient and beautiful buildings, but few people took any notice of that, stripping lead from the roofs and breaking up the walls for building materials. Monastery lands now belonged to Henry. Some he kept and the rest he sold off to the highest bidder amongst his nobles. Soon it was all over. Hundreds of years of religious life were gone forever. And the Crown was richer by far.

Source ⑧

BEFORE

AFTER

These two pictures are both of Fountains Abbey in Yorkshire. It was a great Cistercian monastery making a lot of money through the wool trade. ❓ *Can you work out roughly where on the 'before' picture the photographer of the 'after' picture was standing?*

Beliefs and buildings

In 1534 Henry VIII became Head of the Church in England. But this did not mean that it stopped being a Catholic Church. Most people in England were Catholics and did not want to change. The changes Henry had made to the Church in his Reformation were legal changes. They didn't set out to change people's beliefs, or the ways they worshipped. But sometimes, if you change the way people do things, and the places where they do them, they do begin to think differently.

What did Catholics believe in?

Before the Reformation, just about everyone in England was a Catholic. They believed in the power of God and of God's son, Jesus Christ. They believed that this power worked for good throughout the world. They believed that they had to lead Christian lives, as laid down by the Catholic Church. They believed that, when they died, they would go to either heaven or hell. Which one they went to would depend on how good they had been on Earth. But various other beliefs about how to get to heaven had grown up around those central ideas.

Saints Catholics believed that, by saying prayers to saints, they would more easily get into heaven. The lives of saints were celebrated on holy days.

Marian devotion Mary, the mother of Jesus was a very important person to Catholics. They would pray to Mary to get them into heaven. One of the most popular places of pilgrimage was Walsingham in Norfolk where there was a shrine marking the place where a vision of Mary had appeared some centuries earlier. Most churches had statues of Mary where people would pray to her.

Purgatory Catholics believed that, on the way to either heaven or hell, they would go to purgatory. This was not supposed to be a very nice place and Catholics believed that the best thing to happen would be to pass through purgatory quickly on the way to heaven. One way to do this was to get monks or nuns to pray for your soul.

How do you get to heaven?

Relics Most churches in England owned a relic. This was part of a dead holy person's body or an object that, for one reason or another, was holy. Catholics would say prayers in front of the relics. They would also touch them because relics were a sign of good in the world. The relics that were the bits of saints' bodies were thought to be especially important because the spirits of saints were said to remain in the body after death. Some relics were highly prized, like the flask that was supposed to contain some of Christ's blood, which was placed in Westminster Abbey in 1244.

Pilgrimages The best place to pray to the saints was at a holy place. Making the journey to a holy place was called a pilgrimage. The holiest of the holy places was Jerusalem which was where Jesus was crucified. Very few were able to make the expensive journey to Jerusalem. The most important site for pilgrimage in England was the tomb of St Thomas Becket at Canterbury Cathedral. Many people also went on pilgrimages to seek a cure for an illness or disability.

Indulgences Catholics believed that one way of getting out of purgatory quickly would be to buy indulgences. These were bits of parchment which, if bought, would give the owner less time in purgatory. Indulgences could also be bought by the living for the dead to speed them on their way.

The Mass

At the heart of the Catholic faith was the MASS. This was the service held in a Catholic church. The high point of the Mass was the celebration of the communion (point of contact) of God with man. This happened when the priest blessed bread and wine and, by doing so, turned it into the body and blood of Jesus Christ. This is called TRANSUBSTANTIATION.

The Mass was said in Latin, a language which not everyone understood. The priest said the Mass with his back to the people in the church. He was talking to God, not them. He was acting as the go-between between God and the people.

Churches

The churches reflected these beliefs. They were full of decorations – paintings and statues reminded the people of what they should believe and warned them of the dangers of hell.

Source 9

crucifix

ceiling decorated to represent 'the heavens'

pictures of saints

Massbook

bright colours

alcove for storing the consecrated bread and wine – the body and blood of Jesus

Server

Rood screen

gold

stained glass windows showing stories from the Bible

Chalice

Altar

Priest

Rushes on floor

Artist's impression of a typical church in 1530.

Did you know?

Even though the Church of England freed itself from the Pope's control in 1534, English monarchs still kept the title Defender of the Faith. If you have a £1 coin in your pocket or purse, take it out and have a look. On the side showing the monarch's head you will see the letters F.D. or Fid. Def. which stands for *fidei defensor*, the Latin term for Defender of the Faith.

Did you know?

The spread of printing from the mid-fifteenth century onwards had an important impact on religion. More people learned to read so ideas spread more quickly. This included ideas that the Church did not like and would previously have tried to control. Some compare it with the way that the internet spreads ideas nowadays.

Task

From the information on this page choose three of Henry's measures that you think the Protestants would agree with, and three that they would disagree with.

Martin Luther

Meanwhile in Europe a storm was about to break that was to turn Henry's legal reformation into a reformation of ideas and beliefs. For many years there had been rumblings of complaint against the Catholic Church. People protested about the misbehaviour of priests and bishops, cardinals and the Pope, monks and nuns. Humanists were university scholars who complained about the ignorance of the priests and the ways in which they frightened ordinary people into giving them money to escape purgatory.

On 31 October 1517, a monk called Martin Luther wrote a list of complaints about the Catholic Church called the *Ninety-Five Theses*. He nailed these complaints to the door of a church in Wittenberg in Germany. Luther did not like a number of things that went on in the Church.

- He did not like the idea of pilgrimages or praying to saints.
- He attacked the buying and selling of indulgences.
- Luther believed that all a true Christian needed was faith in God.
- He stressed the need for education of priests and the importance of publishing a Bible in the language spoken in a region, rather than in Latin.

Because of such 'protests' these people became known as 'Protestants'.

What impact did this have on Henry's Church?

Before we look at the impact of Luther's protest, it is important to get one thing straight. Henry was not a Protestant. Far from it: he enjoyed Catholic ceremonies. Indeed, in 1521 the Pope had given Henry the title 'Defender of the Faith' as a reward for an attack he made on Luther. Although Henry had argued with the Pope and taken over control of the Church in England he was very suspicious of the reformers' ideas in Europe. In 1535 in Germany, religious reformers had got rid of their ruler. Henry definitely did not want that happening in England!

However in a confusing series of Acts over the next eight years Henry introduced some Protestant ideas to the Church in England and kept some Catholic ones.

The Act of Ten Articles 1536

These were the three most important:

- During communion, Jesus' blood and body were present. This was called transubstantiation.
- People would go to heaven if they did good works on Earth and if they did anything wrong, they should do penance for the bad act.
- People should be baptised.

Injunctions, 1536 and 1538

- Priests were told to teach prayers and the Ten Commandments to children.
- The number of saints' days/holy days was cut.
- Pilgrimages were discouraged and Thomas Becket's shrine in Canterbury Cathedral, a focus of thousands of pilgrimages, was destroyed.
- Relics were to be removed from churches.
- Mary, the Mother of Jesus the son of God, was no longer to be considered as particularly important.
- Pictures in churches should be taken down.
- All parish churches were to register baptisms, marriages and burials by writing them down in books specially produced for the purpose.

The Great Bible, April 1539

In 1538, Henry ordered the introduction of the Great Bible, translated into English, a process that took several months. Every church should have a copy. This meant that, in theory, everyone could read it. However just to underline how confusing Henry's religious reforms were Henry also decreed in 1543 that only the most powerful people in England were allowed to read it. Henry did not like the idea of ordinary people being able to read the Bible. They might, after all, begin to get ideas above their station!

The Act of Six Articles June 1539

This Act confirmed the belief in transubstantiation, allowed priests to hold private Masses and the hearing of CONFESSIONS by priests. It said that priests could not marry and ordered automatic burning of anyone who denied the doctrine of transubstantiation.

Cromwell goes too far

> ### Task
>
> Your overall question for this unit is, 'What really mattered to Henry VIII?' What does the story of the rise and fall of Thomas Cromwell suggest really mattered to Henry: money, power, religion, or something else? Choose one and explain your choice.

Many of these changes were led by Thomas Cromwell. To start with he had Henry's support. But he began to move well beyond Henry's wishes. For example, the Bible in English was his idea; the smashing of the shrines was too. But Cromwell's most dangerous action was to start negotiations with the German Protestants. He was hoping for political alliances but others distrusted him and thought he was trying to turn England Protestant.

What followed is a pattern you will now be familiar with: a powerful adviser falls from favour, the King turns against him and the adviser ends up on the execution block. And once again, true to the Henry pattern, there is a new woman involved as well.

Things had not gone well between Henry and Anne Boleyn. Now Henry was desperately in love with Catherine Howard, the eighteen-year-old niece of the Duke of Norfolk. Norfolk was one of Henry's army leaders and also one of Cromwell's sworn enemies, and so it didn't take much for Norfolk to convince Henry that Cromwell was a traitor who intended to turn England Protestant. Cromwell was accused of treason and heresy, and executed.

Cromwell fell because he went too far, too fast, in developing Henry's religious policies in ways Henry didn't approve. Like Wolsey, Cromwell had no power base of his own. Henry had made him and Henry broke him.

The Pilgrimage of Grace, 1536

Many people were deeply saddened by the destruction of the monasteries. This was because the monasteries lay at the heart of their communities. They feared that, after the monasteries had been attacked, the parish churches would be next. The year of 1536 was also one of high food prices and many poor people faced starvation. They could no longer look to the monks and nuns for help.

How did the protest start?

In October 1536, thousands of people in Lincolnshire protested against the work of Thomas Cromwell's officials. Soon the protest spread to the north of England and a huge army of around 40,000 rebels prepared to march on London. They were led by a one-eyed Yorkshire gentleman who was a lawyer in London, called Robert Aske. He had contacts with some people at court who were supporters of Catherine of Aragon and who were opposed to everything Cranmer and Cromwell were doing. Throughout the protest, Aske and his followers stressed that they were loyal to the king: all they wanted was to petition him. This was a clever move on Aske's part. As rebels, they would be traitors and treason was punishable by death. By saying they were pilgrims, Aske put Henry VIII in a difficult position. All Catholics were encouraged to go on pilgrimages at this time. Henry could hardly mow them down. Besides, Henry only had a small army – much smaller than the pilgrim army that was making for London, picking up support from the local gentry as they marched south through Lancashire and Yorkshire. Led by monks and priests, they sang hymns and carried religious banners. The most important banner they carried was that of the Five Wounds of Christ.

The 'pilgrims' demanded:

- the removal of Cranmer and Cromwell as Henry's advisers
- the re-opening of all the monasteries and nunneries
- the restoration of the Princess Mary (Catherine of Aragon's daughter) as Henry VIII's heir.

Things were not looking good for Henry. He had never faced a rebellion before. He was used to total obedience from his subjects. He feared, too, that there would be a Catholic invasion from France led by Cardinal Pole in support of the pilgrimage.

Source ❿

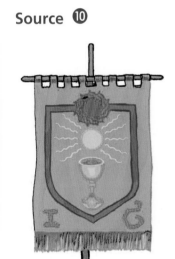

A drawing of the pilgrims' banner. At the centre it shows a chalice (communion cup) and the host (the bread which becomes the body of Christ). ❷ *Why do you think the pilgrims carried banners?*

WHAT WERE THE MOTIVES OF THE 'PILGRIMS'?

Were the supporters of the Pilgrimage of Grace honest people who wanted to preserve the Church and their communities? Or were they rebels who wanted to challenge the power of the King? Look at the evidence and see if you can decide.

Source Ⓐ

Because the rulers of this country do not defend us from being robbed by thieves and Scots, we have to rely on charity, faith, poverty and pity. We must be ready to help one another when thieves or Scots would rob us either by night or by day.

Marchers' Proclamation, October 1536.

Source Ⓑ

When every man rules, who shall obey? Those who are of a worse sort in society should be happy to let the wiser rule and govern them. There must be order in society and we must allow the better people to rule.

By Richard Morrison from A Remedy for Sedition *printed in December 1536. Morrison was a writer employed by Thomas Cromwell.*

Source Ⓒ

During the whole rising, not one leader tried to warn the followers of the pilgrimage that they were committing treason. This was because the leaders thought they were acting in the name of the King and that their rebellion was aimed at his advisers.

By Nicholas Leche, a Catholic priest, giving evidence while in the Tower of London in 1536.

Source Ⓓ

A picture of a bishop leading marchers on the Pilgrimage of Grace. The picture was drawn in the nineteenth century for a book on the history of England.

Source E

A picture of a banner carried by the marchers from Horncastle, October 1536.

Source F

The marchers said that they were defending the faith of Christ, the Church and the well-being of the people. They called this, their traitorous voyage, a holy and blessed pilgrimage. They had certain banners in the field whereon was painted Christ hanging on the cross on one side. I did not believe these banners for one minute. Under these banners marched the troops of Satan [the Devil] with their fake signs of holiness. In doing so they tricked the simple and ignorant people.

Written in the 1530s by the Tudor chronicler, Edward Hall.

Source G

Great God's fame
Does the Church proclaim
Now to be lame
And held in bonds.
Robbed, spoiled and shorn
Of cattle and corn,
House and lands.

A ballad composed by Catholic monks from a monastery near Lancashire, December 1536.

QUESTIONS

1 Look at **Source A**. How do the marchers criticise the government?

2 Look at **Source B**. According to Richard Morrison, how should the country be ruled?

3 Can you trust the evidence of **Source C**?

4 Look at **Source F**. In what ways does this source agree or disagree with **Sources D** and **E**?

5 Look at all of the sources. Which do you think would be least useful to someone studying the reasons why people joined the Pilgrimage of Grace? Explain your answer.

6 'Those who took part in the Pilgrimage of Grace were traitors.' Using all of the sources and your own knowledge, explain how far you agree or disagree with this statement.

How did Henry deal with the pilgrims?

Robert Aske and his army of pilgrims reached Doncaster, where they were met by the Duke of Norfolk, leader of Henry's (much smaller) army. Norfolk played for time, hoping the pilgrims would get fed up and go home, and the support of the gentry would fade away. Norfolk promised the rebels that:

● they would all have a free pardon
● Parliament would meet to discuss the pilgrims' demands
● Henry VIII would meet Robert Aske to talk about the pilgrims' petition.

But he secretly wrote to Henry saying: 'I beseech you to take in good part whatsoever promise I make to the rebels, for surely I shall observe no part thereof.'

Henry gave Norfolk permission to offer Robert Aske a pardon to all rebels, and a parliament meeting in York to discuss the issues they had raised. The pilgrimage was over. Aske's pilgrims, thinking they had won, went home. Aske toured the north of England trying to sell the deal to which he had agreed to the local gentry.

However, Henry had no intention of keeping his promises. He hadn't signed an agreement saying the pilgrims would all be pardoned, and, in any case, he didn't believe that promises made to rebels should be kept.

The following year some of the 'pilgrims' joined a riot in Hull, led by Sir Francis Bigod. The rioters were angry that there had been no moves to set up the promised parliament to listen to their complaints. They hoped to capture Hull and force Henry to set up the parliament. This played directly into Henry's hands: it gave him the opportunity to get his own back. He sent his army north with strict orders to make sure that 'dreadful execution be done upon a good number, by hanging them up in trees and by quartering them'. Henry intended to teach the people of Lancashire and Yorkshire a lesson they wouldn't forget. Robert Aske was thrown into the Tower of London, interrogated and later executed at York. Nearly 200 northerners were hanged, as Henry had ordered, their bodies left rotting in trees as a warning to anyone thinking of rebelling again.

Task

Your overall question for this unit is, 'What really mattered to Henry VIII?' What do you think really mattered to Henry in dealing with the Pilgrimage of Grace: money, power, religion, or something else? Choose one and explain your choice.

2.3 How did Henry try to impress his European rivals?

What... ?

HENRY VIII'S FOREIGN POLICY

Henry was keenly interested in what was going on in Europe. Most of this unit is focused on what was going on at home but that is not how he would have seen his priorities. England was much less important in European affairs than France or the newly unified Spain. Henry wanted to have more influence so he watched events in Europe carefully, looking out for opportunities to win friends or gain an advantage. He never really succeeded – although in the process he did get sucked into some expensive and rather disastrous wars, mostly against France, but also later with Scotland. And these wars are one of the reasons he was so keen to take over the wealth of the monasteries – to pay his war debts. Foreign policy and domestic policy were closely linked – as they so often are in history.

You have seen that Henry, like all great princes of the time, loved show and pageantry. In the days before television and radio, these were two of the ways in which rulers showed off how powerful and grand they were. They did it to impress other rulers as well as their own court and people.

Background: war in Europe

The major powers of Europe had been fighting each other and making and breaking alliances on and off since the 1490s. Their quarrel was long and complicated, and involved lands in Italy. England was a minor power by comparison but Francis I of France and Charles V, the Holy Roman Emperor, were both anxious to have Henry VIII of England on their side before they started fighting each other again. This was 1520. Henry had only been king for eleven years. He was an ambitious young man. Henry was flattered to be courted by the two most powerful rulers in Europe. He and Wolsey started to work out with which ruler they wanted to ally if war between Francis and Charles really did break out.

The Field of the Cloth of Gold

Wolsey planned to impress Francis with Henry's splendour, thus, so the theory went, Francis would want Henry as a rich and powerful ally. Wolsey masterminded the English side of a magnificent occasion that was held in France, just outside Calais. The idea of the event was for each king to display his power by competing to provide the best feasts, music, jousting, and games.

The tents and clothes used so much gold, that the event was named the 'Field of the Cloth of Gold'. It cost the English Treasury an enormous amount of money – the equivalent to its income for a whole year. Was it worth it?

It was really just a fortnight-long jousting tournament and, although Henry and Francis never actually fought each other, both monarchs (very tactfully!) were declared to be the most successful jousters there. Henry declared himself well pleased with the whole event and with the prestige it brought him. Apart from this, nothing of any diplomatic value was achieved. Two years later, France and England were at war with each other.

Source 11

Guisnes – Henry stayed here

Cloth dragon – this was fired into the air to announce Mass

Thomas Wolsey

Henry VIII

The field – where the kings met

Ardres – Francis stayed here

Artificial tree decorated with the English symbol (hawthorn) and the French symbol (raspberry)

The tiltyard – where the jousting tournaments took place

Prefabricated palace made of wood with a triumphal arch for the King to enter through. There was an arch at each end of the field

Fountain flowing with wine

The Field of the Cloth of Gold, *painted by an unknown artist.*

- Religion – so much of what he did was about religion. Was preserving the Catholic faith the most important thing?
- Power – politicians need power. That is the only way to get things done. But did Henry become power-mad? Or did he want power so that he could govern effectively?
- Prestige – was he most worried about what people thought of him?

Work in six groups. Take one topic each and prepare a presentation, using a computer if you can, on your topic. You should aim to prove that this was the most important thing to Henry. Amass as much evidence as you can. Use this book but you might do some extra research as well.

At the end take a class vote – which of the candidates do you think most mattered to Henry?

UNIT 3 Edward VI: unfinished business!

What is this all about?

Henry VIII did, finally, get an heir. His third wife, Jane Seymour, gave birth to a healthy baby boy, Edward, on 12 October 1537. But just nine years later Henry himself died without having had any more children, despite marrying three more times. So a nine-year-old boy became King of England. And in Tudor times that raised a lot of questions: What would happen next? Who would advise him? What would he do? Would Edward be up to the challenge? Most importantly for people at that time: what would he do with the Church? His father's religious policies had seemed confusing, contradictory and disruptive. What path would Edward take?

In part 1 you will examine Edward's religious changes and the reaction to them. In part 2 you will study some other important changes taking place during Edward's reign.

3.1 How did people react to Edward's reformation?

What... ?

PUERPERAL FEVER
A fever caused by infection after childbirth. In the sixteenth century this was the most common cause of death amongst women.

Henry VIII was delighted to have a son at last. He made sure everything possible was done to keep the baby Edward fit and healthy. The walls of his room were washed three times a day; he had only the best quality food, carefully prepared in spotless kitchens; and an army of servants was employed to attend to his every need. Edward's mother had died of puerperal fever giving birth to him so the most important person to Edward was his nurse, Mother Jack. Regular reports on the baby's progress were sent to Thomas Cromwell who, we must guess, conveyed them to Henry.

Edward's education

When he was six, Edward's education began in earnest. He learned Latin and Greek, history and geography, French and German, fencing, lute playing and horsemanship. And he also studied the Bible – a lot.

Henry also wanted Edward to get to know other boys of his own age, and so he ordered a palace school to be set up, where fourteen children of the nobility were taught alongside Edward. Of course people exaggerated his abilities and skills, but he does seem to have been quite a clever boy who was more interested in intellectual things than in sport and games.

Edward's tutors were hand-picked by Henry. Henry chose people who he thought were best at the job of educating a young prince. Henry wanted the best for his son. He wanted forward-thinking people who would

What... ?

HUMANISTS
People who valued the study of Roman and Greek literature and all things to do with the classical world.

Task

Look carefully at Source 1.

1 Can you find: two men fighting with swords; houses along the route hung with colourful banners; people standing on rooftops to get a good view?

2 What can you learn from this painting about:
   a) the attitudes to the coronation of people at the time?
   b) the attitudes of the people who commissioned the painting?

develop the young prince's all-round talents. However it may surprise you, given what you know about Henry's religious beliefs, that these teachers were mostly Protestants or Humanists. They taught the young prince to study the Bible with the eyes of a Protestant, not those of a Catholic.

One of his half-sisters, Elizabeth, was educated in the same way. The other, Mary, was educated by Catholic teachers. This difference was going to become very important in the future. But more of that later...

From Prince to King

King Henry VIII died in the early morning of 28 January 1547. Prince Edward's uncle broke the news to the prince and his half-sister, Princess Elizabeth. The children clung to each other, sobbing and afraid. The terrifying, unpredictable Henry, their father and king, had gone. The future, for the nine-year-old boy and the fourteen-year-old girl, was uncertain and frightening. Edward's uncle knelt in front of him, showing him the loyalty due to a king, and then whisked him off to London before anyone else could try to seize control. No one knows when 30-year-old Mary was told, nor how she reacted.

Source ❶

Edward VI's coronation procession, London, February 1547.

The Council of Regency

When a king is too young to rule by himself a single person is usually appointed regent to rule until he grows up. But in this case it was different. Henry VIII made a will just before he died. In it he laid down that England was to be ruled by a council of regency, consisting of sixteen men he trusted absolutely. They were to rule in Edward's name until he was old enough to rule by himself. There was to be no leader in Edward's council: they were to work together and rule England in his name.

It didn't quite work out like that. Edward's uncle, the Duke of Somerset, quickly took over as leader of the Council and Lord Protector of the young Edward. Somerset and most of the leading members of the Council were 'secret' Protestants – that is, they had Protestant attitudes but they had kept these attitudes secret while Henry VIII was alive. Now they had the chance, if they guided the young king correctly, to bring about some of the changes they wanted to make to the English Church.

But remember...

They were still only Edward's advisers. Edward was a strong, healthy boy of nine years. Everyone's best guess, in 1547, was that in nine years' time, when he reached eighteen, Edward would be ruling by himself. If his advisers had, while he was a child, pushed him to bring in policies with which he really disagreed, they wouldn't have lasted long once he was ruling alone! So it's safe to say that the changes introduced by Somerset and then Northumberland were worked out with Edward and had his approval.

A cautious start

Somerset and Edward at first worked cautiously. They didn't want to risk another rebellion like the Pilgrimage of Grace! But, to be sure, Somerset imprisoned the Duke of Norfolk, the leading Catholic nobleman, in the Tower of London. Somerset didn't want anyone stirring up trouble and perhaps leading a rebellion.

Under Henry Protestants had been persecuted. Somerset worked closely with Thomas Cranmer (see page 29) to change this.

- The Act of Six Articles of 1539 (see page 38) was abolished. Protestants would no longer be burned for refusing to worship in the Catholic way.
- The censorship of books and sermons was relaxed. Protestants could now talk and write about their beliefs in ways that would have been impossible in the reign of Henry VIII.

Protestants who had left England under Henry now began to return. They brought with them other Protestants who were facing persecution in Europe because of their beliefs.

Edward's Protestant Reformation now gathered speed. Over the next three years the following changes were made in English churches.

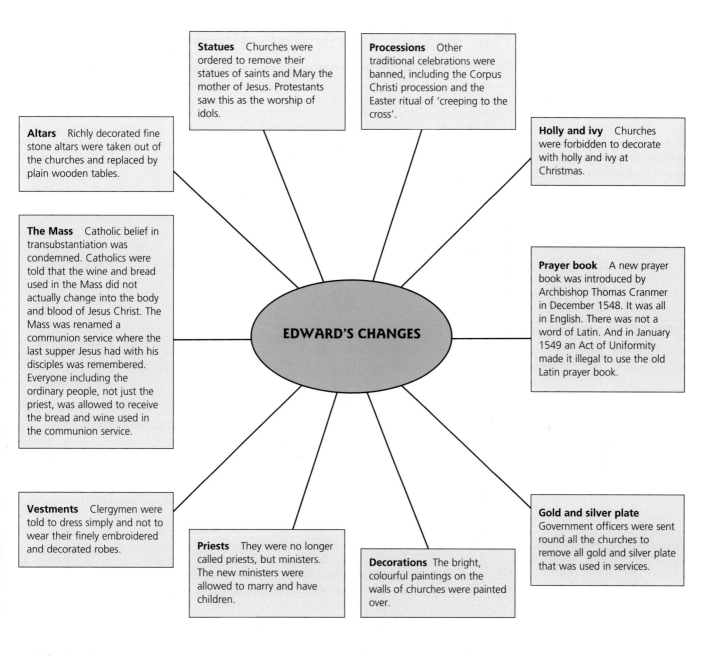

Statues Churches were ordered to remove their statues of saints and Mary the mother of Jesus. Protestants saw this as the worship of idols.

Processions Other traditional celebrations were banned, including the Corpus Christi procession and the Easter ritual of 'creeping to the cross'.

Holly and ivy Churches were forbidden to decorate with holly and ivy at Christmas.

Altars Richly decorated fine stone altars were taken out of the churches and replaced by plain wooden tables.

The Mass Catholic belief in transubstantiation was condemned. Catholics were told that the wine and bread used in the Mass did not actually change into the body and blood of Jesus Christ. The Mass was renamed a communion service where the last supper Jesus had with his disciples was remembered. Everyone including the ordinary people, not just the priest, was allowed to receive the bread and wine used in the communion service.

EDWARD'S CHANGES

Prayer book A new prayer book was introduced by Archbishop Thomas Cranmer in December 1548. It was all in English. There was not a word of Latin. And in January 1549 an Act of Uniformity made it illegal to use the old Latin prayer book.

Vestments Clergymen were told to dress simply and not to wear their finely embroidered and decorated robes.

Priests They were no longer called priests, but ministers. The new ministers were allowed to marry and have children.

Decorations The bright, colourful paintings on the walls of churches were painted over.

Gold and silver plate Government officers were sent round all the churches to remove all gold and silver plate that was used in services.

What... ?

CORPUS CHRISTI
The feast of Corpus Christi was first observed in England in 1318. It became a major event, with processions and miracle plays in many towns. Houses along the route of the procession would be decorated with flowers and lights.

CREEPING TO THE CROSS
On Good Friday, the day on which Christians mark the crucifixion of Jesus Christ, parishioners would make their way on their knees to a cross set up in their local parish church, and kiss it.

Task

Study the diagram above. Place these ten changes on a copy of this line. Which do you expect to be most controversial and meet the most opposition? Which will be the least controversial?

Most _____ Least
controversial   controversial

49

The Prayer Book Rebellion of 1549

In 1547 a Mr William Body arrived in Cornwall. His job was to go from church to church ensuring people made the changes ordered by Edward. His men removed and smashed statues. They painted over decorations. They removed the gold and silver plate. As the news spread of Body's exploits, in 1548 a group of men in the Cornish town of Helston decided to murder him. The gentry quickly dealt with the plot – William Body survived to continue his work – but they couldn't stop the people hating Body and all that he stood for.

The trigger

Then in 1549 along came the English Prayer Book. For the people of Devon and Cornwall this was the last straw. The old, familiar service was gone. They were forced to worship God in English.

The march

Things came to a head in June. In the tiny village of Sampford Courtenay, the people made their priest deliver the Mass in Latin. And ten days later angry people from Devon and Cornwall met at Bodmin and wrote out a list of complaints. They wanted religion to go back to the way it was in Henry VIII's day. They demanded that heretics be punished as they had been in Henry's time. They wanted to see Archbishop Cranmer, whom they regarded as the chief heretic, burned at the stake. Then, led by Humphrey Arundell, they marched towards Exeter. They carried the banner of the Five Wounds of Christ – just as the rebels taking part in the Pilgrimage of Grace had done.

The first victim

The local gentry did their best to control and contain the situation. But they didn't succeed. In Devon, a gentleman called Mr Hellier who tried to stop them, was hacked to pieces. Sir Peter Carew, the head of the most important family in Devon and a Protestant, took over. He did no better. The rebels met with him and, after a pretty tense exchange of views, chased him back to Exeter. By 23 June a rebel army surrounded Exeter.

The negotiator

The Duke of Somerset asked Lord Russell, a Catholic member of the Council, to work out a solution. Somerset had other things to worry about: troubles on the border with Scotland, problems with the French and riots in the Midlands. He offered Russell a small army if he needed it.

Russell first tried to negotiate with the rebels but got nowhere so, on 28 July, he and his army advanced against the rebels. He defeated them at Fenny Bridges and Clyst St Mary, relieved Exeter and finally finished off most of the rebel army at Sampford Courtenay, where it had all begun.

Source ❷

Task

Role play

The rebel leader Humphrey Arundell is face to face with Sir Peter Carew.

- **Carew** knows his job is to do what the King wants. He is a Protestant who believes in Edward's changes. But he also wants to ensure peace in his area. He knows what happened to the last person to confront the rebels. He fears for his life.

- **Arundell** is very unhappy at the way that churches are being changed. Outside he has hundreds of even angrier, armed men. He wants to persuade Carew to see sense, to join his side and to help stop these heretical changes. Or else.

In pairs, work out what might have been said by each side. You can act out for others your discussion or argument if your teacher will let you!

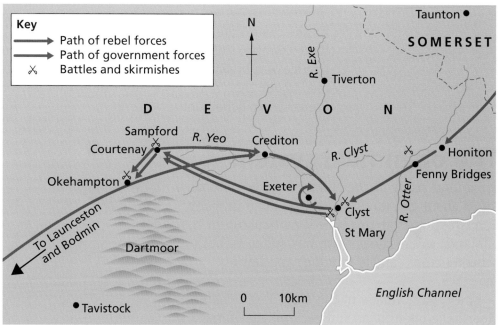

This map shows you where the Prayer Book Rebellion (sometimes called the Western Rising) happened.

The punishments

The rebel army may have been defeated, but small pockets of rebels held out in the villages and moors of the West Country. When they were caught, rebels were hanged without trial and their property given away to government supporters.

Robert Welsh, the vicar of the church of St Thomas in Exeter, was suspected of being a leader of the rebellion. Russell's soldiers dressed him in his vestments and hanged him from gallows they had erected on his church tower, with 'a holy water bucket, a sprinkle, a sacring bell, a pair of beeds, and such other like popish trash hanged about him.'

An estimated 3,000 rebels were executed in all.

The end of Somerset

Were Edward and his Council pleased about all this? No, they were not! Of course they were pleased that the rebels had been defeated, but not the way in which it was done. Introducing the Protestant Reformation was difficult enough for them without having soldiers acting in such a bloodthirsty way. Edward survived the Prayer Book Rebellion, but Somerset did not. The nobles on the Council suspected that he had approved the bloodthirsty punishments. They did not trust him any more. They sent him to the Tower of London in October 1549 and he was executed three years later.

3.2 Trouble in the countryside

At the same time that the Prayer Book Rebellion was taking place in the West Country, 200 miles away in the middle of England a different kind of trouble was brewing for Edward with an apparently different cause. As you read about this, note down any similarities with or differences from the Prayer Book Rebellion.

The open field system

From your study of the Middle Ages you probably know about the way farming was done in many English villages at this time – particularly in the Midlands where the climate was suited to both growing crops (arable farming) and raising livestock.

In a typical village in the early 1500s there were large open fields and each villager farmed strips in each field. They agreed what to grow each year and the crops would be rotated: wheat one year, barley the next, then left fallow for one year (grass was grown and animals were grazed) so the soil could recover and nutrients be replaced.

As well as the open fields there were usually several other shared resources:

- Each villager had the right to rear cattle, sheep, chickens and goats on the common land.
- Often they had rights to harvest hay from the common meadowland to feed their animals.
- If there was woodland nearby, all villagers would have the right to collect fallen trees to be used as fuel in their homes as well as for building.
- Villagers were allowed to keep pigs in the woods, where they ate acorns and other delicacies.
- Many villages had a well for water which everyone shared, and access to a nearby stream or river was also important for washing purposes as well as being a ready source of fish for food.

Source ❸

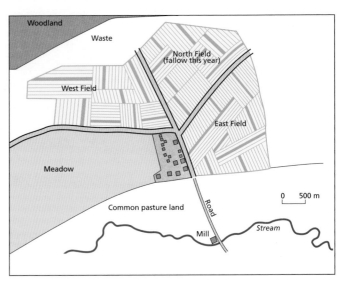

The strip system of medieval farming. One person's strips are shaded green.

Task

Work with a partner to draw up a list of advantages of this system of farming.

Most villagers did not own their land. They rented it from the landowner. The livestock raised by the villagers was an important resource. Many animals were killed in the winter and the meat preserved in salt: this gave people something to eat once last year's harvest ran out in the so-called 'hungry months'.

Enclosure

Enclosing land means putting hedges and fences around land that had once been open countryside, common land or great open fields. During the Tudor period many landowners decided to enclose their land and raise sheep instead of growing crops. This was not a new idea but it was becoming more common in the Tudor period for three reasons.

1 The demand for wool   Wool was Britain's biggest industry, and it was booming. Good wool fetched a much higher price than good grain. English cloth was sold all over Europe.

2 The costs of labour   Gone were the days of the feudal system where the villeins had to work the landowners' land for one day a week. Now if a landowner wanted workers he had to pay them. One worker could look after thousands of sheep in an enclosed field. It would take many workers to grow the same value of corn.

3 Improving your stock   New books were appearing written by experts that helped farmers to raise bigger, better, fitter, woollier sheep through a managed breeding programme. But this all depended on keeping your animals separate from someone else's. You did not want your animals mingling with diseased or inferior animals. Your wool would be less valuable.

Source ❹

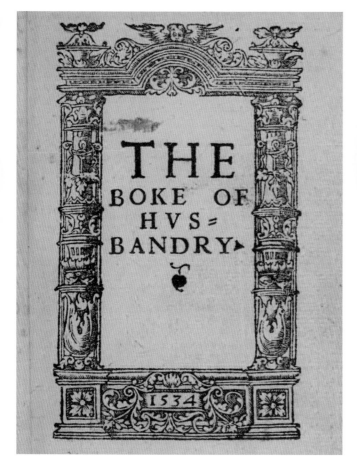

The Boke of Husbandry *by Anthony Fitzherbert gave practical advice on hundreds of topics (see box, right).*

Task

1 Choose two of the following characters and complete the word bubble for them.

> *Enclosure is a good thing because …*

- The sheep farmer
- The landowner
- The sheep improver
- The wool merchant

2 Work in pairs to identify all the reasons why you think a typical villager in the open field system might be against enclosure.

Tips from the Boke of Husbandry:
- Oxen are better for ploughing in tough clay and on hilly ground, as long as you had some nice pasture for them to graze on overnight.
- Sow barley in well-dunged soil, in March.
- Cow dung is much better than horse dung as manure.
- Thistles are an ill weed and prevent shearers working cleanly.
- Make a rake in the winter, when sitting by the fire with nothing else to do.

Visit http://www.gardenhistoryinfo.com /medieval/fitzherbert02.html for more tips!

Who criticised enclosure?

It will be obvious to you that enclosure could spell problems for some villagers. But they were not its only critics.

Source 5

Your sheep that were so meek and tame and such small eaters, now, as I have been told, have become such great eaters that they eat up and swallow men. They take over and devour whole fields, houses and towns. If you look in any part of the country that grows the finest and most expensive wool, there you find noblemen and gentlemen who leave no land for ploughing. They enclose all into pastures for grazing. They tear down houses; they pull down towns; they leave nothing standing except the church to be made into a sheep house.

The husbandmen [peasant farmers] are thrown off the land. They choose to sell their land, either because they are tricked, threatened with violence or simply by being worn down to the point that they give up. These poor, silly, wretched souls: men, women, husbands, wives, fatherless children, widows, woeful mothers, with their young babes, are forced off the land. Away they trudge, from their houses, but finding no place to rest in. They are forced to sell all of their household stuff for next to nothing. The little they get they spend and then what can they then else do but steal? If caught they are hanged, or else go about a-begging.

Sir Thomas More, writing in his book Utopia, *published in 1516.*

Sir Thomas More was not alone in raising objections to enclosure. Church leaders such as Bishop Latimer claimed that enclosure was harming society. Government officials such as John Hales travelled the country in the 1540s and reported back their worries about the impact of enclosure, especially in areas where there was de-population (people leaving the countryside and moving to find jobs). However they did not and could not stop the spread of enclosure, because the gentry were in charge of local government and were the very people who were enclosing the land.

Enclosure riots

More direct opposition to enclosure came from those whose lives were affected by it. Throughout the sixteenth century there were enclosure 'riots' – attempts to stop planned enclosures or reverse enclosures that had taken place. They are called riots but usually the protests were peaceful. Typically a few fences were broken down and villagers put their animals onto enclosed land that had previously been common land. In some cases they ploughed up land that had been enclosed and converted to pasture.

Punishment was rarely harsh. Indeed, in some areas magistrates were quite sympathetic to the protesters' complaints against their loss of ancient rights to use common land – particularly in the 1540s when a series of droughts pushed up food prices and led to starvation in some areas. In Suffolk the Earl of Hertford treated with kindness those brought before him who had pulled down enclosure fences.

Usually enclosure rioters were whipped or fined. These were not considered harsh punishments at that time.

However, occasionally, protests against enclosure got out of hand or became mixed up with other issues. In 1549 the government faced protests in 23 separate counties. In these cases, the government was prepared to act quickly and harshly. The most serious happened in Norfolk in 1549.

Kett's rebellion, 1549

You might not expect a landowner to lead a protest against enclosure but in 1549 Robert Kett, a Norfolk landowner, did just that.

On **8 July 1549**, trouble broke out in Wymondham, Norfolk. A large group of prosperous townspeople, local farmers and ordinary farmworkers started tearing down enclosure fences in the middle of a drunken party. They attacked the property of Robert Kett, a local landowner. But in a strange turnaround, rather than trying to stop them, Kett took charge and on **9 July** he led 16,000 protesters to Norwich, the county town.

On **12 July** the rebels set up camp on Mousehold Heath, outside Norwich. They drew up a list of grievances they wanted King Edward VI to put right (see Source A on page 56). Robert Kett said that they were loyal to the Crown. Their protest was against powerful landowners.

Ten days later, Kett and the rebels attacked and occupied Norwich. They were trying to make the King take notice and listen to them. He did, but not in the way they wanted. A royal army of just 1,500 men arrived. They took Norwich, but after just one day the rebels were back in charge. The government, seriously alarmed, sent a force of about 12,000 men, who recaptured Norwich and held it, despite being bombarded by the rebels for nearly two weeks.

On **27 August** Kett and his men fought the King's troops in open battle at Dussindale and were soundly defeated. About 3,000 men, mostly rebels, were killed.

Robert Kett was charged with treason. He pleaded guilty and was sentenced to death. On **7 December 1549** he was hanged from the walls of Norwich castle. His body was left to rot until, several months later, people complained about the smell and it was cut down.

So, what had supposedly started as a protest against economic conditions had clearly got badly out of hand. The government officials sent to sort it out had made big mistakes.

What... ?

SHEEP-CORN
An area where land was rotated between sheep grazing and barley being grown. There was no enclosure, just open fields.

WOOD-PASTURE
An area where land was rotated between cattle grazing and wheat being grown. This land was already enclosed.

Source **6**

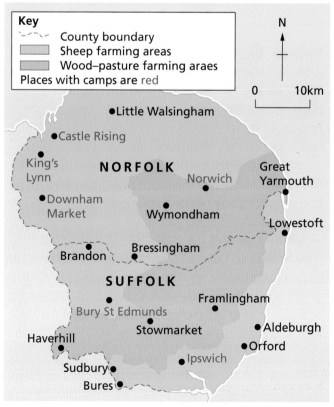

Map of Norfolk and Suffolk showing the rebel camps, types of farming and main towns.

DID ROBERT KETT GET WHAT HE DESERVED?

Source A

1 We ask your Grace that from now on, no man shall be allowed to enclose land any more.

2 We ask your Grace that no lord of the manor shall be allowed to use the common land.

3 We ask that priests from now on shall not be allowed to buy land, and that the lands they have may be rented to ordinary men, as they were in the first year of the reign of Henry VII.

4 We ask that any priest who cannot preach lose his job.

5 We ask that all bond men may be free, for God made all free.

Some of the 29 requests drawn up by Robert Kett and the rebels that were presented to Edward VI in July 1549.

Source B

The people suddenly gathered together in Norfolk and increased to a great number. They began to stay upon a hill near to the town of Norwich, which looked after them. The Earl of Warwick came with 6,000 men and 1,500 horsemen and entered into the town of Norwich. But having won it, he could not defend it. Often the rebels came into the streets, killing his men. The townsmen were given to mischief themselves.

Warwick stopped the rebels' supplies for three days and so forced them to move from the hill.

The Earl of Warwick then overcame them in plain battle, killing 2,000 of them and taking Kett, their captain. In January following, he was hanged at Norwich and his head hanged out.

From the Chronicle, *written by King Edward VI. The King was eleven years old at the time of the rebellion, and wrote this account shortly after it ended.*

Source C

The city began to withstand the rebels. As the rebels came from the hill they were shot at with a great number of arrows. So desperate were the rebels for weapons that their vagabond boys came amongst the shower of arrows and gathered them up. Some of the arrows stuck in their legs. The boys most shamefully turned up their bare bottoms against those who shot. This so insulted the archers that it took the heart from them.

Also for lack of powder they couldn't shoot. And also many of the citizens were in their houses about their business at eleven or twelve of the clock. The ragged boys and desperate vagabonds came in great numbers with spears, swords and some with pitchforks and so were able to enter the city.

From The Commotion in Norfolk *by Nicholas Sotherton, written in about 1559. In 1549, Sotherton was a wealthy citizen of Norwich. He was there at the time of the rebellion, and saw what happened.*

Source D

A large crowd of thieves met together, drawn by the hope of loot. There were almost 16,000 dangerous men in Kett's camp. They entered the houses of gentlemen, robbing them. They took away and carried into the camp what cattle they found in the field, money in the houses, or corn in the barns. Many hid their loot into holes and corners. Everyone heaped up wealth secretly for himself.

When Kett and the other leaders were told this, they agreed to hold a court of justice. There was an old oak with great spreading boughs where Kett and the other governors sat to hear and judge complaints and quarrels. Sometimes they took everything away from the greedy.

From Norfolk Furies, *written by Alexander Neville in 1575. He based it on the memoirs of Archbishop Matthew Parker, who visited the camp at Mousehold Heath on 12 and 13 July. Parker tried to persuade the rebels to disband, but fled when the rebels objected to his sermons.*

Source E

> We, the King's friends and deputies, do grant licence to all men to provide and bring into the camp at Mousehold all manner of cattle, and provision of supplies wherever they may find them, providing that no violence or injury be done to any honest or poor man.

A warrant issued by Kett authorising the collection of supplies for the rebel army on Mousehold Heath.

Source **F**

A picture by Norfolk artist, Samuel Wale, painted in 1746–47. It shows the scene on

Mousehold Heath in 1549 when a herald delivered the King's message, offering a free pardon if the rebels would disperse. This happened before the rebels decided to occupy Norwich.

QUESTIONS

1 Study **Source A**. What does this source tell you about the situation in Norfolk in 1549?

2 Study **Sources B** and **C**. Which account of events in Norwich would you trust the most? Why?

3 Study **Sources D** and **E**. 'Robert Kett ran a well-organised camp at Mousehold Heath that didn't threaten law and order.' Do you agree?

4 Study **Source F**. How likely is it that the artist Samuel Wale has painted an accurate picture of what Mousehold Heath was like on 22 August 1549?

5 Study all the sources. 'Robert Kett was a rebel and a traitor who got the punishment he deserved.' How far do you agree with this view? Use the sources and what you know to explain your answer.

Task

List the similarities and differences between The Prayer Book Rebellion (page 50) and Kett's Rebellion. Which do you think Edward should be most worried about?

Task

1 Edward kept a careful chronicle of what happened during his reign. There is a sample in Source B on page 56. We don't have his account of the meeting with Northumberland in May, but what do you think he would have written? Write an entry describing those events. You will have to decide whether you think:
a) Edward was forced to make a will overruling his father's wishes, or
b) Edward genuinely wanted Lady Jane Grey to be queen instead of Mary his half-sister.

You could start it: 'I was visited by my adviser Lord Northumberland. He asked me…'

Edward dies

By 1552 Edward VI was taking an increasingly active role in government. He was attending Council meetings. In view of his advanced skills Parliament had decided that, instead of waiting until he was eighteen to take full powers as king, Edward would reach 'the age of majority' when he was sixteen the following year.

But in January 1553 Edward became seriously ill. He had a chest infection (probably tuberculosis). Doctors warned the Council that he could die. There was a flurry of worry – who would succeed to the throne? But Edward survived and by May his doctors were predicting a full recovery. No problem. These things happen.

Then at the end of May he got suddenly worse. He could only sleep with the help of drugs and was coughing up foul-smelling mucus.

Henry VIII's will

A monarch's will was very important. It laid down who should be the next monarch. Parliament and the judges had to take notice of it. You will remember how important Henry VIII's will had been in setting up what would happen when the young Edward became king. Henry had also planned even further ahead. Henry's will stated that if Edward had no children, then the throne should pass to Henry's eldest daughter Mary and then his younger daughter Elizabeth. Everyone knew this. It had been agreed by Parliament. But they also knew that Mary had been raised a Catholic. She would want to undo all that Edward had done to make England Protestant. So was Catholic Mary to be the next monarch? Not if Edward and, more importantly, his now most senior adviser the Duke of Northumberland could help it!

Edward's will

When he first became ill in January 1553, Edward made some notes making it clear he did not want his Catholic half-sister, Mary, to succeed him. At the end of May, when things for Edward took a turn for the worse, Northumberland and his law officers visited him. Edward's will was formally drawn up, stating that the throne should pass to Lady Jane Grey and from there to her male heirs. Lady Jane Grey was one of Edward's cousins and the granddaughter of Henry VIII's sister Mary, so she could trace her ancestry right back to the start of the Tudor dynasty. And guess what? She was married to Northumberland's son.

How did Edward (if it was Edward) explain away the claims of his half-sisters Mary and Elizabeth? He said that Henry's marriage to Mary's mother, Catherine of Aragon, and Henry's marriage to Elizabeth's mother, Anne Boleyn, were 'clearly and lawfully undone'. This meant that Mary and Elizabeth were illegitimate and so couldn't inherit. Simple!

Source ⑦

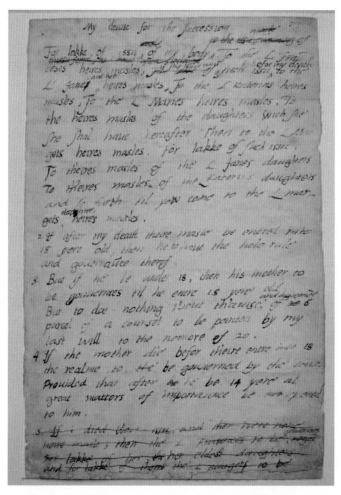

This is part of Edward's will. Look closely. ❓ *Can you see any signs that it might have been altered after Edward had written it?*

The law officers, headed by the Lord Chief Justice Montague, were appalled by what they were asked to do. Edward was not yet eighteen so couldn't make a will. He most certainly couldn't override a parliamentary statute that stated Mary should inherit after Edward if he had no children. Mary was Edward's legitimate heir. Reluctantly, under great pressure from Northumberland Montague agreed to draw up the will, but warned everyone that it wasn't legal.

But on 6 July 1553, before Parliament could confirm the will, Edward died, aged fifteen years and eight months. He had no children. So Henry's will was still valid. What a mess! It was up to Northumberland and Mary to decide what to do next.

Task

2 What do you think will happen next? You may already know but if you don't:
a) Who do you think will be crowned queen – Mary or Lady Jane Grey?
b) Will England become more Protestant or more Catholic?

Summary task

Most Common Entrance essays ask you to a) describe and b) explain.
- A describe question invites you to impress the examiner with your knowledge of what happened.
- An explain question invites you to impress the examiner with your understanding and analysis.

You can get advice about this on pages 190–92. But for now try your hand at this question that asks you to sum up the big issues in Edward's reign.
a) Describe the way Edward and his advisers changed English churches.
b) Explain whether these changes were successful.

Source ⑧

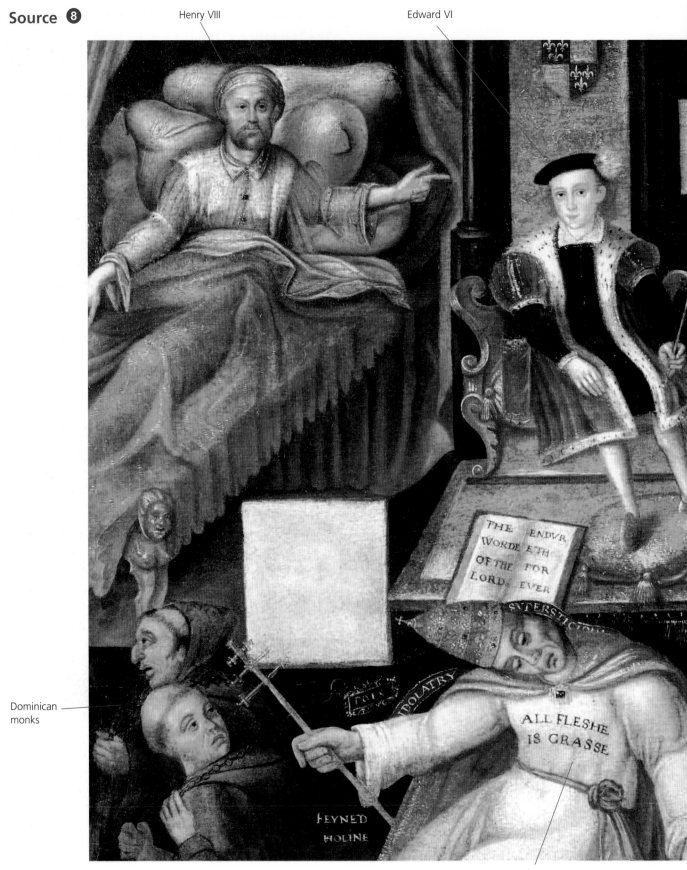

Henry VIII

Edward VI

Dominican monks

Pope Paul III

Protector Somerset   Thomas Seymour   Thomas Cranmer, Archbishop of Canterbury

Edward VI and the Pope, or an allegory of the Reformation under Edward VI. This painting, by an unknown artist c. 1570, includes portraits of all the key people involved in the religious changes during Edward's reign. Like many Tudor paintings, it is loaded with meaning. As the audience, you are meant to discover its message from the clues provided. See if you can decode this painting on the religious situation in Edward's reign.

Task

1 What are the monks in the bottom left corner doing?

2 What is happening to the Pope?

3 Who or what do you think Henry is pointing at and why?

4 What is going on in the background, top right?

5 What do you think is the overall message of the painting?

6 The four blank spaces were supposed to have text written in them but it was never added. Write your own short statements for each blank to give the meaning of the painting.

UNIT 4 Mary I: she did it her way!

> **What is this all about?**
> Mary had not expected to become queen. But when the opportunity unexpectedly arose she seized it with total commitment and with rather unpredictable results.
>
> This unit is all about stubbornness. In part 1 it is about the stubbornness of a woman who was determined to be queen; in part 2 the stubbornness of a queen determined to bring England back to Catholic ways; in part 3 the stubbornness of an English queen intent on marrying the Catholic monarch of her choice.
>
> Where did Mary's stubbornness take her? Could she have succeeded if she had been more willing to compromise? Read this unit and make up your mind.

4.1 'I <u>will</u> be your queen!'

Source ❶

Portrait of Mary Tudor painted in 1554 by the artist Antonio Moro.

We finished Unit 3 with the fate of the Tudors hanging in the balance. Edward VI had done his best to stop his half-sisters, Mary and Elizabeth, from inheriting their father's throne. Most councillors and Members of Parliament were prepared to accept Northumberland's plan for Lady Jane Grey to become queen but the Princess Mary was no pushover.

Northumberland decided he had to capture Mary and imprison her. Two claimants to the throne, both standing their ground, could lead to civil war and that would be a disaster. Northumberland had his golden opportunity on 6 July 1553. Mary was travelling from her home at Kenninghall in Norfolk to Greenwich in London to visit her dying half-brother Edward. No one knows exactly why but, suddenly, nearing London, Mary and her retinue stopped. They turned round and raced back as fast as they could for home and safety. Maybe Mary scented danger. Perhaps someone tipped her off that Edward was already dead; perhaps she guessed what Northumberland was up to. Northumberland had missed his chance. Back in her powerbase of Kenninghall, Mary and her advisers took three days to work out their plan of action.

Mary takes action

Mary had no intention of stepping aside for Lady Jane Grey. Indeed, she had no intention of stepping anywhere at all, except to London for her coronation. She believed she had everything on her side. She was her father's chosen heir. And as a Catholic, she viewed all later marriages of her father as unlawful in the sight of God. She was, she believed, his rightful heir in the sight of God.

On 9 July Mary wrote to the Privy Council asserting her right to the throne. She wrote to cities and towns throughout the country as well as a wide range of powerful individuals telling them the same thing: she was Queen Mary I and she intended to inherit the throne of her father. She quickly gained a whole range of supporters, rich and poor, humble and powerful, which was exactly what she intended. The Duke of Northumberland had been outmanoeuvred, but he wasn't finished yet.

Northumberland reacts

Northumberland continued with his plan. On 10 July, Lady Jane Grey was proclaimed Queen Jane in London. Northumberland set out for East Anglia with some soldiers, determined to arrest Mary. He was treating her opposition as just one more Tudor rebellion. He sent ships to cut off any possible retreat Mary might make from Great Yarmouth. However Northumberland was taking big risks:

- By leaving London he risked losing control of some of the most powerful members of the Council. Some of them had only agreed to Lady Jane Grey becoming queen under his angry bullying.
- The repressive way in which he had helped put down Kett's rebellion made him unpopular in Mary's home territory of East Anglia.
- He couldn't even be sure that the commander of the fleet he had sent to blockade Great Yarmouth was on his side.

He was right to be worried!

- With Northumberland out of the way Sir William Cecil led his colleagues in making a declaration of loyalty to Mary.
- Sir Henry Jerningham organised a mutiny in the fleet against Northumberland and in favour of Mary.
- Northumberland's troops deserted him.

Princess Elizabeth also remained loyal to her half-sister Mary. She wrote an angry and impassioned letter to Lady Jane Grey, asking her what on earth she thought she was doing.

It was clear that Northumberland's gamble had failed. The Duke of Suffolk had to tell his daughter, the Lady Jane Grey, that she was no longer queen. On Tower Hill he proclaimed Mary to be Queen of England. News of this reached Northumberland and, desperate to save his own life, he declared his support for Mary. It was all over.

Queen Mary I

Mary's supporters soon entered London and captured Lady Jane Grey (who had been 'queen' for just thirteen days) and her husband. Northumberland was captured in Cambridge, brought back to London and beheaded. Mary herself entered London on 3 August amid great rejoicing: all the church bells were ringing and the people celebrated with street parties and feasts that went on long into the night.

Mary believed that the rejoicing was because she was a Catholic, come to restore the old religion. It was much more likely, however, that the people were rejoicing because one of Henry's daughters, a Tudor, had succeeded to the throne of England.

> **Did you know?**
>
> Lady Jane Grey was imprisoned in the Tower of London and beheaded on 12 February 1554.

4.2 'England <u>will</u> be Catholic again!'

Mary had a disturbed life as a child and young woman. Born and brought up as a Catholic, she had lived through the time when her beloved Spanish mother, Catherine of Aragon, was cast aside for a younger woman, removed from the throne and banned from court; she had been forbidden to visit her mother when she was dying; she had suffered years of rejection by her father and she had watched while her Catholic religion was scorned and overthrown. Yet throughout her life Mary had remained stubbornly loyal to her mother and to Catholicism. Now she was Queen of England, she ought to be able to return England to the Catholic Church and to force the English people to return to what she regarded as the one true religion. But could she do it? Should she do it?

Task

Mary faced a choice:
1 She could accept the Protestant religion as laid down in 1552 and continue with her own Catholic beliefs and practices in private, as she had been doing for years.
2 She could go all out to reverse the changes made since 1530 and make England a Catholic country again.
Discuss with a partner the arguments for and against each course of action.

Bringing back Catholicism

For Mary, there was no debate at all. She wanted the English Church to return to the old Catholic beliefs and practices and she wanted the Pope to be restored as head of the Catholic Church in England.

- In 1553, all the religious laws passed in Edward VI's reign were repealed.
- In 1554, all the old Heresy Laws were revived.
- In 1555, the anti-Papal laws were repealed.

And with the law on their side once again those people who had never been happy with Edward's changes set about repairing the damage done to their churches by the Protestant reforms. Statues of the Virgin Mary and the saints (which had been kept safe in cellars and outhouses for just such an occasion) were brought out, cleaned up and put back. The Mass was said in churches and the services were once again in Latin. People revived the old ceremonies and processions.

In November 1554, the papal legate, Reginald Pole, officially forgave the whole country for its sin in worshipping in the Protestant way, and welcomed England back into the Catholic fold.

Who... ?

REGINALD POLE (1500–58)

His mother was the Countess of Salisbury so he had royal blood in his veins. As a boy and young man he trained for the priesthood, but his career came to a full stop when he opposed Henry VIII's divorce. He fled into exile in Italy, where he became a leading church reformer and twice narrowly missed being voted in as Pope. He supported everyone who opposed Henry VIII, especially after his mother was executed for treason in 1541. He returned to England as papal legate when Mary became queen. Mary made him Archbishop of Canterbury and together they worked hard to return England to the Catholic faith. In 1557 the Pope took away Pole's legateship, suspecting he had Protestant leanings, and asked him to return to Rome. Mary refused to let him go and he continued as Archbishop of Canterbury until his death in 1558, just two hours after Mary herself died.

This universal forgiveness, however, did not extend to certain individuals who, Mary and Pole decided, had led others astray. What was to be done with them?

- Married clergy were forced to leave their wives. Although most accepted this rule, there were complaints about frequent visits by clergy to their former wives!
- Archbishop Cranmer was sacked and Reginald Pole was made Archbishop of Canterbury in his place.
- Bishops Latimer, Ridley and Hooper along with other leading Protestant bishops were sacked and Catholics made bishops in their place.

A series of staged debates between leading Catholic and Protestant churchmen were held in Oxford. The idea was to show the weakness of the Protestant position, but in fact, for many, it did just the opposite.

What about the monasteries?

Mary even thought about restoring the monasteries but that was impossible. Not only had they been stripped of all their gold, silver and precious jewels, but the roofs had been stripped of lead and the stone used in local buildings. They were well and truly ruined. To complicate matters, most of the monastic land had been sold, and sold to Catholics as well as Protestants. To try to buy all the land back would be very costly and would offend too many people.

Did everyone want Catholicism back?

No, they did not! Indeed, the debates in Parliament in 1553 about repealing all Edward VI's religious laws lasted for five days but in the end, the laws were repealed by 270 votes to 80. At the same time, the Heresy Laws were thrown out by the House of Lords and had to be re-introduced the following year. Most people, however, opted for a quiet life and accepted Mary's changes just as they had accepted Edward's. As for those who did not...

What... ?

HERETICS
People who wrote, spoke or behaved in ways that showed they disagreed with the legally accepted religion of a country.

Source ❷

And so Rogers was brought to Smithfield, saying the psalm 'Misere'. All the people wonderfully rejoiced at his determination, giving praise and thanks to God. And there in the presence of a wonderful number of people, the fire was put unto him. When it had taken hold both upon his legs and shoulders, he, as one feeling no pain, washed his hands in the flame, as though it had been cold water. Most mildly this happy martyr yielded up his spirit into the hands of his heavenly Father.

John Foxe's description of the burning of John Rogers in February 1555.

'Bloody Mary'

The Heresy Laws said that heretics had to be burned at the stake, and so Mary and Reginald Pole set to with a will. The trials and burnings began. The first person to be burned to death was John Rogers in February 1555. Rogers was a minister and divinity lecturer who preached against Mary's proclamations. He was imprisoned in Newgate Prison and was the first 'Marian Martyr'. He had eleven children!

In the next three years there were 283 burnings. Most took place in London and the south-east. One of the most dramatic was that of the two Protestant bishops, Latimer and Ridley. Death by burning at the stake is slow and dreadfully painful. Friends of the two bishops tied small bags of gunpowder around their necks, hoping that the flames would make the gunpowder explode and so kill them instantly. Latimer called out to Ridley 'Be of good cheer, Dr Ridley. We shall this day light such a candle as I trust shall never be put out.' But their deaths weren't quick. It was a wet day and the logs burned slowly. Latimer managed to twist round until a flame caught his bag of gunpowder and it exploded, killing him. Ridley wasn't so lucky. The lower part of his body burned slowly and he was clearly in great pain. Some friends lifted a smouldering log to the bag of gunpowder round his neck which exploded and ended his agony.

Archbishop Cranmer was forced to watch the burnings of his friends, the bishops Latimer and Ridley. Eventually Cranmer signed a confession promising to give up Protestantism. It didn't save him. He too was sent to the stake. When his burning began, Catholics expected him to repeat his condemnation of Protestantism. Instead, he did just the opposite. Clearly and boldly he stated his belief in the Protestant way of worshipping God.

Source ❸

This picture of the burning of Archbishop Cranmer was printed in Foxe's Book of Martyrs.
❓ *What details in the picture make you sympathetic to Cranmer?*

What happened to Protestants who weren't burned?

About 800 of them fled to safety to Protestant countries in Europe. Once in exile, they remained steadfast to their faith, sending back books and messages of support to Protestants who couldn't flee. Queen Mary was only 37 when she was crowned Queen of England. They expected a long exile and many thought they would die abroad. Those who couldn't, for whatever reason, flee to Europe set up their own underground Protestant churches in England, especially in London. They met secretly in houses and inns and worshipped together in the way they thought right. Most, however, simply kept their heads down and watched and waited.

What were Mary's motives?

It might seem that Mary was out for revenge on those who had slighted her, her mother and her Catholic religion. It may be that she really believed that this was the way to restore the 'true faith', Catholicism, to England. She may even have believed that by burning the heretics she was saving their immortal souls from hell. We will never know.

> ## Task
>
> 1 Most of what we know about the burnings of Protestants is taken from John Foxe's *Book of Martyrs* printed in 1563, after Mary's death. John Foxe was an extreme Protestant. Does this mean that these accounts and illustrations are unreliable?
> 2 What does Source 4 tell you about
>   **a)** Protestantism in England at this time?
>   **b)** Mary's motives?
> 3 What do your answers to questions 1 and 2 tell you about Protestantism in England at this time?

See page 194 for a practice source exercise on Mary I.

Source ❹

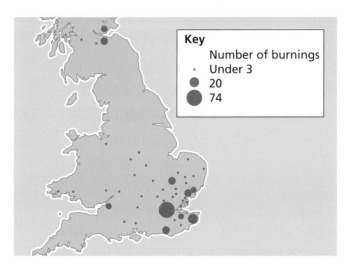

Map to show where those burnt as heretics lived.

Source ❺

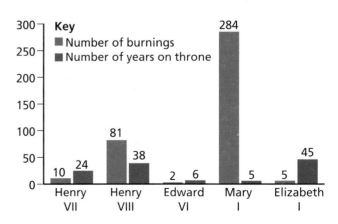

Bar chart to show numbers burned in the reigns of all the Tudor monarchs.

4.3 'I <u>will</u> have Catholic babies!'

Mary hoped the religious changes she was making would be permanent. She had good reason to believe this was possible. England had been a Catholic country for centuries. It had only been Protestant for a few years.

It was, in Mary's mind, absolutely essential that she should marry and produce an heir (or, preferably, heirs) who would be brought up as good Catholics and would reign when she was gone. Otherwise her half-sister, the Protestant Princess Elizabeth, would become queen.

But Mary was 37 and her child-bearing years were coming to an end. She had to find a suitable husband quickly and become pregnant as soon as possible after the marriage.

Enter Philip of Spain

Mary decided that she would marry Philip of Spain. She had never met him, but to her he was eminently suitable. First and foremost, he was Spanish and a Catholic and Mary felt comfortable with both these attributes. Her own mother, Catherine of Aragon, had been a Spanish princess and, of course, Mary could not for one moment consider marriage to a non-Catholic. There was some political sense in the marriage: it did cement relations with the Netherlands, a country that was England's major trading partner but that was effectively under Spanish control; and it did stop arguments amongst the nobility that would have broken out if she had married one of them and so raised him above the other nobles. But that was about all.

Mary's councillors were horrified. They would have preferred her to marry an Englishman and many had been urging her to consider Edward Courtenay, Earl of Devon. Parliament was also horrified. A delegation was sent to persuade Mary to change her mind. Mary was outraged at their impudence. 'Parliaments were not accustomed to use such language to the Kings of England' she thundered. Stubbornly determined to marry the man of her choice, Mary gradually persuaded the majority of her councillors that marriage to Philip would be a good thing.

The marriage treaty

Mary and her most trusted councillors worked out a treaty that they hoped would calm the fears of all those who opposed the marriage. This is what it said:

- Philip was to be called 'King' but he was to have no power of his own: he would rule jointly with Mary.
- Philip could not promote foreigners to positions in England.
- Philip had to uphold the laws of England.
- Any child of the marriage would inherit England and the Netherlands, but not Spain.

Task
Read the clauses of the marriage treaty carefully.
1 Who benefited most from this treaty, Mary or Philip?
2 Can you foresee any problems arising from the treaty?
3 Do you think the treaty did enough to satisfy the people who were opposed to the marriage?

- If there were no children, or if Mary was to die before Philip, he would have no claim to the English throne.
- Philip could not take Mary, or their children, out of England without the permission of the nobility.
- England had to help defend the Netherlands in the event of a French invasion.

Wyatt's rebellion

If you answered 'yes' to question 3, you were wrong! Plans were already afoot for risings in Devon, Kent, Leicestershire and the Welsh borders to take place in the spring of 1554. When the marriage treaty was published in January 1554, these plans were hastily brought forward, but with disastrous results. Only Thomas Wyatt, a wealthy Kent landowner, could raise a reasonable number of men at short notice. They marched on London, determined to remove Mary from the throne and put the Princess Elizabeth there in her place. If Wyatt hadn't delayed his final assault on the city, he might have been successful. But the delay gave Mary time to rally her troops and the Londoners. After some fierce hand-to-hand fighting, it was all over.

Wyatt himself was tried for treason, hanged and disembowelled. His head was put on a spike over one of the gates into London. About ninety of the rebels were hanged, their bodies left to rot on London gallows or on gallows in the villages from which they had come, as a dreadful warning to others. Mary had clearly decided to make a clean sweep of all threats to her position: Lady Jane Grey and her husband, although they had had nothing whatsoever to do with the rebellion, were brought out of the Tower of London and executed.

What of the Princess Elizabeth? Wyatt had clearly wanted to put Elizabeth on the throne. Had she known anything about this plot? There is some evidence that she did, but no evidence that she was directly involved in it. Mary had Elizabeth moved into the Tower of London, just in case.

All rebels and potential rebels were out of the way and the stage was set for the marriage of Mary and Philip.

Source ❻

This is the Great Seal of Philip and Mary, to be used on all official documents.

> ### What... ?
>
> **DISEMBOWELLING**
> This could be part of the process of hanging someone. In some cases, before the person being hanged was actually dead, his (or her) bowels were cut out and held up in front of them.

Love, marriage and babies?

Marriage to a Spanish Catholic prince, with the promise of babies in the years ahead, was, for Mary, a dream come true. She truly believed that, at last, in the 38th year of her life, she would be happy. For Philip, it was different. Aged 26, already a widower with one son, he viewed the marriage as a standard diplomatic marriage that happened in all royal families throughout Europe. So did his father, Charles V. He wanted this marriage because it would strengthen the alliance he was building against France. With Spain, the Netherlands and now England allied, France would be unlikely to cause any trouble on the European stage.

So did the marriage work? Philip, expected in England as early as February, did not arrive until July, forcing a long and tense wait on Mary. He brought with him a large retinue of advisers, courtiers and servants and so the English household prepared for him was not needed. Eventually, on 23 July, Philip and Mary met. They were married two days later in Winchester cathedral. He spoke no English and her Spanish was rusty. Their only common language was French, which Mary spoke well and Philip, more or less, understood.

By the autumn of 1554 Mary was declared pregnant, with the baby due in May 1555. May came and went; so did June; so did July. There was no baby. Philip left England in August 1555. Mary's chances of getting pregnant were growing less and less as the months passed and she was left on her own. In May 1557, Philip returned, with the main aim of gaining English support for a possible war with France. Once again, after a few weeks, Mary declared herself to be pregnant and once again, she was wrong. Philip left England in July 1557. He never returned.

Depression and death

By 1558, Mary was a troubled queen.

- The burnings of Protestants were making her steadily more and more unpopular.
- Although she had succeeded in restoring Catholicism to England, Protestantism was gaining strength in Europe and it could only be a matter of time before it took hold again in England.
- Her marriage had failed to come up to her expectations.
- Some saw her phantom pregnancies as God's punishment for burning heretics. Others mocked her for believing that, at 42, she could still become pregnant.
- War with France had resulted in England losing the French town of Calais.

Ill for most of 1558, by the autumn Mary was a very sick woman. She died on 17 November, lonely, childless and with an absent husband. And her heir was her Protestant half-sister, the Princess Elizabeth.

Summary task

We started this unit by saying that Mary was a very stubborn woman.

Draw up two lists: one giving examples of how this stubbornness worked to her advantage and one giving examples of how this stubbornness worked against her.

Now use those lists to help you write an answer to this 'describe and explain' question:

1 Describe the main events in Mary I's reign.
2 Explain, with examples, how Mary's stubbornness helped or hindered her in what she wanted to achieve.

UNIT 5 Elizabeth I: what made her successful?

What is this all about?

When Elizabeth became queen of England in 1558, she was just 25 years old. She inherited a troubled kingdom. And yet by most criteria Elizabeth had a very successful reign. In this unit you will investigate the different factors that helped contribute to her success – her skills, her good luck, and her sensible decisions.

- Part 1 examines how she dealt with the problem of religion that she had inherited from her brother and sister, Edward and Mary, and how, despite rebellions and the threat of invasion, she emerged intact with England a stronger and more secure country.
- Part 2 focuses on threats to Elizabeth's power and how she dealt with a rebellion, an invasion and a rival.
- Part 3 explores her relationship with Parliament.
- Part 4 investigates how her government dealt with the troubling problem of what to do about poor people.

Source

Lucky to be alive!

This portrait of Elizabeth was painted in 1546 when she was about thirteen, newly restored to favour and to her father's court.

It is a little surprising that Elizabeth even lived to inherit the throne in the turbulent world of Tudor politics. When she was three years old, her mother was executed and her father declared her illegitimate. She was sent away from the only home she knew and was brought up in relative poverty. Her father ignored her. She was finally allowed back to court when she was thirteen, largely due to the efforts of Henry's sixth and final wife, Catherine Parr. But the Tudor soap opera had some episodes to run.

After Henry died, Catherine Parr married Thomas Seymour, the brother of Jane (Henry's third wife), and of the powerful Duke of Somerset, who was Edward VI's protector. But Catherine soon died giving birth to a baby daughter. Seymour then turned his attention on the young Elizabeth who was a lively and attractive 15 year old.

Just one year later Seymour was executed for plotting against his brother. Suspicion fell on Elizabeth – was she involved in the plot too? Her servants were tortured to give evidence against her. They gave none but all the same Elizabeth's reputation was damaged.

Five years later during Wyatt's rebellion in 1554 (see page 69) Wyatt was tortured before being executed. Under torture he said that Elizabeth supported his rebellion. Mary was not wholly convinced but Elizabeth was taken to the Tower of London for several months.

She was eventually released. But, as the next in line for the throne and a Protestant in a country her half-sister was determined to make Catholic, she lived under permanent suspicion of plot and rebellion. Every Protestant plotter saw her as their great hope – whether she knew about them or not. Every Catholic saw her as the great threat.

So by the time the riders galloped up the tree-lined avenue of Hatfield House in November 1558 to tell the Princess Elizabeth that she was now queen, Elizabeth had already shown herself to be a survivor.

Source ❷

Elizabeth was crowned, amid great rejoicing and feasting, in Westminster Abbey in January 1559, at the age of 25. She had this official portrait painted, showing her in her coronation robes.

Task

1 Compare Sources 1 and 2. Choose adjectives to describe Elizabeth as she is shown in the two paintings.
2 Now read the report from the Venetian ambassador. This is a different sort of portrait – a pen portrait. In what ways does it give an image of Elizabeth that agrees with the portraits? In what ways is it different?

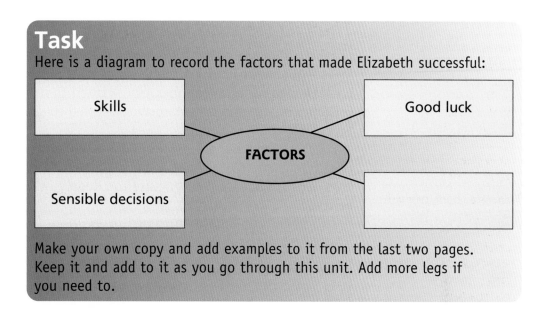

Task
Here is a diagram to record the factors that made Elizabeth successful:

Skills

Good luck

FACTORS

Sensible decisions

Make your own copy and add examples to it from the last two pages. Keep it and add to it as you go through this unit. Add more legs if you need to.

5.1 The big problem: religion – a reason to rebel! A reason to invade!

By far the most urgent problem Elizabeth had to settle was religion. Her father Henry VIII made himself head of the Church of England, yet he lived and died a Catholic; his son Edward VI had tried to turn England into a Protestant country; his daughter Mary I had tried, by her burnings, to turn the people back to Catholic ways and had seen the Pope re-established as the head of the English Church. What would Elizabeth do?

What were Elizabeth's personal beliefs?

This is a difficult question to answer because Elizabeth had survived largely by keeping her own views very private. However, as a girl and young woman she had been taught by Humanist tutors, the most important of whom was Roger Ascham. She had spent the last years of her father's reign at court, very much under the influence of his queen, Catherine Parr, who was a noted Protestant evangelical.

However, she kept a crucifix and candles on the altar of her private chapel. She also liked some traditional ceremonies. She continued to employ the Catholic composers Thomas Tallis and William Byrd because she liked their music.

On the other hand, early in her reign, she walked out of Mass in disgust when a priest tried to ELEVATE THE HOST as a sign of transubstantiation. This belief was at the very core of the Catholic faith.

What... ?

EVANGELICALS
Protestants who believe that all Christian teaching should be based on the basic principles laid down in the Gospels.

The Elizabethan Church settlement

Elizabeth thought that, if Protestants were allowed to preach their new ideas throughout England, they would stir up some sort of popular backlash against the Catholics. She wanted to avoid both extreme Roman Catholicism and strict Puritanism. She tried to find a settlement that was acceptable to most people.

Elizabeth said she did not want to 'make windows into men's souls'. By this she meant that as long as people attended church and obeyed her laws, she did not want to enquire too deeply into what they actually believed.

Two important Acts were passed in 1559:

1 The Act of Supremacy

Every person who had an official position had to swear the following oath:
I do utterly testify and declare in my conscience that the Queen's Highness is the only Supreme Governor of this realm in all spiritual and church matters; and that no foreign prince, person or power hath any authority within this realm.

2 The Act of Uniformity

This laid down that:
- Attendance at church every Sunday was compulsory. Non-attenders would be fined.
- All church services had to be in English, not Latin.
- A new prayer book was to be used that addressed the vital issue of transubstantiation by using words that made it possible to believe in it, or not.
- The 'ornaments' of the church (the clothes the priests wore and crosses, crucifixes and other church furnishings) had to be as they were in Edward VI's reign.
- Priests had to keep a register of baptisms, marriages and burials in their parish.
- Every church had to have a Bible written in English available for all.

Task

1 What would:

a) a strict Catholic   **b)** a Puritan
like or dislike about Elizabeth's new laws?

2 Do you think that Elizabeth's laws were 'a good compromise' or 'a recipe for disaster'? Give reasons for your answer.

Did you know?

Catholics who could not accept the new form of worship laid down by the Act of Uniformity and who refused to attend church were called recusants. They were not persecuted. They were simply fined for non-attendance.

Catholics and Puritans: how did they threaten Elizabeth?

Elizabeth's Church settlement was a compromise between Catholicism and Protestantism. Most people gradually came to accept it, but two groups never did.

- The Puritans – hardline Protestants who wanted to purify the Church and make it more Protestant and less Catholic.
- Hardline Catholics who disliked the changes that had been made and wanted the Church to stay totally Catholic.

Both groups posed problems for Elizabeth throughout her reign.

Task

Draw a timeline of Elizabeth's reign down the middle of a page like this.

Catholic threats	Date	Puritan threats
Mary, Queen of Scots, seen by some Catholics as the rightful queen, arrives in England as Elizabeth's prisoner. Seriousness: 6/10	1568	

As you work through the next section add notes on either side of your timeline to summarise the threats from Catholic or Puritans. For each threat give it a seriousness score out of 10. If it was an extreme danger to Elizabeth (she might be deposed) give it 10 points. If it is no threat at all give it 0 points. It is more likely to be somewhere in between. Remember there are no 'right' answers. This is your opinion. It is up to you to decide.

1 What did they think of Elizabeth's Church of England?	
Catholics	**Puritans**
Elizabeth's 'Church of England' was separate from the Roman Catholic Church. For Catholics that was not allowed. They believed there was only one rightful Church – the Roman Catholic Church – and only one leader – the Pope who was God's representative on Earth – so they could not recognise Elizabeth as head of the Church. Elizabeth tried to get round this by calling herself 'Supreme Governor' of the Church rather than 'Supreme Head'.	Elizabeth introduced many Protestant elements into the Church of England in 1559 but the Puritans wanted even more. They wanted to remove all traces of Catholicism 'to purify the Church'. For example, they wanted to get rid of the vestments worn by the clergy, and holy days and organ music. They wanted bishops to have less power and local congregations to elect their clergy.
All the Catholic bishops and about 300 priests (out of approximately 9,000 parishes) left the Church. Many who stayed probably did so *not* because they agreed with Elizabeth but because they did not want to lose their jobs. Throughout her reign, as clergy died they were replaced by clergy who did support the Church.	At first Puritans stayed in the Church and some became bishops. They were a minority but their aim was to change the Church from within. Puritan bishops tried to stop clergy wearing vestments, but had little success. So they tried to make changes through Parliament. Again, they had little success – Elizabeth was firmly in control of Parliament.
Elizabeth kept vestments and churches still had altars and crucifixes which pleased the Catholics. But there were other changes that Catholics could not accept. Many Catholics obeyed the law and did attend the Church of England services (they did not want to pay the fine for non-attendance) but they then also went on and took part in a secret Catholic service. Some missed the service and risked the 12d fine. But the evidence is that as time passed people got used to the new Church and its services, and Catholics were left alone as long as they did not cause any trouble. In some areas the fine was not even enforced from the beginning.	In the 1570s Puritans then turned to prophesyings. People and clergy met together to pray and discuss. Elizabeth thought these events might encourage people to question the Church of England. She ordered Grindal, her archbishop, to ban them. When he refused, she had him put under house arrest!
	In the 1580s Presbyterianism developed. Puritans formed local groups of ordinary people discussing the Bible and its teachings, together, in secret. They questioned the way the Church was run: were bishops necessary? Why should congregations not elect their own minister? To Elizabeth, these were very dangerous ideas. In 1583 she appointed Whitgift as Archbishop of Canterbury. He started to remove Puritans from positions of power in the Church.
Catholicism might have simply faded away if it was not for the Jesuit priests who arrived in England in 1580. They helped keep Catholicism alive by holding services and trying to win converts. The government suspected they were organising plots and ordered their arrest.	In the 1590s a small minority of Puritans became separatists. They left the Church of England and tried to set up their own Church. However most Puritans stayed inside the Church of England. Elizabeth thought the Puritans were more of a threat than they really were. They really did not want to destroy the Church. They were thankful to have a mainly Protestant Church, and the last thing they wanted to do was to weaken it and allow the Catholics to grow stronger.
The Jesuits failed to convert many people and in 1603 there were only about 40,000 Catholics in England. Most of these quietly worshipped God in their own way while the majority of people supported Elizabeth's Church.	

Discuss: who seems to have accepted the Church of England more – Catholics or Puritans?	
2 What did they think of Elizabeth herself?	
Catholics	**Puritans**
Some Catholics could not accept Elizabeth as rightful queen for reasons that went back to Henry VIII's reign. Henry's marriage to Anne Boleyn was not recognised by the Pope so Elizabeth, who was Anne and Henry's daughter, was illegitimate. She could not be queen. They saw Mary, Queen of Scots (who was Catholic) as rightful queen; what is more from 1568 Mary was living in England.	Some Puritans were not keen on having a woman as head of the Church. However being very anti-Catholic they realised they needed Elizabeth as much as she needed them.
	The only alternative to Elizabeth was a Catholic monarch like Mary, Queen of Scots. Mary would return England to Catholic control – something Puritans dreaded. Most realised that the way the Church of England was run could be a lot worse for them than it actually was.

To make matters worse, in 1570 the Pope issued a Papal Bull announcing that Elizabeth was not the rightful Queen of England. He ordered everyone in England not to obey her. The Pope was almost encouraging Catholics to rebel against Elizabeth! And as you will see, many did.

Most Catholics, however, preferred to ignore these issues. In religion they stayed loyal to the Pope, but in politics they were loyal to Elizabeth. They did not want a foreigner deciding who should rule England. When there were plots against Elizabeth, the vast majority of Catholics did not get involved.

Discuss: Who seems more loyal to Elizabeth – Catholics or Puritans?

3 How did they oppose Elizabeth?

Catholics

Until 1569 there were no Catholic attempts to depose Elizabeth. Mary's arrival in England and the Papal Bull of 1570 changed all that.

The first rebellion was in 1569 (see next page). In 1571 the Ridolfi plot tried again to replace Elizabeth with Mary, Queen of Scots. It was a dismal failure. It had little popular support. Most English Catholics were horrified. But sometimes in history it only takes a few powerful plotters to unseat a ruler. Elizabeth and her advisers were on their guard.

When Jesuits began to arrive in England in 1580 they strengthened the Catholic opposition. They began to make new converts. Although this group remained very small, Elizabeth's government took strong action against them and 200 Catholics were executed. In 1583 there was the Throckmorton Plot (see page 86) and in 1586 the Babington Plot to murder Elizabeth.

An even bigger worry was Catholic Spain. From 1585 England was at war with Spain. The Spanish king, Philip II, saw his war with Elizabeth as a religious crusade. His aim was to remove her from the throne, replace her with Mary, Queen of Scots and so restore Catholicism to England. He gave his support to plots and sent an invasion fleet – the Armada in 1588. But that mission failed (see pages 81–84 to find out why) and so ended any chance of Philip's invasion plan succeeding.

Puritans

The Puritans were not strong enough to mount a rebellion against Elizabeth. They did not want to in any case because that might lead to Catholicism coming back. Even if they did there were no foreign armies waiting to come and help them.

Discuss: How secure was Elizabeth against Catholic and Puritan threats?

Task

1 Look at your completed timeline. Use it to write a paragraph to explain who you think posed the greater threat to Elizabeth: Catholics or Puritans? The answer may seem obvious to you but you will need to explain why. That means you will need to back up what you say with evidence from your timeline.

2 Discuss: Do you think that is how it appeared to Elizabeth and her advisers at the time? Give reasons.

5.2 A rebellion, an invasion and a rival

Case study 1: a rebellion

In 1569 a Catholic rebellion took place. Its aim was to depose Elizabeth – but did it stand any chance of success?

The story starts with the flight of a desperate Mary, Queen of Scots to England in 1568. She had been deposed as Queen of Scotland and her army had just been defeated by her enemies there. She fled to England for safety, expecting support from her cousin, Queen Elizabeth. How wrong she was! The arrival of Mary, Queen of Scots as a fugitive in England gave Elizabeth a difficult security problem. Mary was her rival for the English throne, and she was a Catholic! What should she do with her? She put her under house arrest.

Mary's sudden arrival in England, however, was welcomed by some. It provided a golden opportunity for Catholics to rally round her and to begin to plot to put her on the throne of England instead of Elizabeth. The Rebellion of the Northern Earls was the first of several such conspiracies.

The leading rebels

Thomas Howard, Duke of Norfolk

He was the most important noble at that time. He planned to marry Mary, Queen of Scots and, by having children, secure her succession to the English throne. However, when the conspiracy was discovered, he lost his nerve and begged the Earls of Northumberland and Westmorland not to rebel.

Thomas Percy, Earl of Northumberland

Head of one of the oldest noble families in England, a Catholic family that had been involved in the Pilgrimage of Grace and had lost their estates. Mary I restored these to the family. Percy was willing to rise in support of Catholicism but did not want Norfolk and Mary to marry.

Charles Neville, Earl of Westmorland

Married to Norfolk's sister. Owned enormous estates in the North.

Source ❸

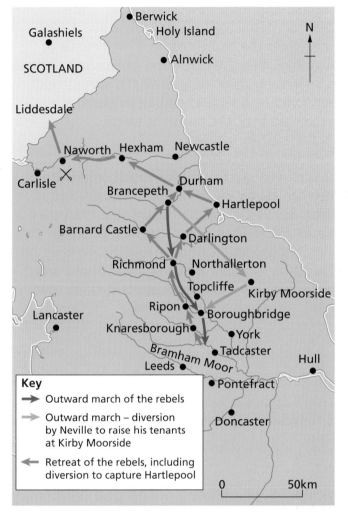

A map of the rebellion.

Key
→ Outward march of the rebels
→ Outward march – diversion by Neville to raise his tenants at Kirby Moorside
← Retreat of the rebels, including diversion to capture Hartlepool

0   50km

Stage 1 The marriage plan

Mary's arrival in England attracted a number of powerful Catholic aristocrats like bees to a honey pot. The most important peer in England, the Catholic Duke of Norfolk, was soon involved in a plot to release Mary from the house where she was being kept prisoner and marry her. Other aristocrats were involved in the plot – Leicester, Sussex, and Arundel. Elizabeth heard rumours about the planned marriage and Norfolk ended up in the Tower of London! He begged for mercy and pleaded with the other conspirators to stop.

Stage 2 The earls rebel before they are ready

However, there were others in the far north of England who were determined not to be stopped. Catholicism had always been strong in the north and the great noble families there had had enough. One historian described their motives:

> The great dynasties told themselves that they had been in Northumberland and Westmorland, when the Tudors were still in the brewing trade in Wales, and they were by now heartily sick of being told by some jumped-up-quill-pusher from the south [this refers to Cecil] what they could or couldn't do. For these people Mary Stuart [an alternative name for Mary, Queen of Scots] was not just a successor. She was a replacement.

However, here is the manifesto issued by two northern earls. Do their motives seem to be the same as those mentioned by the historian?

> Several new nobles about the queen's majesty do daily go about attempting to overthrow and put down the ancient nobility of this realm. They have, in the space of twelve years now passed, set up and maintained a new-found religion and heresy, contrary to God's word. In order to put this right, several foreign powers do purpose shortly to invade these realms. This will be to our utter destruction and so we must ourselves put matters straight.

Elizabeth summoned the Earls of Northumberland and Westmorland to London to explain themselves. Should they go, or not? The Duchess of Westmorland (who was Norfolk's sister) persuaded the earls that they should go ahead with the rebellion and they refused Elizabeth's 'request'. Not a clever move! The uprising had not yet been properly planned and the earls were not really ready to act. However, once they had refused to go to London, they had to go ahead with the rebellion.

Stage 3 Initial success for the rebels

The rebellion started in November and for a time it looked as if the northern earls might win. They mustered 3,800 foot soldiers and 1,600 horsemen, and marched south under the banner of the Five Wounds of Christ, last seen on the Prayer Book Rebellion. The Earl of Sussex had little luck in the north, trying to raise an army in support of the government. At first he had only just over 1,000 foot soldiers and a few hundred horsemen. Could he manage to hold back the northern earls?

Stage 4 Retreat

By the end of November the earls had got as far south as Bramham Moor, near Leeds. At this stage they controlled the whole of the north-east of England, and had captured Barnard Castle and Hartlepool. But then they stopped their march southwards. Why? They were beginning to realise that no one in the south was going to support a Catholic rebellion. So they sat tight and waited, hoping that Philip of Spain would land a Catholic army in the spring with which they could link up. Some historians claim that Philip of Spain had no intention of sending such a force!

Stage 5 Disaster

However, Elizabeth did not sit tight and wait. She had Mary imprisoned in Coventry where the rebels could not rescue her. By the middle of December a royal army of 12,000 men was moving up from the south. As soon as the earls heard this they seem to have lost their nerve and fled to Hexham, and then to Scotland.

Stage 6 Punishment

Hundreds of rebels were executed. Some of them were hanged, cut down while still alive and disembowelled. Northumberland was handed over to the English by the Scots and was executed. Westmorland spent the rest of his life abroad and Norfolk was soon involved in another plot – the Ridolfi Plot – and was also executed.

Task

Here are some of the factors that would have given the Northern Rebellion a chance of success. You are going to work out how many were present in 1569. Take each in turn and look for evidence of this. Write down your evidence under the heading.

- powerful leaders who would attract a lot of support
- a genuine cause that would make people support them
- a good plan
- people reluctant to fight for Elizabeth
- help from abroad
- courage and determination.

Now use this information to write a paragraph of about ten lines in answer to the question 'Could the Rebellion of the Northern Earls have succeeded?'

Case study 2: an invasion

Threats to Elizabeth didn't always come from inside her kingdom. By far the greatest threat to England and to Elizabeth came from Spain in 1588. This threat was closely connected to Elizabeth's religious policies.

The background

Philip of Spain devised his first plan to invade England as early as 1559 – just after Elizabeth turned down his proposal of marriage. Not only was he upset by her rejection but he also felt he had a duty to God to protect the Catholic religion in England. Remember, Elizabeth was turning England into a Protestant country.

However, as king of the most powerful country in the world, Philip had many other things to worry about and it was not until 1586 that the real planning began. By this time English sailors like Francis Drake were attacking Spanish ports in South America and Spanish treasure fleets. They had to be stopped. Even more seriously, Elizabeth I was helping Protestants in the Netherlands who were rebelling against Spanish rule.

Historians have suggested three possible reasons for the failure of the Armada:

1 bad luck
2 the English ships and sailors were better than the Spanish
3 the poor planning, tactics and leadership of the Spanish.

The English at the time had their own theory. They believed that as God was a Protestant he helped them in various ways.

As you read the story look out for examples of any of these reasons.

Task

Look carefully at the map and at the picture of the Ark Royal. Keep them in mind as you read through the story. You will need them both when you write up the task at the end.

The story

Source 4

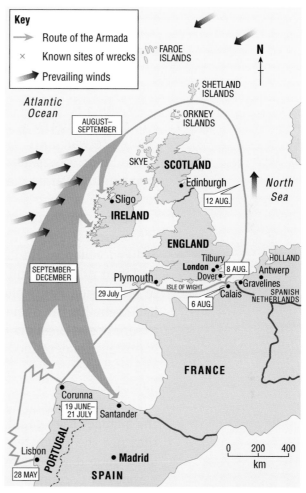

A map showing the route of the Armada.

Source 5

The Ark Royal, flagship of the English fleet. It had fifty guns.

Held up at Corunna

The summer of 1588 was a long one for Elizabeth and her subjects as they waited for the Spanish to make their move. A huge fleet of about 120 ships was gathered together in Lisbon harbour. On board this fleet was the best army in the world; if it landed in England it would be unbeatable. Despite complaints that insufficient provisions had been loaded, the fleet set sail on 20 May, bound for Flanders where it would meet up with the Duke of Parma, who governed the Netherlands for Philip. Parma had an army and a fleet of pontoons and transports waiting there for the attack on England. However, the Duke was very unhappy about the plan and wanted to wait until he had secure control of a port on the coast of the Netherlands. (Remember the Dutch were at that time rebelling against the Spanish, and Parma didn't want to give the Dutch rebels any opportunity to create chaos.)

The man in charge of the Armada was the Duke of Medina Sidonia, one of the richest aristocrats in Spain. However, he was peaceful, gentle and disliked violence. He just wanted to run his estates and live a quiet life. He loved riding around the countryside with the peasant girls curtseying to him. When Philip chose him to lead the Armada he was horrified. He had spent his life avoiding any military experience. He had even less experience as a sailor; in fact he suffered from terrible sea-sickness. One historian has described him as 'a brave bullfighter, with perfect manners and turned-out toes'. Another has written 'he hardly knew a ship from a haystack'.

The Spanish needed good weather for their venture to succeed. As it was the summer they could reasonably expect such weather. Unfortunately they got the opposite – day after day of strong gales. Soon after the fleet left Lisbon it was hit by a fierce storm and had to flee for shelter into the harbour of Corunna.

Unlike English ships, which were small and agile, many of the Spanish ships were big and clumsy. They were hard to manoeuvre and struggled in bad weather. They were held up at Corunna for over a month because they needed the wind behind them to even get out of the harbour. While the fleet was in Corunna the Duke of Medina Sidonia, the Spanish admiral, wrote to Philip suggesting they abandon the expedition. Philip did not agree but the delay at Corunna was potentially catastrophic, because the Duke of Parma gave up waiting for the Armada to arrive and instead sent the crews of his own ships to work on canals inland.

However, the Armada did finally leave Corunna and, on 29 July 1588, people on the coast of Cornwall sighted the fleet. Beacon after beacon was lit sending the news along the south coast.

Source ❻

An engraving showing the beacon system on the English coast warning of the Spanish approach.

The race down the English Channel

This warning allowed the English commander, Lord Howard of Effingham, to get the English fleet of about 60 warships out of Plymouth in time. (Remember, although the Spanish fleet was 120-strong many of these were transports or supply ships. The Spanish had about the same number of warships as the English.) As the Spanish fleet made their way along the English Channel in a crescent formation they were followed by the English ships. The Spanish were reluctant to engage in a battle because they knew the English gunners were far superior. There were several skirmishes and the Spanish lost two ships. However, the English found it difficult to inflict any major damage on the Spanish and failed to stop them. The crescent formation had worked – the Spanish looked unstoppable! Then on 6 August the Armada, to the surprise of the English, anchored off Calais. The English, of course, did not know about the Spanish plan to join up with the Duke of Parma's army in the Spanish Netherlands.

The fireships

Anchored off Calais, the Duke of Medina Sidonia received some bad news – the Duke of Parma would not have his army ready for nearly another week. The Armada would have to wait. Lord Howard took his chance. He ordered seven of his ships to be emptied and filled with pitch and tar and other things that would burn. He had the cannon on these ships filled with gunpowder and shot, so that they would go off when the ships were burning well. He waited until it was dark and then set fire to the ships and allowed the wind and tide to drift them into the Spanish fleet.

The Spanish panicked – just imagine the fire and explosions, in the dark of the night. Many of the Spanish captains cut their anchor ropes and fled.

The Battle of Gravelines

The next day there was a fierce battle at Gravelines. The Spanish lost some ships but amazingly the Armada managed to get back into formation. It was by now very low on food and ammunition and needed to return to Spain. Sailing down the English Channel would mean having to defeat the English fleet that was blocking their escape, and so Medina Sidonia decided to sail home by going round the north coast of Scotland.

The terrible journey home

The English fleet followed the Armada as far as the east coast of Scotland but had to return because of a lack of food. Howard was still worried that the Armada was heading for Norway or Demark for provisions and would then return. However, the Spanish experienced terrible weather. With every storm they encountered, more ships were lost along the coasts of Scotland and Ireland. They had no charts of these waters, they were short of food, and remember that many of the ships had lost their anchors. On 13 September, the Duke of Medina Sidonia managed to reach Spain – behind him, limping home, was just half of his fleet.

Source ⑦

Both sides of a medal made soon after the defeat of the Armada. The words on the right say 'God blew and they scattered'.

Source ⑧

The Armada portrait of Elizabeth I.

Source **9**

This portrait of Mary, Queen of Scots was painted when she was fifteen, just before her first marriage.

Task

Mary was 26 years old when she arrived in England, asking for help. Quite a lot had happened to her in those 26 years. What impression do you get of Mary so far? Do you think she had been unlucky or simply stupid?

Case study 3: a rival

Mary, Queen of Scots was involved in dramas, plots and deaths for almost the whole of her life. But none of them was quite as dramatic as the plot that led to her execution in 1587. In order to understand the part she played in Elizabeth's life and in the politics of England, we have to go back to the beginning.

Mary became Queen of Scots when her father, King James V of Scotland, died soon after she was born. Mary's mother was French, and Mary spent most of her childhood in France. She ended up as Queen of France, married to Francis II. He died in 1560 as the result of an ear infection and, aged eighteen, Mary decided to return to Scotland as its queen.

But things were not that simple. Mary was a Catholic. She had to face the Scottish nobility, many of whom had become Protestants, and the formidable Protestant preacher, John Knox, who hated women rulers almost as much as he hated Catholics.

In 1565 Mary added to her problems by marrying Lord Darnley. This infuriated Elizabeth because both Darnley and Mary had a claim to the English throne and it looked to Elizabeth as though they were planning a takeover bid. She tried, and failed, to stop their wedding. To make matters worse for Mary, Darnley turned out to be a stupid, vain, boastful drunk. Jealous of her secretary, David Rizzio, Darnley convinced himself that they were having an affair and in 1566 he killed Rizzio in front of Mary.

The following year, Darnley himself was killed. The house he was staying in was mysteriously blown up and Darnley was found dead in the garden. He had been strangled, and the prime suspect was the Earl of Bothwell, Mary's lover. Mary, now a widow for the second time, promptly married him. The Scottish nobles were horrified. They had had enough. With English support, they rose up against Mary, who was cornered and her forces defeated at the Battle of Carberry Hill, outside Edinburgh, in 1567. Her baby son was taken away from her, proclaimed King James VI of Scotland and brought up as a Protestant. Mary never saw him again.

Mary herself was imprisoned in Lochleven castle, in the middle of Loch Leven. Escaping dramatically in a rowing boat, and defeated again at the battle of Langside, by May 1568 Mary was in England. Arriving in Cumbria and moving from Carlisle Castle to Bolton Castle in Wensleydale, she asked Elizabeth for help.

Elizabeth's dilemma

Mary's arrival in England put Elizabeth in a very difficult position. Mary was a queen and a cousin. She was also a threat to Elizabeth herself and to the security of her realm. What was Elizabeth to do? She had three main options, and each one had a snag:

- Imprison Mary in England for the rest of her life. **But** Mary was a Catholic and heir to the English throne. English Catholics might murder Elizabeth, release Mary and put her on the throne.

- Force Mary to return to Scotland. **But** she might be killed by her enemies there and Elizabeth would be held responsible.
- Send Mary to France. **But** she might persuade the French to invade England and force Elizabeth from the throne, so making herself queen.

If you had been a Privy Councillor, what would you have advised Elizabeth to do? Eventually, Elizabeth decided that Mary must stay in England, but under guard. This was probably the most sensible decision. Elizabeth had more control over Mary than she would have done had Mary been despatched elsewhere. But this didn't stop Mary from becoming the focus of a number of Catholic plots, whether she knew about them or not.

Plots, plots and more plots

In 1569, the Rebellion of the Northern Earls (see pages 78–80) aimed to re-establish Catholicism and put Mary on the throne. Although the revolt was easily suppressed, it nevertheless showed that a major Catholic rising against Elizabeth was possible. Worse was to come. The following year came the Papal Bull that excommunicated Elizabeth. The Pope further stated:

> I reject Elizabeth's false claim to the throne. English nobles and subjects are let off all promises, loyalty and obedience to her. I forbid nobles and subjects to obey her orders or laws.

This looked as if the Pope was encouraging Catholic plots to overthrow Elizabeth. Nothing was safe or certain any more.

- In 1571 the Ridolfi Plot aimed to murder Elizabeth, to free the Duke of Norfolk from the Tower and Mary from imprisonment in Tutbury Castle in Staffordshire and set them up as King and Queen of England. All this was to be backed by a Spanish invasion force. The plot was discovered and the Duke of Norfolk executed.
- In 1583, Walsingham uncovered the Throckmorton Plot, which aimed to do the same thing. Francis Throckmorton, a Catholic, confessed under torture that Mary knew about the plot and was involved in it. But Elizabeth refused to have her tried.

Now thoroughly alarmed, the Privy Council drew up a Bond of Association. This said that if Elizabeth was murdered, anyone who benefited from the murder would be killed. It was clearly aimed at Mary, Queen of Scots. The bond was signed by thousands of Elizabeth's loyal subjects.

- In 1585, Walsingham uncovered the Parry Plot. This was a plot by an MP to murder Elizabeth. Walsingham couldn't prove, to Elizabeth's satisfaction, that Mary was involved and so, again, she refused to have her tried.

However, these plots were nothing compared to the Babington Plot that was to be Mary's undoing.

What... ?

EXCOMMUNICATION
Being forbidden by the Pope to attend Mass and from mixing with other Catholics.

The Babington Plot

Mary sent messages in code to Anthony Babington. He was a Catholic living in Paris and very sympathetic to Mary and her plight. Together they planned to recruit six men who would kill Elizabeth. But Walsingham was several steps ahead of Mary. In December 1585 he had got hold of the secret code.

Source ❿

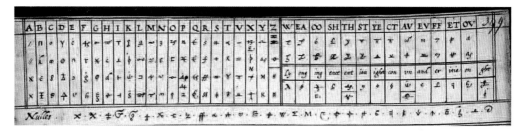

This is the code Walsingham uncovered. ❓ *Try to write a message to a friend using the code.*

He decided to trap her once and for all so that Elizabeth would have no alternative but to put her on trial. Mary sent her messages to Babington written on cloth, wrapped in waterproof material and hidden in beer barrels. Walsingham's own agents had told her this was the best way to get messages through to Babington. But they were intercepting every single one. Only when Mary had fully implicated herself in the plot to murder Elizabeth did Walsingham put a stop to the enterprise. He had gathered all the evidence he needed.

Elizabeth decided to have Mary tried by a special court. In October 1586 she was taken to Fotheringay Castle in Northamptonshire and put on trial for 'imagining and encompassing Her Majesty's death'. There, 31 specially selected commissioners (peers, Privy Councillors and judges) heard all the evidence against her.

Mary conducted her own defence. The main points she made in her defence were that:

● the court had no right to try her
● none of the letters was in her own handwriting. They were either written by one of her secretaries, or copied out by a scribe working for Walsingham. They could have written anything, just to make her appear guilty.

It was no use. Mary was found guilty, with only one peer disagreeing with the verdict. Her sentence had to be execution, but would Elizabeth agree to it?

The execution of Mary, Queen of Scots

Elizabeth dithered. Mary was plainly guilty of treason, but could she sign her death warrant? Many European monarchs were Catholic and did not believe that Elizabeth had any right to the throne of England. If she ordered the execution of the woman they believed to be England's rightful monarch, would they invade England to overthrow her? Did she have any right to order the murder of a fellow monarch – an anointed sovereign? If she did, wouldn't she be making a statement to the effect that the murder of monarchs by monarchs was acceptable and so open the way for her own murder? These thoughts must have gone through Elizabeth's mind as she decided what she should do.

The Privy Councillors were very clear as to what Elizabeth should do. So were both Houses of Parliament, who petitioned Elizabeth to have Mary executed. At the end of 1586 a deputation went to see Elizabeth to urge her to put Mary to death. The reply Elizabeth gave must have puzzled them:

> As for your petition, your judgement I condemn not. But I pray you to accept my thankfulness, excuse my doubtfulness, and take in good part my answer, answerless.

What did she mean? Cecil and the other Privy Councillors were getting increasingly impatient. For weeks Cecil had had Mary's death warrant prepared, ready for Elizabeth to sign. And still she wouldn't make a move. Eventually, the pressure on Elizabeth was so great that she had no option but to sign, and this she did on 1 February 1587. Even then Elizabeth dithered. She asked William Davison, the secretary who was given the signed death warrant, not to seal the document in case she changed her mind; she called him back as he was leaving to ask if perhaps Mary could be killed quietly, so that a death warrant with her signature on it wouldn't be necessary. The answer was no. Cecil and Walsingham had Davison rush to Fotheringay with the warrant. They didn't want Elizabeth having any second thoughts until it was too late. Mary, Queen of Scots was executed on 8 February 1587.

Elizabeth's reaction

Elizabeth flew into a rage, declaring that she had never intended the death warrant to be sent and had not ordered it to be taken to Fotheringay. She turned William Davison into a scapegoat and threw him into the Tower of London; she talked about putting members of the Privy Council on trial for murder; she refused to speak to Walsingham for weeks, and she ordered a royal funeral for Mary. Eventually, relationships went back to normal. Davison was released from the Tower, Walsingham was restored to favour and all talk of murder charges was ended.

In Scotland, Mary's son, King James VI, made only the briefest of protests. He was, after all, now Elizabeth's heir and, before long, would come into his inheritance.

Discuss

1 Why did Elizabeth take so long to sign the death warrant of Mary, Queen of Scots?
2 Are you surprised at Elizabeth's reaction to Mary's execution?
3 Should Mary, Queen of Scots have been executed? Explain your answer.

Source ⑪

The execution of Mary, Queen of Scots at Fotheringay castle in 1587. ❓ *What do you think is happening at each of the numbered points 1–6?*

Task
Add more notes to your diagram about Elizabeth's successes.

5.3 Did Elizabeth share power with her parliaments?

Certainly not! At least, that is what Elizabeth would have said. Parliament, on the other hand, was always trying to have a greater say in matters of state than Elizabeth and her ministers liked. But in order to understand how Elizabeth used her parliaments, we must first look at how the country was governed.

How did Elizabeth rule?

Elizabeth, like her father, half-brother and half-sister before her, ruled with the help and advice of a Royal Council of about 58 important and influential men. However, Elizabeth decided to take only general advice from them. She chose, from her Royal Council, a small group of twelve or so men, her Privy Council, whom she trusted to give her detailed advice about the running of the country. It was their job, too, to keep in touch with the influential people who held power in the cities and counties throughout England and Wales. They had to make sure Elizabeth's wishes were understood and carried out, and they had to be able to warn Elizabeth if trouble was brewing. She didn't want any surprise rebellions!

Who were Elizabeth's Privy Councillors?

The most important of Elizabeth's Privy Councillors were:

● William Cecil, Lord Burghley (1520–98), who was Elizabeth's Principal Secretary from the start of her reign until the time he died. She trusted him absolutely. He was a cautious, moderate man and an excellent administrator. He looked after the Queen's finances, too. Working together, Elizabeth and Cecil made her reign the success it was. The only time they fell out was when he persuaded her, against, so she said, her better judgement, to sign the death warrant of Mary, Queen of Scots.

> **Who...?**
>
> **WILLIAM CECIL, LORD BURGHLEY (1520–98)**
> Cecil became an MP in 1543 and learned a lot about politics by working in Edward VI's Privy Council. During Mary's reign, although he offered her his diplomatic services, he seems to have been part of a group of MPs who were critical of the Crown.
>
> Under Elizabeth I, Cecil's career flourished, and the two formed a formidable partnership that ensured the success of her reign. Cecil was Elizabeth's private secretary, her principal secretary and, from 1572, her lord treasurer. He was the key link between Elizabeth and her Privy Council. He worked hard, collecting and analysing information from foreign diplomats, preparing council agendas and drafting papers for Elizabeth. But his position also gave him the opportunity for pressing his own concerns and presenting them to the Queen.

Source 12

Source 13

Source 14

Task

Tudor portraits were usually painted very carefully to present a certain image. Work in pairs. Use the bullet pointed text to help you decide which of the above portraits (Sources 12–14) is William Cecil, Robert Dudley and Francis Walsingham.

- Robert Dudley, the Earl of Leicester (1533–88), was Elizabeth's favourite. There were strong rumours about their relationship and at one time it seemed possible that she might marry him. He was dashing, handsome, vain, arrogant as well as being incompetent as a military commander. Despite all this, Elizabeth listened to his advice and they remained devoted to each other until his death.

- Francis Walsingham (1530–90), a strict Puritan, was Elizabeth's spy-master. He organised a vast intelligence service involving networks of spies. They worked mainly abroad, finding out if there were any plots developing against Elizabeth and reporting back to their master what they found. Although the security of her realm depended on him, Elizabeth respected Walsingham rather than liked him.

How important was William Cecil?

In a word – very! He was very clever, managed people well and was aware of his own limitations. He spoke his mind to Elizabeth, even when he knew she would disagree with him. He also knew that, once he had given his opinion, it was his duty to enforce whatever the Queen had decided should happen. But, as her reign progressed, William Cecil developed strategies for getting Elizabeth to accept his advice.

Source ⓯

Just look at what Cecil had achieved by the time of his death in 1598:

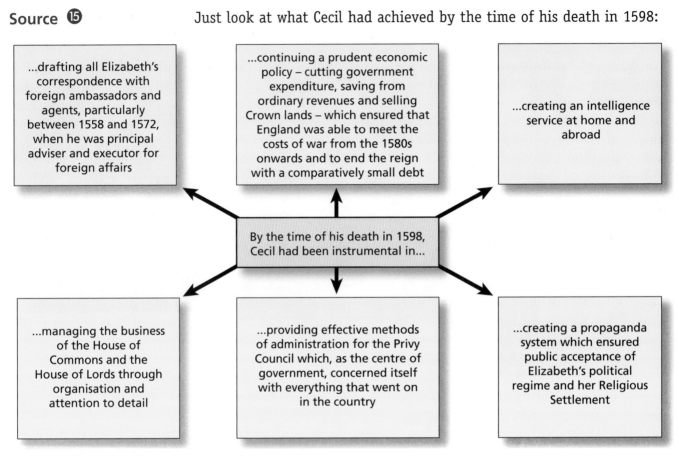

...drafting all Elizabeth's correspondence with foreign ambassadors and agents, particularly between 1558 and 1572, when he was principal adviser and executor for foreign affairs

...continuing a prudent economic policy – cutting government expenditure, saving from ordinary revenues and selling Crown lands – which ensured that England was able to meet the costs of war from the 1580s onwards and to end the reign with a comparatively small debt

...creating an intelligence service at home and abroad

By the time of his death in 1598, Cecil had been instrumental in...

...managing the business of the House of Commons and the House of Lords through organisation and attention to detail

...providing effective methods of administration for the Privy Council which, as the centre of government, concerned itself with everything that went on in the country

...creating a propaganda system which ensured public acceptance of Elizabeth's political regime and her Religious Settlement

Summary of William Cecil's achievements.

What about Parliament?

Elizabeth didn't have to call any parliaments at all. There was no rule that said Parliament had to meet a certain number of times or sit for a certain length of time. If Elizabeth wanted something to happen, she simply issued a proclamation saying it was to be so. But if she wanted to be really certain, it was best to call a parliament and get the House of Commons and the House of Lords to pass a law. In 1565, Sir Thomas Smith wrote a book called *The Governance of England*. In it he said:

> The most high and absolute power of the realm of England consists in the Parliament. Every bill or law is read and discussed three times in both Houses of Parliament. Therefore no man can complain but must accept and obey it. And the consent of Parliament is taken to be the consent of every man.

The only other reason Elizabeth would have to call a parliament would be because she needed money. This was because Parliament had to agree to taxes being collected from the people.

Members of Parliament, however, had other ideas! Henry VIII had used Parliament to make his dissolution of the monasteries legal. Edward VI and Mary I used the power of parliament to legalise their religious changes.

MPs began to think that, if they were this important, Parliament should have a greater say in royal policies, and not just meet when the monarch fancied it.

MPs had another problem, too. Parliament could (in theory, at least!) only discuss those issues that the monarch thought appropriate for them. Elizabeth didn't think it right, for example, that Parliament should discuss religion, the succession or foreign policy, and she certainly didn't think it was any of their business to discuss the possibility of her marriage. Many times Elizabeth had to warn them that they had overstepped the mark. Too often she had to say: 'Take heed what you do, the Queen's Majesty liketh it not.'

Throughout Elizabeth's reign of 45 years, Parliament met just thirteen times:

January–May 1559	January–April 1563	September 1566–January 1567	April–May 1571	May–June 1572	February–March 1576	January–March 1581	November 1584–March 1585	October 1586–March 1587	February–March 1589	February–April 1593	October 1597–February 1598	October–December 1601

Even though it met relatively few times, Parliament was one of the most important ways for a monarch to communicate with his or her people. The men who met from time to time as a parliament in the Palace of Westminster came from the upper section of society that dominated politics. The House of Lords consisted of 26 bishops and 60 peers. Members of Elizabeth's Privy Council who were also peers attended regularly. Important though it was, the House of Lords became even more important when the Queen's chief minister, William Cecil, was made Lord Burghley in 1571 and took his seat in the House of Lords. In the House of Commons, MPs were 'knights of the shire', who represented the counties, and 'burgesses' who represented the towns. They informed the Queen of their wishes and those of the people living in their own parts of the country; they returned to their homes and told people what had been agreed. This line of communication was very important because Elizabeth had no police force or standing army to enforce decisions made by Parliament.

What... ?

STANDING ARMY
A regular, paid army that exists all the time, not one that is put together when danger threatens.

Source ⓰

Queen Elizabeth

bishops and lords

clerks taking notes

MPs from the House of Commons

speaker

Discuss

1 What did Elizabeth think Parliament was for?
2 Why would many MPs disagree with her?
3 Describe and explain the role of William Cecil in Elizabeth's government.
4 Explain how the Queen, her Privy Council and Parliament could work together to make sure the country was well-governed.

An engraving of Queen Elizabeth on her throne in Parliament. Members of the House of Commons are presenting their speaker to the Queen. ❓ *What does this engraving tell you about the relationship between Elizabeth and her parliament?*

Were there arguments between Elizabeth and her parliaments?

By and large, the business of parliament ran smoothly. Taxes were granted and laws passed. This was partly due to good management and partly because Parliament and the Queen agreed on their two main objectives: maintaining the Protestant religion and defending the country against its enemies. It was also due to the personality of the Queen. She had a terrible temper and, too often for Cecil and her parliaments, refused to make up her mind on what they thought were important issues. Perhaps, though, above all, she knew how to charm in order to get her own way! This is part of a speech she made to Parliament in November 1601. Even as an elderly lady she could turn on the charm and win hearts and minds:

> Although God hath raised me high, yet this I esteem the most glory of my crown, that I have reigned with your loves. .. it is not my desire to live nor reign longer than my life and reign shall be for your good. And though you have had, and may have in the future, many mightier and wiser princes sitting in this seat, yet you never had, nor shall have, any that will love you better.

However, there were two linked areas where Parliament and the Queen came into conflict. These were the Queen's marriage and the problem of who was to succeed her.

Why was the Queen's marriage and the succession such a problem?

When Elizabeth came to the throne she was unmarried and had no children. Her closest living relative, and the person with the best claim to the throne after Elizabeth herself, was Mary, Queen of Scots. Mary was a Catholic and everyone's great fear was that, should Elizabeth die without children, Mary would try to turn England back to Catholicism. There would be even more religious upheavals! The obvious thing to do was for Elizabeth to marry and have children of her own, who would be brought up as Protestants. But who was Elizabeth to marry? Mary I's marriage to Philip of Spain had been something of a disaster and if Elizabeth was to marry a foreign prince he might well try to take over ruling the country from her. On the other hand, marriage to an English nobleman would bring a different set of problems, if a man from one of the leading families in the country was raised above all the others.

Time and again the Privy Council and Parliament tried to discuss Elizabeth's marriage and the succession; time and time again Elizabeth refused to let them do so. Elizabeth had no intention of being 'bounced' into marriage. Indeed, she probably had no intention of marrying at all. Maybe she didn't want any suggestion of power-sharing with a husband; maybe she didn't want to produce an heir, remembering how opposition to the reigning monarch had gathered around her when Mary I was on the

Discuss

1 Why did Parliament keep trying to persuade Elizabeth to marry or name her successor?
2 Why do you think Elizabeth refused to be pushed into marriage?
3 Why do you think Elizabeth didn't want to name her successor?

throne, and what a dangerous time this had been for her. Maybe her own childhood, in which her father had had her mother executed, had put her off marriage for good.

Elizabeth, in fact, played the 'marriage game' very cleverly. She was quite a catch. Although at the beginning of her reign, England had an empty Treasury because of expensive wars with France, England was of great strategic importance. It controlled the sea routes from Spain to the Netherlands, and from the North Sea to Europe. Marriage to Elizabeth would give her husband considerable power in foreign affairs. Elizabeth knew this, of course. She managed to string along quite a few suitors – Archduke Charles of Austria, King Erik XIV of Sweden, the French Dukes of Anjou and of Alençon , for example – in order to gain friends for England.

There remained the problem of the succession. Elizabeth steadfastly refused to name her heir, even though everyone had a dreadful scare in 1562. She caught smallpox and the doctors thought she would die. People, even royal people, often died if they caught smallpox, which was then a killer disease. Even on what her Privy Council thought might be her deathbed, she would not say who she wanted to reign after her. Miraculously, Elizabeth recovered, so the problem was solved. But that didn't stop Parliament and her ministers pressing her to name her successor. The next time they might not be so lucky. Elizabeth would have none of it. Even in 1601, when she was 68, she still refused. Only when she was dying in 1603 did she whisper the name of the Protestant King James VI of Scotland – son of Mary, Queen of Scots.

Source 🄱

Task

You have looked at a lot of portraits of Tudor people. So far, you have been asked what you think the portraits are suggesting about the character of the people they are portraying. But there's a hidden agenda. Many portraits contained hidden messages.

1 Now look carefully at the portraits of Elizabeth, Source 17A and B opposite. What can you see in them? What is their hidden message?
2 Design your own portrait of Elizabeth. What message do you want to convey? What symbols will you put in?

Task

Add some more details to your diagram of Elizabeth's successes.

Pelican
Legend has it that the mother pelican pecks at her own breast and feeds her young on her own blood so that they might live. Elizabeth, as the mother pelican, will sacrifice her life for her people and for her Church.

Tudor rose
The emblem of the Tudor family, it shows Elizabeth's regal status and her right to the throne.

Fleur-de-lis
The royal emblem of France, it symbolises Elizabeth's claim to the throne of France which she did not renounce, despite the loss of Calais.

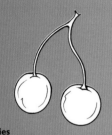

Cherries
This fruit represents sweetness, the fruits of paradise and the delights of the blessed.

Thornless rose
Symbolising the Virgin Mary, it suggests that Elizabeth, the Virgin Queen, was married to her country in the same way that Mary was married to the Church.

Fan of feathers
The exotic feathers, imported from the New World, represent England's overseas expansion.

Gloves
A sign of elegance, Elizabeth was fond of holding them to show off her long white hands of which, it is said, she was very vain.

Ermine
Legend tells that the ermine was willing to die rather than dirty its pure white coat, and it therefore symbolises Elizabeth's virtue and purity.

Clothing and jewels
Elizabeth's sumptuous clothing and her jewels reflect power, and the choice of colour and stone sometimes mirrors the heraldry of a particular suitor. A white dress and pearls represent chastity.

Phoenix
A mythical bird that was believed to rise from the flames unscathed, the phoenix represents the Protestant Church's rise from the flames of Mary's reign.

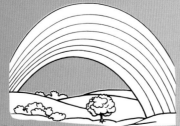

Rainbow
A rainbow reinforces an old Latin motto, 'no rainbow without the sun', and illustrates peace.

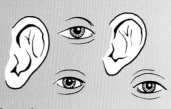

Eyes and ears
They are thought to refer to *Hymns to Astraea*, composed by Sir John Davis – 'eye of that mind most quick and clear' – and illustrate Elizabeth's ability to see and hear all.

5.4 Paupers and vagabonds: how did Elizabeth I's government deal with poverty?

One of the problems that most worried the Queen, the Privy Council and Parliament, as well as JPs in towns and cities, was the growing number of poor people in the country. Most worrying were the vagabonds, who wandered, sometimes in large gangs, from village to village and town to town. They were beggars, and often their begging became menacing. Thomas Harman, a JP in Kent, told of a gang of over 200 vagabonds who roamed Essex, Kent, Middlesex, Surrey and Sussex, terrorising local people. Edward Hext, a JP in Somerset, wrote to William Cecil complaining about gangs of between 40 and 80 vagabonds travelling through his county.

Why were there so many beggars in Elizabethan England?

There had always been beggars in England, but in Elizabeth's reign their numbers increased sharply. This was for several social and economic factors:

- There were a series of **bad harvests.**
- **Prices** of basic goods, like bread, were rising.
- **Wages** were not going up at the same rate as food prices.
- The **population** was growing.
- **Demand for food** was increasing.
- More land was being used for **sheep farming**, less for crop growing.
- Sheep farming needed **fewer workers** than crop growing.
- **Unemployment** was increasing.
- **Monasteries** that had once supported the poor had been closed.
- In the 1590s, England was at **war** with Spain. Soldiers and sailors who got injured could no longer work. After the wars finished, soldiers and sailors came home looking for jobs.

Stage 1: the authorities get worried

The authorities were growing more and more worried about the increasing numbers of poor people for two main reasons:

- Vagabonds were suspected, often with very good reason, of being petty criminals and therefore of bringing about a decline, or even a collapse, of law and order.
- There was a growing feeling, especially amongst the Puritans, that it was wrong to be idle. Everyone should be encouraged to work and punished if they did not. But there was a growing understanding that a difference should be made between those who could not work through no fault of their own, and those who could work, but refused to.

Task

1 Choose one 'scam' and make a poster to be pinned on a village wall warning people against this kind of beggar. Remember not everyone can read so make it visual!

2 Why do you think beggars resorted to scams like these?

Things were not always what they seemed!

Many people were desperately poor and begging was the only way they stood a chance of surviving. Some of these attempted different sorts of scams in order to persuade people to give them money. Some beggars were not poor at all and turned to begging as an easy way to make money. How were ordinary people to decide between the tricksters and the genuinely destitute?

Clapper dudgeons covered themselves in artificial sores and wrapped these in blood-soaked cloths.

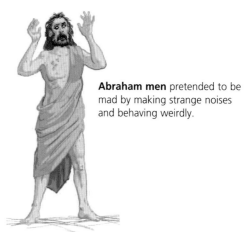

Abraham men pretended to be mad by making strange noises and behaving weirdly.

Bawdy baskets were women who sold lace and pins from door to door, stealing clothes that were laid out to dry and persuading ladies' maids to give them food in exchange for cheap jewellery.

Courtesy men were smartly dressed men who persuaded people to lend them money, and then vanished without paying it back.

Counterfeit soldiers pretended to be wounded war heroes.

Freshwater mariners claimed to have been wounded fighting with a famous sea captain.

Dummerers were beggars who pretended to be deaf and dumb.

This is what the Council of the North had to say about the situation in 1572:

Instructions drawn up by the Council of the North to the Justices of the Peace:
Order is to be given in market towns and other places, that all suspected vagabonds, beggars and rogues, because they trouble the quiet of the realm, be punished with severity and speed.

Source check

The Middlesex county records tell us what happened to five vagabonds caught at Harrow-on-the-Hill:

John Allen, Elizabeth Turner, Humfrey Fox, Henry Bower and Agnes Wort, being over fourteen years old and having no lawful means of livelihood were vagrants and had been vagrants in other parts of the country. Sentenced to be flogged severely and burnt on the right ear.

Stage 2: The towns take action

It was the towns that tackled the problem first. This was because many of the poverty-stricken unemployed went to towns in search of work.

The 'sturdy beggars' or 'vagabonds'

They decided that not all the poor were helpless. Some of them were what Elizabethans called 'sturdy beggars', people who were fit enough to work but chose not to. The way to deal with them was to whip them and publicly disgrace them.

Vagabonds could then be sent to 'houses of correction', usually called Bridewells, where they were trained in the sort of skills they needed to fit them for work. But many returned to their vagrant life!

The deserving poor

Some poor were genuinely in need of help. London led the way in providing for the 'deserving poor':

- St Bartholomew's Hospital was restored, with the help of the Bishop of London for poor people who were sick and bedridden.
- The bishop also helped restore St Thomas' Hospital, which was for poor people who were old as well as being ill.
- Christ's Hospital cared for orphan children.
- Bedlam Hospital looked after the poor who were insane.

Although this only touched the tip of the iceberg, it was a start. Other towns followed. Ipswich and Norwich set up Bridewells for sturdy beggars and hospitals for the deserving elderly and infirm poor. The city authorities gave badges to genuine beggars so that people would know they were not being tricked if they gave them money or offered them work. They did not allow children to beg. In order to pay for the help they were giving to people in genuine need, the authorities collected a tax from all those who were in work. The Privy Council was impressed.

Task

1 What do you think of the idea of punishing some poor people and helping others?
2 What problems do you think the towns will face in following these policies? Make a list.
3 How far do you think these measures will solve the problem of poverty?

Stage 3: The government acts

A bad harvest in 1571 led to even more hardship for poor people and a rapid increase in the number of roaming beggars. Members of Parliament debated the subject at great length and passed two Acts. These Acts tried to apply to the whole country the experiences of towns like Norwich.

What?

RELIEF
Giving help to the poor.

IMPOTENT POOR
Those who were too sick, old or young to look after themselves.

Task

A Common Entrance style essay question:
1 **Describe** the changes that were made in Elizabeth's reign to the ways in which the poor were treated.
2 **Explain** why these changes were made.

Summary task

Look at the diagram you have been compiling throughout this unit. Which leg has the most examples attached? Was this the key to Elizabeth's success?

• In 1572 an 'Act for the Punishments of Vagabonds and for the Relief of the Poor and Impotent' laid down that when a vagabond was caught begging, he or she was to be whipped and a hole burned through their right ear; vagabonds who were twice caught begging were to be hanged unless someone would agree to give them a job. If a vagabond was caught begging a third time, hanging would be an automatic penalty. The Act also said that every 'city, borough, town, village and hamlet' had to raise money so there was a local fund to support the local poor.

• In 1576 an 'Act for the Setting of the Poor on Work, and for the Avoiding of Idleness' introduced a system whereby the poor would be given work, like weaving or spinning, to do in their own homes. If they refused, they would be sent to a 'house of correction', which was to be set up in every county, where they would be forced to work. Working people who refused to contribute to the cost of poor relief had to pay twice as much as the amount they were first asked for!

The Privy Council tried to make sure that the regulations were followed throughout the country, but it wasn't easy. Then in 1586 there was another bad harvest. This time the government took special measures to make sure corn was available for the poor and needy. By now the Privy Council and Parliament were beginning to see that giving relief to the poor would help to stop people from becoming beggars. A long period of famine in the mid 1590s led to a number of laws being passed. The death penalty for vagabonds was abolished; instead they were to be whipped and sent out of the parish in which they were begging. Overseers of the poor were appointed in all parishes to collect and administer poor relief.

Finally, in 1601, all the laws and regulations for dealing with the poor were gathered together into a great Poor Law Act. This Act was the basis of England's Poor Laws for more than two hundred years.

Source 18

This woodcut, made in the sixteenth century, shows a beggar being whipped through the streets.
❓ *How can you tell this woodcut was made before 1590?*

Section 1: Summary task 1

The Tudors: Successes and failures

You have studied five Tudor monarchs and it is time to compare them.

1 Make notes about their successes and failures using a table like this:

Monarch	Successes	Failures
Henry VII	Established the Tudor dynasty	
Henry VIII		
Edward VI		
Mary I		
Elizabeth I		

Use note form but include as many points as you can on both sides. An example has been done for you.

2 Choose a portrait of each monarch (from this book or from your own research on the internet), to make a Tudor Gallery. Under each portrait write a paragraph, or some bullet points summarising the key events of this person's reign and mentioning at least one of their successes or failures.

3 Find some way for your gallery to show who was most successful. You could hang the most successful highest, or make it biggest, or number them 1–5, or put them in order of success. Then write a paragraph to explain who you put top and another about who you put bottom and why. Support your argument with evidence.

Section 1: Summary task 2

Who holds the power?

One of the big themes you are studying in this book is the changing relationship between monarchs and Parliament.

At the end of the Tudor period, how far had power shifted away from the Crown? How would you redraw this to show what had changed by 1600?

SECTION 2

The Stuarts: Civil War and Commonwealth

THE

Worldturn'dupfidedown:

OR

A briefe defcription of the ridiculous Fafhions
of thefe dultacted Times.

By T. J. a well-willer to King, Parliament and Kingdom.

This picture comes from a pamphlet published in 1647. The artist who made it signed himself simply, 'A well-wisher to the King.' He called his picture: 'The world turned upside down.' As you look at it can you see all the things that are 'wrong' in the picture? What do you think the artist was trying to say?

By the end of this section you should be able to explain this picture very well. Through the section you will find out how some of the problems that had rumbled on through the Tudor century – particularly arguments over religion – turned very serious indeed and led to a bloody civil war between King Charles II and his Parliament.

Unit 6 is a short unit setting the scene; Unit 7 examines the causes of the Civil War in detail; Unit 8 then tells the story of the Civil War – and explains why the King lost, and why he was executed. Finally Unit 9 examines the period known as the interregnum (when England had no monarch) and assesses the reputation of the man who led England in this period – Oliver Cromwell.

Your final task will be to review this turbulent period through the eyes of different characters.

6.1 Who planned the Gunpowder Plot?

Did you go to a bonfire party last November? If you did you would have seen fireworks as well as a 'guy' being burned on the bonfire. Why do we do this every year? And who is the 'guy' meant to be? You probably know the answers to these questions but do you know that the usual story about the Gunpowder Plot is not believed by some historians? They believe it was a put-up job by the King's chief minister, Robert Cecil, to discredit Catholics. As you will see it all revolves around a mysterious letter...

The background to the plot

You have already seen that during Elizabeth's reign England became a Protestant country. Catholics were sometimes persecuted but most stayed loyal to Elizabeth and were allowed to quietly get on with their lives. If they refused to attend church services the worst that happened to most of them was that they had to pay a recusancy fine. When James I became king in 1603 many Catholics hoped that he would abolish these fines. James himself was probably happy to leave the Catholics alone but there were many people in England, and in his government, who saw them as traitors and wanted them to be persecuted. James could not afford to be seen to be weak and in February 1605 he ordered a purge against recusants. By November 1605 over 5,500 Catholics had been arrested and convicted of recusancy.

The official story

This is the story you might already know. It is certainly the story the government at the time wanted everybody to believe!

Source **1**

A drawing of the alleged plotters. ❓ *The caption is German. What does this tell you about the interest created by the plot?*

A group of Catholics (you can see them in Source 1) decided that they had had enough. They planned to blow up the House of Lords when the King, his ministers and MPs were all present. They would then seize James' daughter Elizabeth, and Charles, his son, and proclaim one of them as the new Catholic monarch.

The plotters started their preparations early in 1604. They rented a house next to the House of Lords and began tunnelling. However, they could not dig their way through the thick foundation wall of the House of Lords and had to give up. They then found out about a cellar that was right under the House of Lords. Its advantage was that it had a door that opened onto the River Thames. In February 1605 they rented the cellar and over the next few months gradually filled it with 36 barrels of gunpowder that were transported by river. Soon they were ready for the state opening of Parliament on 5 November.

However, things went badly wrong for the plotters. During the night of 26 October, one of Lord Monteagle's servants was given a letter by a stranger. When Monteagle read the letter he was puzzled. The fact that there was no clue as to whom the letter was from made it even more mysterious. To be on the safe side, he decided to show it to Robert Cecil. Here is part of the letter:

> My Lord, out of the love I bear to some of your friends, I have a care for your safety. Therefore I warn you, as you value your life, to make up an excuse for not attending at this Parliament. Do not ignore this warning, but go back to your country where you may await the event in safety. For though there be no appearance of any trouble, yet I say they shall receive a terrible blow this Parliament; and yet they shall not see who hurts them.

Did you know?

The cellars of the House of Lords are still searched by the Queen's Bodyguard of the Yeoman of the Guards on the evening before every Opening of Parliament.

Cecil immediately ordered the cellars of the House of Lords to be searched. They didn't find much although there was a huge pile of firewood heaped up in the cellar. The King ordered another search, which took place in the early hours of 5 November. They found a man in a cloak and dark hat skulking beneath the House of Lords. He said his name was John Johnson, but they later discovered his real name – Guy Fawkes. The plot had been discovered!

The other plotters fled to the Midlands to try and start an uprising but they were easily rounded up. Some were killed while others were captured. They were put on trial and in January 1606 were hanged, drawn and quartered. When Parliament met in the same month Cecil was able to use the plot to get more severe laws against Catholics passed. And the fireworks and bonfires that we still have today? Well, James wanted the plot to be remembered and asked people to light bonfires on 5 November. They put effigies of the Pope on their bonfires to show their hatred of him.

There are two possible explanations of the Gunpowder Plot.

Explanation 1: It was a Catholic plot

The official story that you have been reading about is correct. The letter to Lord Monteagle was sent by one of the plotters, his brother-in-law Francis Tresham. He simply wanted to save Monteagle from being blown up.

Explanation 2: It was a government plot

The letter to Monteagle was just too much of a coincidence. The plot was planned by Robert Cecil who wanted an excuse to persecute Catholics. His agents made Guy Fawkes and the other plotters believe it was a real plot. They did not know the government was behind it. He had the letter written as a way of letting the government pretend it had discovered the plot.

Source 2

A seventeenth-century drawing of Guy Fawkes showing him preparing the gunpowder. This was made by Protestants who wanted the reader to think Guy Fawkes was guilty and a traitor. ❓ How do the numbered features in the picture show this?

106

The evidence is below. Some of it you already know, but some of it is new. It can all be used to work out what really happened.

Task

1 You are going to use the following evidence to decide which explanation is correct. Copy the grid into your exercise books. For each piece of evidence put a tick in one of the columns.

Evidence	It was a Catholic plot	It was a government plot
1		

2 What do you think? Which of the explanations does the evidence favour? It may not be the explanation with the most ticks. Some of the evidence may carry more weight than other pieces. When you have made your decision there will be a secret class vote and you will have the chance to explain why you chose the explanation you did.

Evidence 1
Catholics were angry because in 1605 the government started to punish Catholics more harshly.

Evidence 2
Robert Cecil wanted an excuse to persecute Catholics even more harshly.

Evidence 3
All of the plotters were Catholic and two of them, Robert Catesby and Francis Tresham, had been involved in the 1601 rebellion against Elizabeth.

Evidence 4
The night the letter was sent to Lord Monteagle was the only night in 1605 that he stayed in his London house.

Evidence 5
Lord Monteagle is a mysterious figure. He was from a Catholic family and was involved in a plot against Elizabeth in 1601. He was let off surprisingly lightly and from that moment appears to have been loyal.

Evidence 6
The government seemed to know where the plotters had fled to after the discovery of the plot. On 8 November they cornered them at Holbech House in Staffordshire. Even though the plotters put up little resistance, the ringleader Catesby and three other plotters were killed. This meant they could not tell their story.

Evidence 7
Guy Fawkes and the other plotters who were arrested confessed under torture to being involved in the Plot.

Evidence 8
During the trial of the plotters, Robert Cecil told the government lawyers to praise Lord Monteagle and make it clear that he was not one of the plotters.

6.2 What were the issues facing James and Charles?

1 Anti-Catholicism

The belief which united most Protestants in England, Scotland and Ireland was a hatred and fear of the Catholic Church, called anti-Catholicism. The impact of anti-Catholicism on events throughout the reigns of James I and Charles I was very important. Most Protestants treated anything that reminded them of Catholicism with real suspicion. All non-Catholics feared a return to power and influence of the Roman Catholic Church.

- Their grandparents remembered the burning of Protestants by the Catholic Queen Mary, the memory of which was kept alive in the pages of the most popular book of the day, *The Book of Martyrs* by John Foxe.
- The failed Spanish Armada of 1588 was proof to most English people that Catholic countries such as Spain hoped to take England and force its people to become Catholics.

2 Fear of absolutism

At the start of the seventeenth century, some foreign kings and queens, such as the King of France, had the power to make laws and raise taxes without asking for the approval of any of the people in their country. This was absolutism. In England, the king or queen was expected to ask the leading nobles and gentry for approval for taxes to raise an army by calling a parliament. An English king and queen could not override a law passed by Parliament, nor could he or she take away the basic rights of the people, such as the right to a fair trial.

Closely related to the fear of Catholicism was a hatred of absolutism. Many English people put the two things together. The English monarchy was a personal monarchy. This meant that kings or queens such as Elizabeth had the power to make decisions about things like going to war without asking Parliament. They could surround themselves with advisers who had quite a lot of power themselves because they were close to the king or queen.

As we have already seen (page 93) Elizabeth did not call Parliament often. But when Parliament was not meeting, she made sure that contact with the important people in the country was maintained at her Court.

3 Divine Right of Kings

The Divine Right of Kings was based on the idea that kings and queens were God's representatives on Earth. So, the thinking went, their power came from God and could and should not be questioned. Both James I and Charles I believed in the idea of the Divine Right of Kings. Here is an extract from a speech made by James I to Parliament in 1610:

> The State of monarchy is the supremest thing on earth; for kings are not only God's lieutenants upon earth and sit on God's throne, but even by God himself they are called Gods.

Not surprisingly, kings and queens all over Europe also generally approved of this idea. But what was significant was what they did about it. Some, like James I, were happy to believe in the idea in theory. But James realised that it did not mean that he had the right to challenge the power of Parliament. Charles was a little different in his attitudes, as we shall see.

4 Court and Patronage

How could the monarch ensure that he or she had the support of the leading nobles and gentry? He or she could give them presents of cash, new jobs or land. This was called patronage. Whether Parliament was sitting or not, it was important that the monarch kept in touch with his or her leading subjects. This was best done by inviting them to Court where they would attend parties, dinners and balls as well as take part in activities such as hunting. The important point was this: contact between monarch and subjects reduced suspicion. There was a downside for kings and queens in giving out all of this patronage. What do you think it was?

5 Money

You have probably guessed right. Patronage cost money. So did fighting wars. One of the main problems faced by the monarchs in the seventeenth century was the issue of raising money. Their main sources of income are shown in the chart below. By the time James had become king in 1603, there was a problem with each one of them.

Source of income	Problem
Crown lands (renting them out or selling what was grown there)	Many Crown lands had been sold so overall income from these lands was going down.
Grants from Parliament known as subsidies	Parliament often did not grant all the money that the King wanted.
Customs – taxes charged on goods brought into the country	The way these were collected was that the King sold to merchants, for a fixed price, the right to raise customs duties. The King got his money but the merchant kept any extra. So it was hard for the King to ever increase the amount of customs duties even if trade was increasing.
Feudal dues such as wardship	Wardship was a right left over from the feudal times. If someone who owned an estate died and his successor was still a child, the Crown had the right to hold the estate (and take money from it) until the successor had grown up, when the successor could claim the lands back. The problem was that the Crown had to find someone to look after the child.
Other taxes	Parliament was supposed to approve all new taxes. If a monarch really wanted to they could raise taxes without the consent of Parliament but they would have to cope with the consequences.

One of the problems that James faced was that Elizabeth had not died on the best of terms with Parliament. In her last years she had fought expensive wars with Spain and in Ireland and had tried to raise taxes without Parliament's consent. So many in Parliament already felt that their liberties and position were under threat. Elizabeth did not leave behind an easy or effective system for the monarch to raise money.

6 Religion

At the heart of the debate about religion was the future of the Church of England. Elizabeth had not tolerated any debate about her Settlement of 1559. But many wanted to reform the Church further.

- Some, like the Puritans, wanted to make it more Protestant (see pages 75–77).
- Others thought that Protestantism had gone too far.

The problem for James and Charles was how to manage this debate without either causing divisions in the Church or allowing the religious debate to spill over into Parliament.

7 Foreign policy

The challenge for James and Charles was to avoid costly wars. It was also important for them to be seen to be backing the Protestant side in European wars. This was because many people believed that Catholic Spain was now England's number one enemy.

8 A united Britain?

This issue emerged when James I became King of England in 1603. Before coming south to England, James had been King James VI of Scotland. Although James was now King of England, Wales, Ireland and Scotland, there was no such thing as a united Britain. Indeed, there were real problems to face.

- In the lowland areas of Scotland, the Protestant faith had taken a far stronger hold than in England. Many Scots were Presbyterians which means that they believed in a much stricter Protestantism than that practised by most people in England.
- Scotland had a different legal system from England and a separate Parliament.
- There was religious tension in Ireland where a large number of Irish people were Catholics.

James and Charles had to address these and other issues in the 'Three Kingdoms' which made their governing England much more difficult.

UNIT 7 The causes of the English Civil War

What is this all about?

In 1642 Civil War broke out in England between the armies of King Charles I and the forces of Parliament. Such a dramatic turn of events could not have been foreseen in 1603 when James I came to the throne or even in 1625 when he was succeeded by his son, Charles I.

It is our task to find out **why** Civil War broke out, and why it broke out **when** it did.

In part 1 you compare the reigns of James I and Charles I and see if you can see any long-term explanations for conflict between king and Parliament. You will see there were certainly tensions during that period, but even in 1640 Civil War was not expected, so part 2 examines in depth what happened between 1640 and 1642 to bring the country to the brink of war.

Source ❶

James I. This said to be the marriage portrait sent to the Danish Court in order to attract Anne, his future wife.

7.1 James and Charles: successes and failures

James I

Issue 1: Image and court life

James encouraged the nobility and the gentry to visit his Court to discuss their problems with him. In return he visited their estates in the summer months. James was also generous with his money. As a result he got lots of political support. He was experienced at balancing the demands of different groups or factions at Court: when he became king in 1603, he immediately promoted Henry Howard to become Duke of Northampton to counterbalance the power of the Cecil family.

Not all aspects of James' rule were so positive: he had favourites to whom he gave too much money and power such as Robert Carr, whom he made Earl of Somerset. He was also quite lazy; leaving the paperwork to others such as Robert Cecil or Lionel Cranfield.

Elizabeth I had been very good at presenting a good image of herself as queen but James did not care about his image. Some visitors to James' Court, including King Christian IV of Denmark, arrived to find everyone was completely drunk!

Did you know?

The Overbury Scandal, 1615–16, seriously damaged the reputation of James' Court. His favourite, Robert Carr, was having an affair with Lady Essex. The affair was encouraged by Sir Thomas Overbury. To cut a long story short, it all went terribly wrong and Lady Essex killed Overbury with the use of a poisoned pie that she sent him. None of this looked too good to those in or outside Court.

Did you know?

James had a rather strange way of talking to his courtiers. He gave many of them nicknames: he called Robert Cecil 'my little wiffle-waffle' and George Keith, who was Earl Marshall of Scotland – a very important job – 'my little fat pork'. To make it worse, he called them these names in front of everybody. How embarrassing!

Issue 2: Religion

For many people in England, the most important fact about James I was that he and his wife, Anne of Denmark, were Protestants. Almost as importantly – they had two sons so the next king would be too!

During Elizabeth's reign the Puritans had been excluded from influence over the Church but now that a new king was coming the Puritans could not wait to ask for changes. On his journey from Scotland they presented him with suggestions known as the Millenary Petition, including these requests:

Source ❷

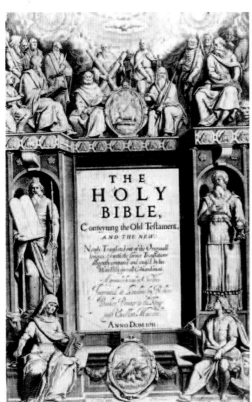

Authorised version frontispiece.

* We want to see an end to priests making the sign of the cross.
* Rings should be banned in weddings, they are religious symbols.
* We want to see our priests wear ordinary clothes, not Catholic robes.
* Priests must stop bowing when the name of Jesus is mentioned. This is what the Catholic priests do.
* It is about time that all priests were given a good Protestant education.
* All people should be allowed to read the Bible.

James was happy to discuss these ideas and called a conference at Hampton Court in 1604. James was not unsympathetic but like Elizabeth he did not like being pestered by Puritans. At the end of the Hampton Court conference James refused to carry out the reforms. He appointed Richard Bancroft Archbishop of Canterbury who insisted that Puritans tow the line. Most accepted Bancroft's wishes.

James did agree with the Puritans that the Church of England needed a new Bible translated into English that could be understood by everyone. By 1611, this new Authorised Bible was complete and out in the churches.

Puritans liked to hold discussions about the sermons that were delivered in churches. These groups were called 'exercises'. James agreed that this was a good way of teaching both ministers and the public about the Protestant religion.

In 1611, James appointed George Abbott to be Archbishop of Canterbury. He was more sympathetic to the Puritans than Bancroft. For example, he did not insist that ministers wore gowns in church.

⌐ What... ? ¬

THE AUTHORISED BIBLE, 1611

This translation of the Bible was the work of 47 scholars who translated it from the original Hebrew and Greek. The Authorised Version was the only version of the Bible available in English until 1881 and became the most printed work of all time. James ordered that the Bible be chained to the pulpit in every church in the land so that no one could steal it and everybody had access to it. It is still one of the most widely used English translations of the Bible today – 400 years later.

Godly lives

Puritans did not think religion was just for Sunday. They wanted to see people in England live more godly lives, every day.

Drunkenness is an evil sin. It would be best to shut down the alehouses.

Dancing around the Maypole is ungodly and should be stopped.

People who work hard have been chosen by God. Laziness is a sin.

People should be careful with their money.

Godly people should pray every day. All families should hold daily prayer meetings.

Dancing, football or bowling are ungodly and lead to drunkenness and sin.

People should only have sex when they are married.

People should not work on the Lord's Day (the Sabbath).

James did not give ground on these issues. For example in 1618 he had published the Declaration of Sports that specifically allowed activities such as archery and dancing. Many Puritans felt that to live godly lives they would have to leave the country. Some emigrated including the Pilgrim Fathers who set sail for America on the *Mayflower* in September 1620.

Issue 3: Parliament and money

One downside of James's open court was its cost. For example, James spent four times as much on clothes in 1610 than Elizabeth had in 1603 – £36,000 compared to £9,000. The cost of running the royal household also went up from £64,000 a year to £114,000.

The main way Parliament controlled a king was that he needed Parliament's permission to raise money. They wanted to know where James was going to get this extra money from. Their main worry was that the King was raising too much money using feudal rights of PURVEYANCE, wardship and IMPOSITIONS, and the sale of monopolies.

The King's minister, Robert Cecil, Earl of Salisbury, and Parliament discussed better and fairer ways of raising royal income but did not get far. James wouldn't cut down his spending and he argued that the money offered to him by Parliament (£200,000 a year) wasn't enough to get him to give up money-raising feudal rights like wardship.

Did you know?

James, as ever, was out to make money. In 1615, a London merchant called Cockayne came up with a project that involved selling cloth to Europe. James became involved. The project failed, lots of people lost money and James was blamed.

Issue 4: Foreign policy

The most expensive pastime for a monarch at this time was making war. Luckily for Parliament, although James spent a fortune on his court he saw himself as a peacemaker. The wars in Europe during this time were usually about religion and James tried to stay on good terms with all sides:

- In 1604 he made peace with Catholic Spain.
- In 1608 James joined with other Protestant countries in a Protestant Union.
- In 1612 James married his daughter to one of the leading Protestant princes, Frederick, ELECTOR PALATINE.
- James even tried to marry his son Charles to the daughter of the King of Spain. This plan was known as the 'Spanish Match'.

Issues 3 and 4 together: Parliament, money and foreign policy

James' first Parliament lasted from 1604 to 1610 and they argued to the point that James thought that he would rule without Parliament for a while. However, he had to call Parliament back in 1614 because he needed money to pay off the costs of his son Henry's funeral and the wedding of his daughter Elizabeth to Frederick, Elector Palatine. Parliament refused to vote him money and, instead, argued again about the Crown's feudal dues. In June 1614 Parliament was dissolved.

The Parliament of 1621 met in more difficult times. The harvest of 1621 had been a poor one, trade was bad and many MPs were not happy with the King raising money through monopolies. James' foreign policy had failed. War had broken out in Europe and James's son-in-law, Frederick, Elector Palatine, had been defeated in 1620 by the Catholic Habsburgs at the Battle of White Mountain near Prague. This was a crushing blow for Europe's Protestants.

Many people in Parliament began to criticise James' 'Spanish Match' plan to marry his son Charles to the Catholic princess of Spain. James' Lord Chancellor, Sir Francis Bacon, was attacked in the House of Commons for corruption, was fined £40,000 and put in prison. This was the last straw for James. He felt that his foreign policy was none of Parliament's business (unless he wanted money out of them) and he dissolved Parliament in January 1622.

By the time of the Parliament of 1624 James was very ill and it was really his son, Charles, and the Duke of Buckingham who made the running. James asked Parliament to vote him a £1 million subsidy to clear his debts. Parliament refused. James died in 1625.

What... ?

MONOPOLIES
A monopoly was something that was supposed to be granted to someone who had invented a new product. In practice, monopolies gave people the right to be the only person or company to sell the product. Many courtiers were given monopolies by the monarch and then made a lot of money issuing licences to companies, giving them the right to produce a product. Monopolies could also be granted to companies giving them the right, for example, to be the only company to trade with India.

Did you know?

The Duke of Buckingham was not much liked. A popular rhyme went as follows: 'Who rules the Kingdom? The King. Who rules the King? The Duke [of Buckingham]. Who rules the Duke? The Devil.'

Issue 5: Scotland and Ireland

One of James' priorities was to unite England and Scotland; he was, after all, king of both countries. In 1604 he asked the English Parliament to consider the matter. It was clear from the start that the English were not keen on the idea. The Scots were the old enemy and they had different laws. By 1607, the matter had been buried, although James managed to introduce a union flag to be carried by all British ships from 1606. However, the flag was not widely adopted and the two countries remained independent states. James also managed to draw the Scottish Church closer into line with the Church of England; from 1607 bishops were re-introduced into Scotland and in 1618 they accepted practices such as baptism (which had been banned). Ireland was a different issue. Elizabeth had experienced real problems in keeping Ireland under control. James' answer was to set up plantations. In 1608, he ordered that plantations be set up in Ulster in the north of Ireland. The plan was that the mainly Catholic Irish who lived on this land would be cleared off and it would be given to Protestant settlers from Scotland and England. New towns, such as Londonderry, were to be built.

Source ❸

The 1606 union flag. ❓ *Can you see how it is different from the flag used today?*

What... ?

PLANTATION
This is when people are forced off their land, which is then divided up and granted to settlers.

Task

You have now studied how James tackled these five issues. Make notes about what he did then give him a success rating.

Issue	Notes	Success score out of 5
1 Image and court life		
2 Religion		
3 Parliament, money and taxes		
4 Foreign policy		
5 Scotland and Ireland		
	Total score	

5 – Highly successful in this area
4 – Generally a strong performance in this area
3 – Satisfactory performance

2 – Not a very successful performance
1 – A disastrous performance

Task
Make another copy of the table from page 115 and fill it out for Charles I.

Charles I

James was succeeded as king by his son Charles.

Source

Charles I painted by van Dyck.

What... ?

THE COURT
This was a close-knit group of people of influence around the monarch. Even though the routine business of government was done in Council, by ministers and by administrators, crucial decisions were made by the monarch and his/her immediate advisors at Court. It was at Court that careers of men like Buckingham could be made or broken.

STAR CHAMBER
A royal Court first set up by Henry VII in 1487. It often dealt with cases related to the Crown and was often seen as biased in the Crown's favour. It was abolished in 1641.

Who... ?

THE DUKE OF BUCKINGHAM 1592–1628
He was a talented young man who impressed James I. It is said that James fell in love with him, and called him his 'sweet child and wife.'

He made himself very rich by corrupt land deals in Ireland then, as James got more senile, he began to be the key influence on the King's foreign policy and the most powerful person outside of the royal family. It was he who took James' son to Spain to secretly arrange a marriage to a Spanish princess. That went disastrously wrong. He later led an attack on the Spanish port, Cadiz, which actually ended up not with a battle but a booze-up as his soldiers enjoyed a warehouse full of wine!

When Charles became king, Buckingham was the only royal adviser to keep his job. But his military failures stacked up, one by one, as did his enemies, and he was stabbed to death by an army officer who had a grudge against him.

Issue 1: Image and court life

Charles' court was much more organised than James'. Members of the gentry could not just turn up as they did in James' reign. In 1632, Charles threw the gentry out of the Court and refused to visit them. If anyone objected, they were sent for trial at the Star Chamber.

Charles was not as generous as his father; patronage was controlled by a handful of people including the Duke of Buckingham. They tended to hand out all of the goodies to their family and friends.

Did you know?

Charles was not very tall, especially for a king. Indeed, he was only five feet tall. He was not much fun either; people at Court were not allowed to tell jokes because he never found them funny. Charles was a shy man, he spoke with a stammer and he did not like any kind of criticism.

Who... ?

WILLIAM LAUD
Born in Reading in 1573. His father was a clothier who had enough money to send the young William to Reading School and then to St John's College, Oxford. In 1601, he became a priest. He also was ambitious to the point that by 1617 he had become one of King James I's chaplains. Laud's career really took off when, in 1622, he became the chaplain to the very important George Villiers (soon to become Duke of Buckingham). He was James' favourite courtier and he was a very powerful man. He was also to become, from 1625 until his death in 1645, Charles I's closest adviser.

Issue 2: Religion

In 1625 Charles married Henrietta Maria, a sister of the French King, Louis XIII.

Henrietta Maria was a Catholic and she set up a private Catholic chapel at court. From the start she had a strong influence on Charles. She surrounded herself and Charles with advisers who were Catholic or had Catholic sympathies. Charles' actions raised suspicion that the Court was dominated by Catholics, for example in December 1634, Charles became the first English monarch for nearly a century to receive an ambassador from the Pope.

A group called the anti-Calvinists believed that the Church of England had become Protestant enough. They were strongly influenced by the Dutchman Jacob Arminius. They were a minority in the Church but Charles agreed with them. Here are two examples of their ideas.

Church of England belief	Anti-Calvinist
Most people in the Church of England accepted the Puritan idea of Predestination: only God's chosen people would go to heaven and these 'elect' had been chosen by God before they were born. Nothing you could do on earth could make a difference.	Anti-Calvinists believed that anyone could go to heaven; as long as they did good things in their lifetime. They could choose to do good or bad that would affect what happened in the after life. This was known as Free Will.
The sermon given by the minister was the most important part of the service.	The Holy Communion was the most important part of the service.

William Laud

The leading anti-Calvinist priest was William Laud. In 1633, Charles gave him the top job, Archbishop of Canterbury. Laud would not tolerate opposition or criticism. Whenever a bishop died he would replace him with a bishop that shared his views. By 1640, most bishops in England were Laudians although most people in England did not like the Laudian ideas at all. One historian has written that Laud became: 'the most hated archbishop in English history'. Let us see why that might have been.

Laud's churches

Laud wanted to restore what he saw as the 'beauty of holiness' in the Church of England. He believed that churches should be decorated and full of symbols, and that there should be mystery and ceremony in church services. On page 118 is his ideal church. These were changes you could see. Laud insisted that they were carried out in every church. He sent round inspectors to check that it was happening.

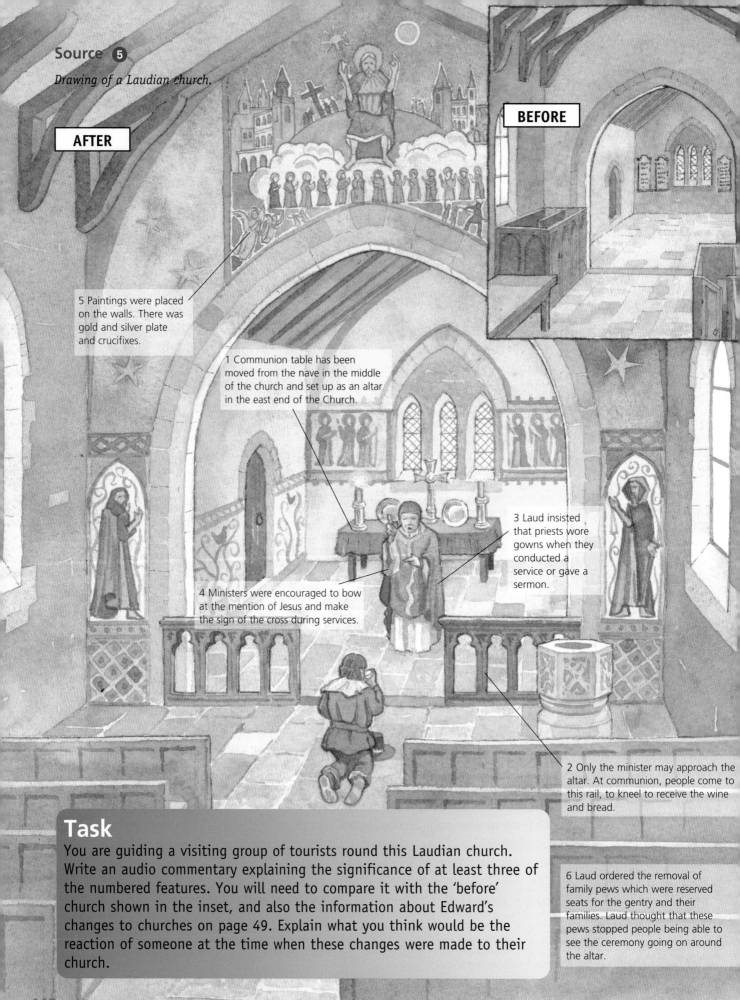

Drawing of a Laudian church.

AFTER

BEFORE

5 Paintings were placed on the walls. There was gold and silver plate and crucifixes.

1 Communion table has been moved from the nave in the middle of the church and set up as an altar in the east end of the Church.

3 Laud insisted that priests wore gowns when they conducted a service or gave a sermon.

4 Ministers were encouraged to bow at the mention of Jesus and make the sign of the cross during services.

2 Only the minister may approach the altar. At communion, people come to this rail, to kneel to receive the wine and bread.

Task

You are guiding a visiting group of tourists round this Laudian church. Write an audio commentary explaining the significance of at least three of the numbered features. You will need to compare it with the 'before' church shown in the inset, and also the information about Edward's changes to churches on page 49. Explain what you think would be the reaction of someone at the time when these changes were made to their church.

6 Laud ordered the removal of family pews which were reserved seats for the gentry and their families. Laud thought that these pews stopped people being able to see the ceremony going on around the altar.

Laud's other changes

Laud believed that people should be allowed to enjoy themselves on Sundays. In 1633 he reissued James I's Declaration of Sports which allowed people to take part in dancing and some sporting activities after they had been to church. He encouraged ministers to teach the idea of Divine Right, that the King was God's representative on Earth and therefore could do no wrong. He also strengthened the powers of the Church courts such as the High Commission and got his supporters appointed to other top jobs.

Laud was a member of the Star Chamber and he used this court to punish his opponents.

- In November 1630, the Puritan preacher Alexander Leighton was arrested for drawing up a petition against the power of bishops. The Star Chamber ordered that Leighton be whipped, that bits of his body be cut off and that he be put in prison for life.
- In June 1637 three Puritans, Henry Burton, William Prynne and John Bastwick were found guilty of writing pamphlets attacking Laud and his beliefs. All three were found guilty. They were branded with a hot iron on the cheeks, their ears were CLIPPED and they were placed in the PILLORY. Laud got his way but the popular support was with the three gentlemen.

- Anyone who even handed out Puritan pamphlets was in danger. In December 1637 the Puritan John Lilburne was arrested for handing out illegal Puritan pamphlets in London. He was sentenced to be tied to a cart and whipped throughout its journey from the Fleet Prison to Westminster. At Westminster he was ordered to stand in the pillory. He was then imprisoned. Those who turned out to see the sentence carried out on 18 April 1638 cheered Lilburne and booed Laud.

Laud may have been powerful but he and his ideas were not popular.

Source 6

Front sheet of Bastwick's attack. ❓ *Can you see what is on the dishes?*

What... ?

TONNAGE AND POUNDAGE

This was a tax that was paid on goods coming into the country. In theory, the money raised was to be spent on improving the navy.

What... ?

IMPEACHMENT

What happens when Parliament charges someone with breaking the law and turns itself into a law court to try them.

What... ?

PETITION OF RIGHT, 1628

Charles was not very happy to sign this Petition (agreement). His problem was that, if he did not sign, he would get no money. The Petition said the following things were illegal: forced loans, billeting, putting people in prison without giving them a trial – all the things that Charles had done since 1625!

Did you know?

Buckingham was stabbed to death in Portsmouth by John Felton. Felton had been a soldier on one of Buckingham's feeble expeditions to France. Although Felton was a hero in the public's eyes for having killed the hated Buckingham, he was hanged at Tyburn on 29 November 1628.

Issues 3 and 4 together: Parliament, money and foreign policy

Charles had already fallen out with Parliament even before he became king. During the Parliament of 1624 his father had been so ill that Charles and his adviser Buckingham had been in charge. They wanted to fight a war against Spain so they needed to persuade Parliament to vote them the money necessary. In the end Parliament agreed for a £300,000 subsidy for war against Spain. This was enough for the war at sea that most MPs approved, but not enough for the land war wanted by Charles and Buckingham.

After he became king, Charles asked again but MPs still did not agree. It was normal at the start of a reign for Parliament to grant the monarch the right to collect a tax called Tonnage and Poundage for life. The House of Commons did not trust Charles so they voted Charles Tonnage and Poundage for one year only. Members of Parliament also started criticising Charles' favourite, the Duke of Buckingham, so Charles dismissed Parliament.

Charles still needed money so in 1626 he had to recall Parliament. For many MPs, Buckingham was still an issue. In September 1625 he had led an attack on Cadiz (in Spain) that was a dismal failure; the English soldiers did little apart from get drunk. In 1626, he decided to lend the Catholic King of France some English ships with which he could attack French Protestants (known as Huguenots). Parliament had had enough and both Houses of Parliament voted to impeach Buckingham. To save Buckingham, Charles dismissed Parliament.

Buckingham's record did not improve: in 1627 he decided to attack the French king's forces at La Rochelle. Another disaster followed; and England was now at war with two of the strongest countries in Europe – Spain and France. By the time Charles called the 1628 and 1629 Parliaments, he needed about £500,000 from Parliament to pay debts.

In return for money, MPs wanted Charles to start showing that he believed in Parliament and to promise that he would obey the law. So they made Charles sign a Petition of Right which listed the things that they thought he had done wrong so far:

● The King was raising money without asking them.
● Buckingham was a terrible man who should be tried.

He signed but just as they were about to impeach Buckingham, he was assassinated.

Many MPs did not like Charles' attitude towards religion and tax. One MP, Sir John Eliot, pinned the Speaker to his chair while the Commons passed the Three Resolutions which attacked Charles' policy. Eliot and his friends feared that Charles wanted to rule without Parliament. They were right. Charles had had enough. In March 1629 he dissolved Parliament and decided to rule without it.

THE SPEAKER
The person who tries to control the House of Commons. He or she is the person who shouts 'Order, order!' In 1629 the Speaker was probably shouting 'Get off me'.

Personal rule, 1629–40

With or without Parliament, Charles still had the same old problem; how to raise enough money? He used two methods to increase his income from £600,000 a year in 1629 to £900,000 a year by 1640 (see below) but in the process he upset quite a few people. The money raised was just about enough as long as Charles did not go to war. Charles realised this and made peace with France in 1630 and Spain in 1631.

How Charles raised money

• Ship Money

Counties in coastal areas of England were supposed to provide ships in time of war to protect England from invasion. Instead of sending ships they sent money called Ship Money. In 1634, Charles asked that coastal counties pay Ship Money and in 1635 he insisted that all counties pay it. Nearly everyone paid up, but lots of people did not like the tax. In 1637 a Buckinghamshire gentleman called John Hampden challenged Charles' right to raise the tax. The judges who tried the case disagreed with Hampden but only by seven votes to five.

• Monopolies

A monopoly is when one company controls a market. Charles used the system of selling monopolies despite the fact that Parliament had kicked up such a fuss about it. He even sold a monopoly for soap so that only one company could make and sell soap.

• Forest fines

The forests belonged to the King. So Charles had the boundaries of the forests fixed as they had been in the reign of Edward III nearly 300 years earlier. Anyone living inside the boundary had to pay a fine. The Earl of Salisbury had to pay £20,000 in fines; he was not very pleased.

When a king wanted money he would often first go to the wealthy City of London for a loan. However, if the City disapproved of or distrusted a monarch, it would not lend much money. Such was the case with Charles. In 1640 he asked for a loan of £100,000 and was offered £10,000 instead!

Charles was not the first king to rule without Parliament but such a long time without Parliament made people suspicious of the King. Many believed that he should ask Parliament before he raised taxes.

Issue 5: Scotland and Ireland

In 1633, Charles sent one of his most trusted advisers, Thomas Wentworth, to Ireland as Lord Deputy. He managed to gain control of the Irish Parliament in 1634. Wentworth then forced the Irish Protestants to have Laudian churches, which most of them hated. He also managed to upset both the 'old English' (who had settled in Ireland before Elizabethan times) and the 'new English' (who had settled there more recently) by making them give up some of their lands and pay feudal taxes.

Charles believed that Scotland should be more like England in religion. In 1637, Charles decided to impose the new Laudian style *English Prayer Book* on the Scots. Their response in 1638 was to draw up a Covenant rejecting Charles' proposals. Both sides raised an army and in 1639 the First Bishops' War began.

Charles' finances had been fine as long as he did not have to fight a war but now he needed money. Fighting the Scots would cost £600,000 in 1640 alone. The only way he could raise that sort of money was to call a Parliament.

So in 1640 Parliament was called. What will happen next?

Who... ?

THOMAS WENTWORTH, EARL OF STRAFFORD 1593–1641
As an MP he was an opponent of Buckingham and a critic of his military failures. In his early years he was also an opponent of Charles I – particularly over taxes – although a moderate not a radical. Then in 1629 with Parliament dividing into the King's supporters and King's opponents he opted to support Charles, and became one of his key advisers through the eleven years of personal rule.

Wentworth was rewarded for his loyalty by being made Lord Deputy (the most senior position) of Ireland but he became a symbol of all that Charles' opponents hated in Charles – particularly the dismissive way of dealing with Parliament. He became Earl of Strafford in 1640.

You can find out how Wentworth met his end on page 124.

Task

James and Charles: successes and failures
You should now have two completed tables for James I and Charles I. Add up the totals in column 3. Use the totals to think about these questions:

- Which king ran the better court?
- Which king dealt better with religious division?
- Which king worked better with his parliaments?
- Which king had the more successful foreign policy?
- Which king had the better policies on Ireland and Scotland?
- What was James' single biggest success and his single biggest mistake?
- What was Charles' single biggest success and his single biggest mistake?

Essay
It may be obvious to you whom you think was more successful out of James and Charles but you still have to explain it using evidence to back up your argument.

Choose the King, James or Charles, whom you think was more successful as a ruler.

a) Describe the main events of his reign (if you have chosen Charles then only go up to 1640).
b) Explain one reason why he was more successful than the other.

7.2 Why did Parliament and the Crown go to war in 1642?

By 1640, Charles was viewed with suspicion by many in England. But as the MPs headed for London very few could have imagined that in two years Parliament would be at war with Charles. But that is what happened so our task is to track the events of these two years.

It will be clear from the last few pages that two of the main disagreements between the King and Parliament were:

- **Money** – the King needed lots and he had to ask Parliament for it. Parliament held the whip hand here.
- **Religion** – always an issue but now it was the extreme Protestants who resented Laud's changes and they were getting stronger in Parliament. John Pym emerged as the leader of this group.

Over the two years 1640–42 a third crucial disagreement emerged.

- **The army** – just as in the Middle Ages the person who controlled the army held power. Charles was in control here. But Parliament did not trust him.

Task

How damaging?

The text that follows describes some of the main developments that led to Civil War. They are all important. Each one increased mistrust between the King and Parliament in some way. Your task is to judge how much each event damaged relations between the two. For each one you have to explain:

a) How did this damage relations between the King and Parliament?

b) Who was most to blame for it in this case: the King, Parliament, or both of them equally?

c) How damaging to the relationship was this on a scale of 1–5?

1 = not very damaging
2 = quite damaging
3 = damaging
4 = very damaging
5 = the damage cannot be repaired

We have given you ideas for the first row.

Event	How this damaged relations	Who would you blame?	How damaging (on a scale of 1–5)	Explanation of score/evidence
The Short Parliament	The MPs criticised Laud and praised the Scots so Charles was annoyed.	The MPs because they came to criticise the King.	2	This was quite damaging because it meant that a number of issues were not dealt with.

EVENT 1

The Short Parliament, 1640

As you have already read, Charles needed money to fight the Scots so in April 1640 he called a parliament. Many MPs admired the fact that the Scots had rejected the new Prayer Book and looked on them as Protestant heroes. These MPs criticised Laud and Parliament and refused to vote Charles any money until he listened to and dealt with their complaints. Charles dissolved the Parliament in May 1640.

> **Did you know?**
>
> The Short Parliament is so called because it was short! It lasted only three weeks.

EVENT 2

The trial and execution of Strafford, 1640–41

Charles still needed money – in fact he needed a good deal of money – because in the summer of 1640 the Scots invaded again in what was known as the Second Bishops' War. They defeated the English and demanded Charles pay £850 a day. Charles had to call another parliament. In November 1640 the Long Parliament met. Most MPs were still loyal to the King but saw the fact that Charles needed money as their opportunity to get Charles to do some other things they wanted. In particular they wanted to remove Charles' 'evil counsellors' (as they called them). If they blamed anyone for what had happened in the past twelve years they blamed Charles' advisers rather than Charles himself.

Parliament ordered that Archbishop Laud be arrested and sent to the Tower of London. That left enemy number one – the Earl of Strafford (previously known as Wentworth) who had been running Ireland for Charles. Parliament particularly disliked him because in May 1640 it was he who advised Charles that he should go on ruling without Parliament and promised that, if needed, he would support Charles with an army that he could bring over from Ireland.

Parliament passed an Act of Attainder accusing Strafford of being a traitor. Charles was now faced with a real problem. If he signed the Act, then one of his most loyal friends and advisers would be executed. If he did not sign, he feared that the people in London, the mob, would remove him from the throne. He signed and Strafford died.

> **Did you know?**
>
> Later Charles said that signing the death warrant of his trusted adviser was the 'one true sin in his life' and believed that Civil War was God's punishment on him and the kingdom for this sin. Strafford for his part wrote to Charles releasing him from his pledge to protect him and saying he hoped his death would restore order in England. On the other hand he privately confided to friends: 'Put not your trust in princes'.

Source ❼

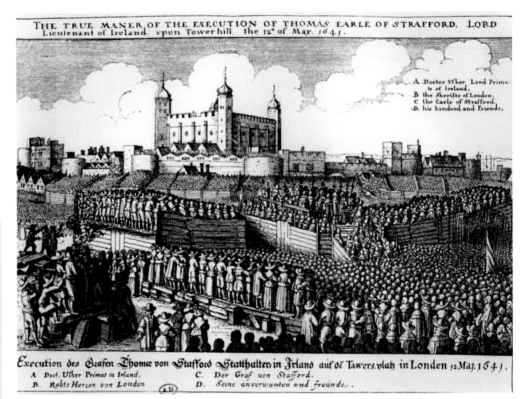

A German engraving showing Strafford's execution on Tower Hill in May 1641. It is estimated that nearly 200,000 attended.

Task

1 Study Source 7.
   a) Why might such a large crowd turn out for this event?
   b) Why might people in other countries be interested in this event?

EVENT 3

Parliament strengthens its position and reduces royal power, 1641

Having achieved a significant victory over the King, MPs, led by John Pym, then passed a series of laws to reduce or control his power.

- In May, they passed the Triennial Act, which said that Parliament had to be called **every three years** whether or not the King wanted it.
- Parliament also passed an Act which said that Parliament could **not be dismissed** without its own agreement.
- In July Parliament **abolished the King's Courts** – the Star Chamber and High Commission.
- Pym also suggested, in the Ten Propositions, that **Parliament should choose the King's ministers** from now on.

Charles had heard enough. He went off to Scotland for six weeks. When he came back, Parliament carried on where it had left off.

- It passed the **Grand Remonstrance** which repeated Parliament's demands that from now on they should choose the King's ministers. The Remonstrance was used partly as an attempt by Parliament to win control of the army from Charles.

Who... ?

JOHN PYM
An MP from Somerset, and a Puritan. He had been a critic of the King since the 1620s, although not extreme in his attitudes. In the run up to the Civil War he emerged as the most important parliamentary leader from 1640 to his death in 1643.

EVENT 4

The Irish Rebellion, 1641

Meanwhile in Ireland serious trouble was brewing.

In November 1641 the Catholic Irish rose up and massacred thousands of Protestant settlers. There was panic in England. Rumours spread that the Irish Catholics were about to cross to England where they would massacre the Protestants. Many people thought Charles was sympathetic towards the Catholics. It was clear that an army was needed to crush the Irish rebellion: the army would cost money that Parliament would have to raise but Parliament did not trust Charles with an army. They thought that he might use it against them.

The Irish Rebellion was the most powerful event so far in polarising attitudes. The previous developments were about political manoeuvrings between King and Parliament but this generated deep fear through the country.

Source ⑧

From a Protestant pamphlet about the Irish Rebellion. These are just two of a series of dozens of pictures and text detailing the atrocities committed by the Catholics. These accounts exaggerated the number of dead and probably invented some of the stories but the graphic imagery and shocking violence affected attitudes in England.

EVENT 5

The attempted arrest of five MPs, January 1642

Charles thought that some MPs were plotting to make a deal with the Scots behind his back. He was also fed up with criticism and personal insults directed to his wife – there were even rumours that Parliament intended to impeach her. Charles decided to seize the initiative. He demanded that Parliament impeach five MPs whom he blamed for the supposed plot. Parliament refused and so, on 5 June 1642, the King entered Parliament with 300 soldiers intending to arrest the MPs. But someone had tipped them off and they had fled into London. Many MPs were angry that the King had entered the House of Commons, which he was not supposed to do. Some MPs, who had previously thought that Pym and the radicals were too extreme, now started to support them. At the end of January, Charles left London.

EVENT 6

Militia Ordinance, March 1642

In March Parliament passed a Militia Ordinance which told the militias in the country to prepare themselves for a fight on Parliament's side. This was the first time in English history that Parliament had issued a law without the King's approval. This was new territory for Parliament. On 11 June Charles issued his own order that the militias had to obey him.

EVENT 7

The Nineteen Propositions, June 1642

Issued by Parliament, the Nineteen Propositions suggested that Charles give up some of his powers such as the right to make war; that Parliament should choose the King's ministers; decide on religious matters, and even arrange the education of the King's children. Charles was not prepared to sign this and Parliament probably knew it.

EVENT 8

Parliament raises its own army, July 1642

Parliament passed a resolution raising its own army under the command of the Earl of Essex. It called on Charles to 'enter into a good accord with Parliament to prevent a Civil War', that is, to agree to the Nineteen Propositions.

EVENT 9

Charles raises his Standard – August 1642

Instead of accepting the Nineteen Propositions, Charles went to Nottingham and, on 22 August, he raised his Standard. By this symbolic action he was declaring to Parliament that he was ready to fight them if necessary. He only had about 800 supporters with him – but he expected much of the country to support him – and most people expected that if there were a war the King would win.

EVENT 10

Parliament's Declaration

On 6 September Parliament declared that anyone who did not support Parliament would have to pay for the war. This pushed many gentry into supporting Charles because they disapproved of this levy. The war had begun.

What... ?

RAISING THE STANDARD
Raising the Standard means raising a flag around which your supporters would rally.

Did you know?

Today we have a Prime Minister who is the head of the government. In theory he or she is the monarch's Prime (meaning first) Minister but nowadays is chosen by the party with the most MPs in the House of Commons. In Charles' time, the monarch chose his ministers. Any suggestion that Parliament should do so was very new.

Summary task

a) Describe the events that led to the outbreak of the English Civil War

b) Explain who you think was more to blame for the war: Charles, Parliament or someone else.

Top tips – planning your answer to part a)
One good way to tackle this question is to divide your answer into long- and short-term causes.

Long-term causes: For the purposes of this essay these are developments between 1625 and 1640 that caused mistrust between Charles and Parliament. They could not cause a Civil War on their own, but they helped to make it possible. For example:

- Personal rule – Charles ruling without Parliament
- Scotland 1637–38
- Trials of Laud's enemies 1637–38

Short-term causes: For the purposes of this essay these are developments between 1640 and 1642 that harmed the relationship so much that compromise was impossible. The problem is that you have many events to pick from. Choose the ones that you think are particularly important. Your chart from page 123 will help you. Choose no more than three. These could be:

- Parliament reduces royal power in 1641
- The Irish Rebellion
- The arrest of the five MPs
- The Nineteen Propositions
- The raising of armies and Standards

Writing your answer
Here is a possible structure for your answer.

- Introduction: write just one or two sentences explaining that there are short- and long-term causes that contributed to the Civil War.

- Paragraph 1: describe three long-term causes – but really importantly say why each one helped cause distrust between the King and Parliament.
- Paragraph 2: describe the three most important short-term causes – again explaining why each made war more likely.

Top tips for part b)
Your answer should be clearly structured. Before you start you should try to plan your answer. Above all else you should try to decide who or what was most to blame. The part of the question that suggests that someone else might be to blame gives you an opportunity to include information about another individual. Can you think of anyone else? When you have decided, you should structure your answer like this:

Introduction In two sentences answer the question.
Paragraph 1 Explain who or what was most to blame and the reasons for your choice.
Paragraph 2 Explain who or what was less to blame. You might still want to explain why they cannot be totally let off the hook.
Paragraph 3 Any other reason or person who might possibly be to blame.
Conclusion Go back to the start and sum it all up.

See page 195 for a practice source exercise on the causes of the English Civil War.

UNIT 8 The English Civil War

8.1 How and why did Parliament win the Civil War?

What is this all about?

Strictly speaking there were actually **two** English Civil Wars. The first lasted from 1642 to 1646, after which the King was taken prisoner although he did not ever accept defeat. This was followed two years later by a much shorter and bloodier Second Civil War in 1648. This ended with a crushing defeat for Charles' supporters in August 1648.

In 1642 almost everyone in England would have said that Parliament stood little chance of winning the Civil War. So the key question to ask in part 1 of this unit is how and why Parliament managed so convincingly to win a war that most expected them to lose.

After Parliament won there was a big dilemma facing them – what should they do with the King now? In part 2 you will find out what they did and why they did it.

In 1642 support for the King was strongest in the west and north of the country, and for Parliament it was strongest in London and the south-east.

Source ❶

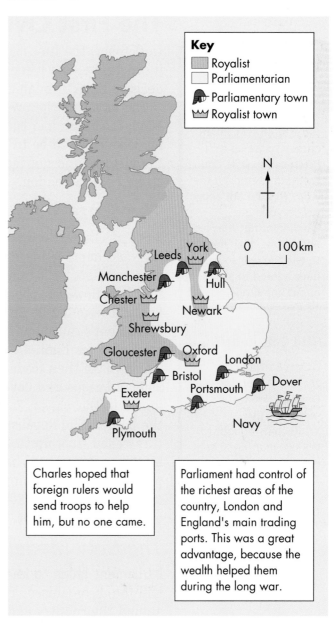

Charles hoped that foreign rulers would send troops to help him, but no one came.

Parliament had control of the richest areas of the country, London and England's main trading ports. This was a great advantage, because the wealth helped them during the long war.

Map showing the main areas of loyalty to the King or Parliament.

But this is only a generalisation. In many areas of the country people stayed neutral. In others people switched sides during the war according to whom they thought was going to win. They did not want to be on the losing side!

There is no doubt that the King held the early advantages. His army was experienced and he had a better cavalry led by the dashing Prince Rupert of the Rhine. However Parliament controlled London (which was important as a source of money) and it controlled the navy which would mean they could prevent troops from other countries being sent to reinforce Charles' army.

The First Civil War, 1642–46

In October, the first major battle was fought at Edgehill. It was inconclusive. The troops battled it out for three hours but no one made a decisive breakthrough. It was more a testing out of each other's strength.

The Royalists then won a series of smaller battles in 1643 and early 1644. If Charles had been thinking strategically you would have expected his next move to be to head southwards to try to seize London. However, the victories did not feel decisive enough to let him attack Parliament's stronghold in London.

The Scots enter the war

Some of Charles' army were fighting a war in Ireland. Charles thought that he could improve his chances of beating Parliament by bringing some of these soldiers back from Ireland. So he struck a deal with the Irish to stop fighting. However, the plan went wrong. The soldiers who came back to England were led by Sir William Brereton who was sympathetic to Parliament's cause and they changed sides and fought against Charles instead of for him!

John Pym then made matters worse by persuading the Scots to sign the Solemn League and Covenant in September 1643 under which they also joined in the war on Parliament's side. In January 1644 the Scots crossed the border. The Royalist army under the Duke of Newcastle was now threatened from north and south. He retreated to York. There he was met by Prince Rupert who was so confident of victory he decided to take the parliamentary army on there and then. He made a mistake! At the battle of Marston Moor the Royalist army was soundly defeated. This was another bitter blow for Charles.

The New Model Army

Parliament failed to follow up its victory at Marston Moor; its armies were still too disorganised. There were different leaders, leading different armies around the country and they were not working together. So instead of finishing the Royalist army off and capturing more of their soldiers, equipment and supplies, the Earl of Essex took his army off to lay siege to

What... ?

THE SOLEMN LEAGUE AND COVENANT
The Scots agreed to join the war and in return the English Parliament agreed to set up a Presbyterian style Church (without bishops) if they won. This did not appeal to everyone in Parliament but that did not matter; they needed to win the war so would have agreed to just about anything.

Did you know?

At the Battle of Marston Moor, the Duke of Newcastle's regiment, the Whitecoats, fought to the last man. Only one person survived: the Duke who escaped and went abroad! That was the end of his Civil War.

Lyme Regis; the Earl of Manchester went east; and the Scots attacked Newcastle.

Parliament saw the problem and by the Self-Denying Ordinance, Essex and Manchester were sacked in the winter of 1644 and, in February 1645, Parliament created a new army: the New Model Army. Its leaders were Sir Thomas Fairfax and, in charge of the cavalry, Oliver Cromwell. This new army had a number of features that were to make it a formidable fighting force:

- **One army** The New Model Army merged three armies into one, thereby creating one fighting force of 22,000 soldiers under one command. Officers were chosen on merit (who was best), not because of their background.
- **Leadership** The leadership of this new army was experienced. Sir Thomas Fairfax had fought in Europe in the Thirty Years War and had proved to be an effective commander in the first two years of the Civil War. Cromwell instilled discipline into his cavalry and the leader of the infantry, Philip Skippon, was a great leader who was much liked by his men.
- **Religion** Many of the soldiers in the New Model Army were Puritans; they were really motivated. For them this war was not about money or fame but about serving God – the most important thing in the world.

Source ❷

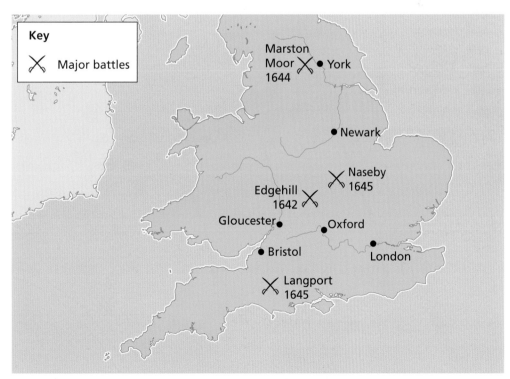

Battles were fought all across the British Isles. The major battles shown on this map involved thousands of troops on each side, but there were also hundreds of minor skirmishes or sieges, some involving just a handful of troops.

Task

Study Source 2. Find the nearest battle site to where you live or go to school or, if you know of a local battle that is not mentioned on this map, choose that one. For that battle find out:

- the exact date
- who won
- how large the armies were
- how long the battle was
- what the casualties were
- any other information that interests you.

You could start by looking at the margin boxes through this unit or by looking up your battle on an internet site such as www.historyonthenet.com.

The Battle of Naseby, 1645

The Battle of Naseby was the decisive battle of the English Civil War. It decided Charles' fate. In June 1645, Charles' army had seized Leicester and was awaiting the arrival of Colonel Gerrard, who was leading a 3,000-strong Royalist army from Wales. But news reached Charles that the New Model Army was about to lay siege to the loyal city of Oxford. He decided to march his weary army of about 3,500 men to Oxford.

But the New Model Army had not reached Oxford. It was instead approaching Buckingham. Charles was confident that he could defeat Fairfax's army and marched to Daventry. On 11 June, the Royalist Sir Marmaduke Langdale arrived at the King's camp with news that Fairfax's army was approaching. A skirmish took place at Borough Hill. Both sides retreated and considered their next move.

Soon Fairfax was joined by Cromwell and his 'Ironsides'. Cromwell advised Fairfax to attack the King's army. On the morning of 13 June, the New Model Army set out in the direction of Market Harborough. By evening, Charles had been made aware of the approaching army. Charles decided to stand and fight, although this was against the advice of Prince Rupert.

Source ❸

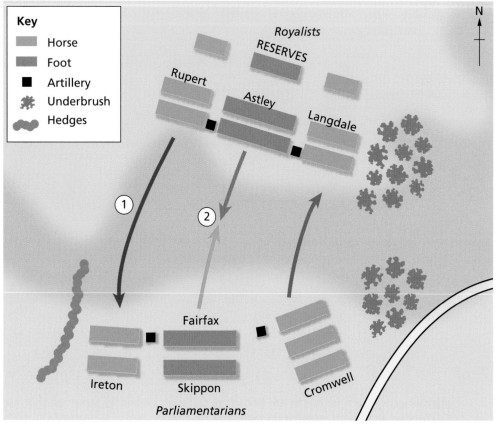

Naseby Stage 1: a plan showing the preliminary moves.

On the King's side, the King's infantry were led by Lord Astley. To the right was the cavalry led by Prince Rupert. To the left the 1,600 men led by Sir Marmaduke Langdale. Drawn up behind these forces were the reserve led by the Earl of Lindsey.

The Parliamentary forces however were nowhere to be seen. Prince Rupert took the initiative and went to find them. After riding for a couple of miles he caught sight of the enemy. Thinking that they were retreating, he called forward the rest of the Royal army.

Fairfax had positioned his troops well and waited. Slowly but surely the King's army came into view.

Fairfax had positioned 300 musketeers ahead of his main forces. To the right he placed Cromwell's cavalry and to the left positioned more cavalry under Ireton. In the middle Fairfax and Skippon were in charge of the foot soldiers.

Source ④

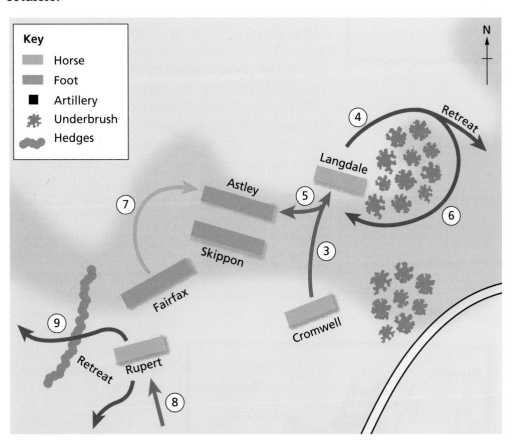

Naseby Stage 2: a map of the battle itself.

The battle

Prince Rupert led his cavalry uphill (move 1) and smashed it into the left wing of the Parliamentary army. The impact of this charge was devastating. Ireton was wounded and taken prisoner. His men retreated towards their artillery. However instead of destroying them Rupert and his cavalry rode on towards the baggage camp – to plunder it.

Meanwhile in the centre the infantry battle had proved an even match (move 2). It began with the usual musket fire followed by infantry charge with pikes. To start with the Parliamentary front line broke under a Royalist charge, but their second line proved stronger. They advanced and drove the Royalists back. Then the King got the upper hand again. In fierce fighting all but one of Skippon's regiments broke and fled. However this one regiment did hold its ground giving the others time to reform their ranks and return to the fight. Where would the decisive move come from? Cromwell perhaps?

What... ?

IRONSIDES
This was the nickname that Cromwell was said to have given to the soldiers in his cavalry. He called them this because they were so tough in battle.

On Parliament's right wing Cromwell's cavalry charged the Royalists' left (move 3). The attack was short but fierce. Langdale's troops fell back in disarray (move 4). Then, instead of charging after the defeated enemy as Rupert and his undisciplined cavalry had done earlier in the day, Cromwell's Ironsides smashed into the Royalist infantry in the centre (move 5). They also held back the attempts of Langdale's Royalist cavalry to return to help their infantry (move 6). The Royalists were surrounded. Fairfax personally led an infantry charge from one side (move 7) while Cromwell led a cavalry charge on the other. The Royalists fought on but against the fierce onslaught regiment after regiment surrendered. It was clear to Charles that the battle was lost.

What about Prince Rupert? In previous battles Rupert's cavalry had never returned for a second charge. On this occasion however, they abandoned their plunder and returned to the battlefield intending to charge again (move 8). However when they saw the hopeless situation, with the infantry surrendering, the remains of the Royalist cavalry fled from the battlefield (move 9). The King escaped to Leicester and then on to Lichfield.

It was the most conclusive victory of the war so far. In an evenly matched and serious conflict, the discipline of Cromwell's troops in comparison to the indiscipline of the King's had proved decisive. Charles had lost his main army: 600 Royalist soldiers had been killed, and another 5000 were taken prisoner. The King's baggage and artillery had been captured.

From this point the Royalist armies suffered defeat upon defeat until, in March 1646, what remained of the Royalist infantry surrendered at Stow-on-the-Wold. In May, Charles gave himself up to the Scots and in June, Oxford surrendered to Parliament. The First Civil War was over.

Source ⑤

Prince Rupert. ❷ *What has happened to Birmingham?*
Do you think this was made by a supporter or an opponent
of Prince Rupert?

Summary task

Here are five possible reasons that Parliament won the Civil War:

- the New Model Army
- effective leadership
- Royalist mistakes
- the Battle of Naseby
- religion.

1 Write a sentence about each one to explain how this helped them win.
2 Find some evidence from the chapter to support your sentence.
3 If you think there are other reasons that should be listed, write a sentence about them and add some evidence.
4 All these reasons are important but some are more important than others. Organise these into an order of importance – in your opinion which of these was most critical in giving Parliament victory. Write a paragraph to explain your top two reasons – why do you think they are more important than others.

If you now put your sentences together you will find you have the basis of an essay on why Parliament won the First Civil War.

Interlude 1646–48: who should run England now – and how?

The First Civil War had determined who had the stronger army but it had not determined what should happen next. The aim of the war had not been to get rid of Charles. It was to make him share power with Parliament. Now that Parliament held the military upper hand it could in theory tell Charles what to do. But what should they tell him to do? And how should they tell him to do it? Divisions were beginning to show in the parliamentary ranks.

- Most MPs were Presbyterians. They wanted Charles to agree to the creation of a national Presbyterian Church, that is, a Church without bishops.
- However, most of the New Model Army – those who had actually won the war for Parliament – were Independents. They did not want a national Church at all. They wanted total religious freedom.
- Some army officers also wanted a say in how the country was going to be run and some of them, known as the Levellers (see feature box on page 136), had very radical ideas.
- For his part the King did not seem to understand fully that defeat had changed things. He still thought that all of those whom he had fought against were traitors. He did not intend to negotiate with them at all.

The Levellers

One of the results of the Civil War was that, for the first time, people could write and say what they wanted about religion and politics. Many more people were able to worship as they wanted. Others put forward new ideas about how the country should be run. Pamphlets were written spreading these new ideas.

Source ❻

The True
Levellers Standard
ADVANCED:

OR,

The State of Community opened, and Presented to the
Sons of Men.

By

William Everard,
Iohn Palmer,
Iohn South,
Iohn Courton.
William Taylor,
Christopher Clifford,
Iohn Barker.

Ferrard Winstanley,
Richard Goodgroome,
Thomas Starre,
William Hoggrill,
Robert Sawyer,
Thomas Eder,
Henry Bickerstaffe,
Iohn Taylor, &c.

Beginning to Plant and Manure the Waste land upon
George-Hill, in the Parish of *Walton*, in the
County of *Surrey*.

LONDON,
Printed in the Yeer, MDCXLIX.

THE
Declaration and Standard
Of the *Levellers* of *England ;*
Delivered in a Speech to his Excellency the Lord Gen. *Fairfax*,
on *Friday* last at White-Hall, by Mr. *Everard*, a late Member of the
Army, and his Prophesie in reference thereunto ; shewing what will
befall the Nobility and Gentry of this Nation, by their submitting to
community ; With their invitation and promise unto the people, and
their proceedings in *Windsor* Park, *Oatlands* Park, and severall other
places ; also, the Examination and confession of the said Mr. *Everard*
before his Excellency, the manner of his deportment with his Hat on,
and his severall speeches and expressions, when he was commanded
to put it off. Together with a List of the severall Regiments of Horse
and Foot that have cast Lots to go for *Ireland*.

Imprinted at *London*, for *G. Laurenson*, april 23. 1649.

An example of a pamphlet circulated at the time.

In the mid-1640s one group emerged who became known as the Levellers. Their ideas came out of pamphlets written by John Lilburne, William Walwyn and Richard Overton. On the next page are some of their ideas.

> **Did you know?**
>
> The Levellers did not call themselves Levellers. It was a nickname given to them by the people who did not like them, including Oliver Cromwell. They accused the Levellers of wanting to level things down by making everyone have the same amount of money. The Levellers said that this was not the case but the name stuck.

We want a new constitution (set of rules) outlining how the country should be run.

We want to see the abolition of the monarchy and the House of Lords.

We believe that all people are born free, are equal in God's eyes and should be treated equally throughout their lives.

We believe that people should be able to follow whatever religion they like.

We believe that all men over 21 should be able to vote in elections for the House of Commons. Parliament should be responsible to the People.

We suggest that magistrates and Justices of the Peace should be elected.

We believe there should not be a central army but local militias.

Who... ?

COLONEL RAINSBOROUGH
The most senior officer belonging to the Levellers, he believed in natural justice. He was famous for arguing that 'the poorest in England hath a life to lead as the greatest'.

Did you know?

The Levellers used to meet at a pub in London called the Whalebone Tavern. Here their members would read the newspaper they printed called *The Moderate*. Oliver Cromwell would not go there for a drink!

By the end of the First Civil War, Leveller ideas were quite well known in London. But they were particularly popular in the ranks of the New Model Army. And as the New Model Army was the reason for Parliament's power it meant that Parliament had to take it seriously.

Arguments about the New Model Army

At the end of the war in 1646, many soldiers in the New Model Army wanted to go home. However:

● Many had not been paid. Parliament owed the soldiers nearly £3 million in unpaid wages – a massive amount of money in those days. The soldiers refused to go home until they were paid at least some of their money.
● Some soldiers were also worried about their own security if they disbanded. Soldiers had done some terrible things in the war and they wanted Parliament to give them a promise, known as an indemnity, that they could not be arrested for these actions after the war.

Parliament however did not trust the New Model Army. Indeed the majority of MPs, led by Denzil Holles, wanted the army disbanded immediately. It was expensive and they did not like the radical political ideas of the Levellers and the radical religious ideas of the Independents.

1647–48

The final piece in the jigsaw was Charles himself. He was held prisoner by the Scots. They agreed to hand him over to Parliament in return for £40,000.

So with the King held prisoner, there was a chaotic set of three-way negotiations through 1647–48 between the King, Parliament and the army. This timeline shows you how the negotiations developed.

1647

February
- Parliament suggested that the New Model Army should disband. They would keep some soldiers who could continue to serve in Ireland.
- Parliament ordered that all officers in the army had to be Presbyterians.

March
- The soldiers sent a petition to Parliament asking for their money and the indemnity. Parliament accused them of treason.

April–May
- Negotiations took place. Again, Parliament threatened to disband the army with only eight weeks' pay.

May
- **The Solemn Engagement** Inspired by Levellers in the army, the soldiers refused to disband until they were satisfied that their demands had been met.
- They also suggested setting up an Army Council which would include ordinary soldiers as well as officers.

June
- Many in the army feared that Parliament would make a deal with Charles. Their solution: capture him! A band of soldiers, led by Cornet Joyce, seized the King and brought him to Newmarket.

July
- The leaders of the army, such as Oliver Cromwell and Henry Ireton, now put their ideas forward to the King in the Heads of the Proposals on how a settlement could be reached. The Levellers did not like these ideas and the King did not respond.

October
- The Levellers in the army put forward their own ideas in The Case of the Army Truly Stated and The Agreement of the People. These demanded:
  - a new constitution
  - that all men over 21 had the vote
  - that there be Parliaments lasting two years
  - that Parliament had all of the authority and power
  - that there should be changes to Parliamentary constituencies.

October–November
- The leaders of the army did not like the Leveller ideas, which they thought too extreme. In October and November they discussed their ideas together at the Putney Debates. The leading Levellers, John Wildman and Colonel Thomas Rainsborough, argued their case but no agreement was reached.

November
- Some Levellers started a mutiny in favour of their ideas but they were crushed by Cromwell at Ware.

November–December
- Still the army leaders and Parliament needed to come to some kind of agreement with the King. But on 11 November 1647 Charles escaped from captivity at Hampden Court and, the following month, he made an agreement with the Scots to fight again, this time on his side. War began again.

Task
Look back to the picture on page 103. Now that you know what happened in 1647, write a paragraph about this picture explaining what it shows and what the message is.

The Second Civil War, 1648

Between January and August a number of Royalist uprisings took place in England but they were all crushed and their leaders executed. In August Cromwell led an army north which defeated the Scots. So ended the so-called 'Second Civil War'.

If this sounds like a bit of a non-event, it was really. People suffered and died but from the military point of view Charles never had a chance of winning. The really important thing about this war is not explaining the military outcome but the political outcome. The Second Civil War is important because it convinced many powerful people – army leaders in particular; those who had previously been willing to give the King the benefit of the doubt and to negotiate with him – that Charles could not in fact be trusted. He had to be dealt with. So on with part 2 – the trial and execution of King Charles I.

Did you know?

Cromwell had no time for the Levellers. In March 1649 he had the leaders – Lilburne, Overton and Walwyn – and others arrested for criticising the new government. In April and May 1649 there were Leveller mutinies which were crushed by Cromwell and Fairfax. By the end of 1649 the Leveller movement was finished.

8.2 What shall we do with the King?

Charles fled to the Isle of Wight where he was imprisoned. Many in Parliament still wanted to negotiate with him, but the army did not. They had had enough. And force won the argument although what happened next was to shock the country.

Pride's Purge

A number of soldiers led by Colonel Pride marched into the House of Commons and threw out all the MPs who wanted to negotiate with the King. They marched them out of the Parliament building, under armed guard, and told them not to come back – or if they did they would face the consequences.

The Rump Parliament

That left about 60 MPs (known as The Rump) who, on 1 January 1649, voted to put the King on trial. They had come to the conclusion that Charles had to go. He was charged with destroying the laws and liberties of England and with deliberately making war on the Parliament and people of England. The House of Lords refused to agree to these charges so the Rump declared that they would make the rules from now on without the agreement of the King or the Lords.

The King on trial

Source ❼

A nineteenth-century picture of Charles' trial.

Source 8

A seventeenth-century picture of Charles' trial.

The trial was held in the Painted Chamber of the Palace of Westminster. Security was tight as the trial opened on the afternoon of 20 January 1649. Charles refused to answer any of the charges against him and stayed silent. He therefore watched as events unfolded.

- 24–25 January: 33 witnesses gave evidence against the King that was read out in public. They stressed Charles' involvement in the wars and his desire to see the wars continue.
- 26 January: Charles was accused of being a 'tyrant, traitor, murderer and public enemy to the Commonwealth of England'.
- 27 January: President of the Court John Bradshaw spoke to the trial. He claimed that even the King had to obey the law made by Parliament. He argued that Charles had broken the sacred bond between a king and his people. He declared Charles guilty of the charges against him, and sentenced him to death by execution.
- At the end of the trial, as had happened every day, John Bradshaw ordered the army to remove Charles. After Bradshaw had spoken Charles was forbidden to speak and was led away from the court to await execution.

Task

Sources 7 and 8 can't both be accurate! Which do you most trust to tell you what it was like at the King's trial? How would you set about finding out which was more accurate?

Did you know?

Security at Charles' trial was so tight that the President of the court, John Bradshaw, wore a steel-lined bullet-proof hat in case of an assassination attempt.

Discuss

Kings had been killed before by their subjects. In your study of the Middle Ages you might have come across at least four such as Edward II or Richard III who were murdered by political opponents or powerful barons. But what is different about this occasion? What is so shocking or unusual? This is a difficult question and you have to think across time. Discuss this with a partner.

THE EXECUTION OF CHARLES I

Source Ⓐ

On the day of his execution, which was Tuesday 30 January, I stood amongst the crowd in the street before Whitehall Gate, where the scaffold was erected, and saw what was done. The blow I saw given, and I remember well, there was such a groan by the thousands then present, as I never heard before and desire I may never hear again.

Philip Henry, 1649.

Source Ⓑ

The King's head was thrown down by him that held it up. His hair was cut off. Soldiers dipped their swords in his blood. Base language [swearing] was used over his dead body.

Eyewitness, 1649.

Source Ⓒ

He took off his doublet [a type of jacket], but being in his waistcoat he put on his cloak again. Charles turned to the executioner and said: 'When I put out my hands, then'.

He said a few words to himself and then laid his head upon the block. The executioner again putting Charles' hair under his cap, which made his majesty think he was about to strike. 'Stay for the sign,' he said, to which the executioner said, 'Yes I will and it please your Majesty'.

So, after a short pause, his majesty stretching forth his hands, the executioner (who was all the while in a mask) at one blow cut his head from his body, which being held up and showed to the astonished people, was with his body put in a coffin covered with black velvet, and carried into the Lodging Chamber in Whitehall.

Adapted from White Kennet, 1706.

Source Ⓓ

The execution of Charles I drawn by a German observer.

Source **E**

The Execution of Charles I, *published in 1660 (note that the executioner is wearing a mask).*

Source **F**

From The Confession of Richard Brandon the Hangman, *1649.*

Task

Stage 1: Studying the sources carefully

1 Common information: Some points of information are mentioned or shown in more than one source. Study all the sources and pick out three points that are common to at least two sources.

2 Unique information: Some points are mentioned in only one source. Pick out one point from each source that is unique to that source.

3 Suggest three pieces of information in any of the written sources (Sources A, B and C) that are backed up by any of the pictorial sources (Sources D, E and F)?

Stage 2: Evaluating the sources

4 a) Are Sources A and B written by Royalists or Parliamentarians?

b) How can you tell? Suggest words or phrases in the sources that support your view.

5 The author of Source C is writing in the eighteenth century.

a) Where do you think he has got his information from?

b) What might be the problems if you were using this source to work out what happened at the King's execution?

6 Do you think that Source F is likely to be more trustworthy than Sources D or E?

Stage 3: Using the sources to write an account

You are writing for the *Inquirer*, a news-sheet that is published once a week in the seventeenth century. The date is 31 January 1649. Using all of the sources above, write a detailed description of the execution of the King.

UNIT 9 Oliver Cromwell: hero or villain?

> **What is this all about?**
> From 1649 until his death in 1658, Oliver Cromwell was the most powerful person in England. He was the leader of the army and the army was the most powerful force in England. People at the time and historians since have been strongly divided in their opinions of Cromwell. Some see him as a hero – a principled and godly man who guided England through the most difficult time in its history, and did the best he could. Others see him as a villain – a tyrant who grabbed power and ruled England selfishly and badly! The debate continues to the present day and you are going to join in. You may have already reached a view from what you read about Cromwell in the previous units. But now you are going to look in depth at how he handled six key issues. As you study what he did you will gather evidence that shows he was a hero or a villain. Let's start with some varying interpretations.

Impressions of Cromwell

Source ❶

A Royalist print in 1649 showing Cromwell surrounded by his cabinet.

Task

1 Study Sources 1–6.
  a) For each one decide if it is pro- or anti-Cromwell.
  b) Identify words or features that tell you whether it is for or against him.
2 Choose two sources that take different views. Explain in a paragraph how they disagree about Cromwell, and suggest reasons why they disagree.

Source ❷

In Ely Fen in 1638 Cromwell made a fair deal with the local people. They would pay him a GROAT for every cow they had on the common and he would pay for the drainage of the land. This meant that the land could be enjoyed by all.

From a report written in 1638.

Source ❸

No man more wicked ever tried to do things as wickedly as Cromwell. No person ever acted more against religion and honesty.

The Royalist Lord Clarendon, writing in the 1660s.

Source ④

An engraving of Cromwell by William Faithorne.

Source ⑤

Look into those strange deep troubled eyes of his with their wild deep sorrow. On his wild face, a kind of murky sorrow.

Thomas Carlyle, writing in the nineteenth century.

Source ⑥

Cromwell was so honest and godly that he contacted a man called Mr Carlton whom he won £30 off in a bet 30 years before. He told Mr Carlton to come and take his money back [because] for him to keep any money won in a bet was a sin.

James Heath, writing in the 1650s.

Cromwell's life: an overview

Beginnings

Oliver Cromwell was born in 1599 in Huntingdon where he went to school before spending a year at Sidney Sussex College Cambridge. He was forced to leave university because his father died in 1617. In 1620, Cromwell married Elizabeth Bourchier and moved to St Ives and then to Ely, where the house that he lived in can still be seen. In 1628 he was elected MP for Huntingdon but it was not until the 1630s that he became a Puritan. Cromwell was elected MP for Cambridge in the Short and Long Parliaments. He supported the opposition leaders such as John Pym and his own cousin, John Hampden.

The Civil War

A reminder of what Cromwell did in Unit 8:

1645: He became the leader of the Parliament's cavalry.

1645: Decisive role at the Battle of Naseby.

1647: Debated with Levellers (radicals) in his own organisation.

1647: Crushed a mutiny led by Levellers in his own army.

1649: Was one of the MPs who signed the death warrant for the execution of King Charles.

The Protectorate

1653: appointed Lord Protector

That is the focus of the next ten pages.

> **What... ?**
>
> **LORD PROTECTOR**
> Ran the country instead of a king. He was to be advised by a Council of State. Cromwell was declared Lord Protector at Westminster Hall on 16 December 1653.

Issue 1: Cromwell and Parliament

Cromwell did not work well with any Parliament between 1649 and 1658. At some times he chose to rule without Parliament altogether. Does this remind you of anybody?

The Rump Parliament

This was the Parliament that sat after the execution of Charles I. They had been prepared to approve killing their king, and they abolished the House of Lords but they did not give Cromwell what he wanted concerning religion. They were mostly Puritans who thought they knew the right way to worship God. But Cromwell believed in religious freedom. In April 1653, Cromwell led a group of soldiers into Parliament and they closed the Parliament and sent the MPs home. That was the end of the Rump Parliament.

> **What... ?**
>
> **INTERREGNUM**
> The period between the reigns of Charles I and Charles II when England had no king. It means 'between kings'.

Barebones Parliament

The question for Cromwell and the army was what to do next. If they held an election for a new parliament, they worried that people might elect MPs who were Royalists. On the other hand rule by the army was not seen as an option because it would be too unpopular. So the decision was made to call a parliament full of MPs chosen by army officers. The Barebones Parliament lasted from April to December 1653. It did some good work but it began to come up with some very radical and (in Cromwell's view) dangerous proposals, for example, to abolish tithes (payments to the church). Cromwell agreed that it should be dissolved.

First Protectorate Parliament

Cromwell ruled the country without Parliament for nine months under the title of Lord Protector. He issued a constitution called the Instrument of Government. When a new parliament finally met in September 1654, many MPs objected to aspects of Cromwell's new constitution including the fact that he had passed laws when Parliament was not meeting. Many MPs were sent home from Parliament because they objected to Cromwell taking the title of Lord Protector without an election. When Parliament also suggested cutting the size of the army, Cromwell dissolved Parliament.

Second Protectorate Parliament

In August 1655 Cromwell introduced eleven Major-Generals (see page 149) to rule the country. Then he called an election for a new parliament. There were many in this Second Protectorate Parliament who objected to the rule of the Major-Generals and so Cromwell got rid of the Major-Generals rather than getting rid of this parliament. But later, when Cromwell faced difficulties with members of the old Rump Parliament who wanted their original parliament restored – saying that it had never legally been closed – he closed the Second Protectorate Parliament altogether.

Can you see the pattern here? Cromwell tries to work with Parliament but when Parliament does not do what he wants (or is it what he thinks is right for the country?) he closes it down. The two problems for Cromwell throughout this period were that:

- Most MPs accepted his leadership, but they did not trust the influence of the army (and Cromwell was a leading member of the army).
- Most MPs did not like the idea of religious freedom.

(see page 149)

Task

Hero   Villain

Here are a set of scales. What can you find in Issue 1 that goes on either side? Here are some suggestions – on which side will you put each statement?

- He tried hard to work with Parliament.
- He dissolved Parliament whenever it went against him.
- He wanted religious freedom for all.
- He ruled by force – he was strong because of the army.

Source **7**

Portrait of Cromwell showing him as a king.

Issue 2: King Oliver?

In March 1657 the Second Protectorate Parliament suggested to Cromwell that he become King Oliver. Many MPs felt that this would be the best way of keeping the country stable. England had always had a monarchy, they argued, and even though Charles was rotten at the job it did not mean that someone else should not do it. Cromwell thought about the offer. On the one hand he wanted stability, on the other hand he had had the last king's head chopped off and he knew that his old friends in the army would not like the idea. After consideration Cromwell told Parliament that God did not like the idea of kings, so he rejected the offer in May 1657.

However, although Cromwell turned down the offer to become king, he certainly behaved like one. People called him 'Your Highness', he knighted people and he used the royal palaces. In April 1654 he moved into Charles' old house, Whitehall Palace. The ceremony to mark his reinstallation as Lord Protector was like a royal coronation. Cromwell wore a purple robe lined with ermine fur and he carried a golden sceptre. Cromwell even took a kind of royal oath and he left the ceremony at Westminster Hall in a golden state coach. The Humble Petition and Advice allowed him to choose his successor. To some in the army, Cromwell might as well have been called a king as he was a 'king in all but name'.

> ## Did you know?
>
> Cromwell refused the Crown by saying 'I will not build Jericho again'. This is a reference to one of the most famous stories in the Bible. The children of Israel had been waiting 40 years to enter their promised land. One strong city stood in their way – Jericho. If they could defeat this city the promised land would be theirs. God told them to march round the city of Jericho seven times with loud trumpets. They did so and miraculously the walls of the city crumbled. The city was theirs. Can you see the connection with Cromwell's situation?

> ## Task
>
> Look at this source. It was probably made by a Dutch artist in around 1657. What can you see in it? Have a close look at what is going on in the background. What does it tell you about attitudes towards Cromwell in 1657?
>
> Find this image on the internet. There is one at: www.wsu.edu/~dee/ENLIGHT/HISTORY.HTM. Print out the image, then add labels to summarise the key features.

Issue 3: The rule of the Major-Generals

In 1655 there was a rebellion in Wiltshire. The so called 'Penruddock Rising' was easily crushed by the army but it convinced Cromwell that there was still a threat from Royalists. Then, when he heard in the middle of 1655 that his English ships sailing to the Caribbean had been defeated by the Spanish at Saint Domingo, he was in no doubt as to why this had happened. Cromwell believed that God had punished England for its sins. His response was to appoint eleven Major-Generals. They were given three main jobs:

- They were to make sure that the Decimation Tax that had been imposed on those who had fought for the Royalists was collected.
- They were to make sure that England was more 'godly'. This meant that they were to shut alehouses (pubs) and prevent gambling, swearing and drunkenness.
- They were to keep a close eye on how the regions were governed.

Some Major-Generals such as Charles Worsley in Lancashire took to the second task very keenly. He shut down anything that he did not think was 'godly'. The people of Lancashire hated him. Others were not so extreme but on the whole the Major-Generals were very unpopular and Cromwell abandoned the experiment in January 1657.

Should we judge Cromwell a tyrant for introducing them in the first place or a wise leader for getting rid of them so quickly?

Task

Here are the scales again. What can you find in Issues 2 and 3 that goes on either side? For example: was he a hero or villain to introduce the rule of the Major-Generals? Was he a hero or a villain to get rid of them when they proved so unpopular?

Issue 4: Cromwell and Ireland

At the end of the Civil War in England, a number of Royalists escaped to Ireland. Throughout 1649, the Royalist leaders, the Marquis of Ormond and Lord Inchiquin, seized a number of towns in the name of the King although in August they failed to take Dublin. Parliament decided to send Cromwell and an army 15,000-strong to Ireland.

Did you know?

The town of Drogheda was surrounded by a 20-foot high wall which had 29 guard towers. The Royalist leader, Ashton thought that Drogheda was so well defended that he said, 'he who could take Drogheda could take Hell'. He underestimated Cromwell.

Did you know?

When Cromwell's troops caught up with Sir Arthur Ashton they killed him by beating him to death with his own wooden leg. They thought it contained gold coins and they were trying to break the leg open.

Source ❽

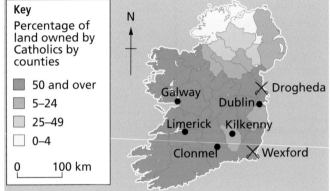

A map of Ireland.

On landing in Ireland, Cromwell immediately marched on the well-protected town of Drogheda. The leader of the 2,300 strong Royalist army in Drogheda was a veteran of the English Civil War, Sir Arthur Ashton. When Cromwell arrived at the town he demanded that Ashton and his army surrender but they refused. Cromwell bombarded the walls and ordered his troops to storm the town. Twice they were thrown back suffering many casualties but at the third attempt they were successful. Cromwell was furious that so many of his soldiers had been killed and he ordered that the Royalists be slaughtered. Not just soldiers but civilians were caught up in the massacre that followed. In all, up to 3,500 people were killed in cold blood including hundreds who were burned alive in St Peter's Church.

Neither Cromwell, his soldiers nor Parliament had a problem with the massacre. Cromwell saw it as revenge for the 1641 slaughter of Protestants (see page 126). His army was full of 'godly' Puritans who saw nothing wrong in killing Catholics. Many of the victims were English Royalist and, by the rules of war, a town that refused surrender laid itself open to such a massacre. None of this meant much to those killed in cold blood. Cromwell's army did not stop there; the following month the people of Wexford got the same treatment. Fearing the dreaded Cromwellians, many of the people in Wexford tried to flee by crossing the River Slaney but they drowned in the process.

Cromwell's army suffered great losses during the winter of 1649–50: up to 1,000 died due to diseases such as malaria. This did not stop Cromwell.

In March 1650 Kilkenny fell (paying £2,000 to avoid the 'Drogheda treatment') to be followed by Clonmel and, eventually, Limerick and Galway. The Royalists and Catholic Irish had suffered a crushing defeat. Land was taken away from the Catholic Irish and given to English settlers. Cromwell's name was hated in Ireland for evermore.

Source ❾

The siege of Drogheda.

Did you know?

After Cromwell had finished his work in Ireland, the only remaining resistance to English dominance came from outlaws who were nicknamed Tories. Have you heard of that word before?

Issue 5: Religious tolerance

Cromwell was an Independent. He believed in a state Church but that people had the right to opt out of it if they wished.

During the Protectorate, all religious groups were allowed to worship freely – *apart* from Catholics. Cromwell remained strongly anti-Catholic and did not think they should share in religious freedom. Some other extreme Protestant groups such as the Quakers were prevented from meeting together and their pamphlets were seized when it was felt that they went too far. But there was greater religious freedom in England between 1653 and 1658 than immediately before or after, during the reigns of Charles I and Charles II.

Issue 6: Foreign policy

Up until 1653, foreign policy was controlled by the Rump Parliament. Thereafter, until 1658, it was made by Cromwell. Both the Rump and Cromwell faced real problems.

- The execution of Charles I sent shockwaves across Europe. Only Spain would recognise the Commonwealth government of the Rump.
- The Rump and Cromwell needed to get control over Scotland and Ireland as well as England.
- England's wealth depended on trade. The Protestant Dutch posed the greatest threat to England's trade.
- Many of the 'godly' wanted a foreign policy based on religion, that is, war against Catholic countries such as Spain. This view was shared by Cromwell.

What did Cromwell do?

Peace with the Dutch   The Rump went to war against the Netherlands over trade. In 1654 Cromwell made peace with the Dutch by the Treaty of Westminster. The Dutch accepted the Navigation Act which said that all goods being carried to the British Isles or English colonies had to be carried in English ships.

War against Spain   Although Cromwell's ships in the Caribbean failed to win Hispaniola, they secured Jamaica in 1655.

The war is marked by the brilliance of the leadership of Admiral Robert Blake. The British navy and shipping was threatened by not only the Spanish but pirate ships. In October 1654, Blake set sail for the Mediterranean. He caught up with the fleet of pirate ships in 1655, sinking the lot.

Blake then led the navy to a famous victory against the Spanish off Cadiz in 1656 which led to the seizure of the Spanish treasure fleet. Blake's most famous triumph was the destruction of the Spanish West Indies fleet that was harboured at Santa Cruz in the Canary Islands. Blake's ships were blown into the harbour, and destroyed all of the Spanish vessels (for the loss of one ship); the wind changed and they were blown out again. No wonder Blake and his sailors claimed that they had been blown by a 'Protestant wind'.

> **Did you know?**
>
> The Spanish treasure fleet captured by Blake was carrying gold and silver back from the Americas, said to be worth £2 million. In the 1650s it was a huge amount of money – enough to run the government for a few years.

Alliance with France   In order to beat the Spanish in Europe, Cromwell made an alliance with France. At the Battle of Dunes in 1658, Cromwell's army impressed their French allies with their discipline in helping to defeat the Spanish. As a result the English were given Dunkirk.

The Baltic   The Baltic Sea was very important to English trade. The strongest country in the region was Protestant Sweden, much admired by Cromwell. In 1656, the two countries made a trade agreement that protected English trading rights in the Baltic.

Summary task

1 Look again at your hero/villain scales. What can you find in Issues 4–6 to put on either side of the scales? Where does Drogheda go? Or religious tolerance?

2 Sort through the evidence you have assembled. You should have some things on either side, but you probably think they have different weights. Even if you have three things on one side you might think that those three things outweigh the six things on the other side! Now is the time to come to a conclusion. Which way does the balance tip for you? Cromwell the hero? Or Cromwell the villain?

3 Now write up your opinion in an essay. Here is a structure for your writing:
   • First, explain what you think was Cromwell's greatest achievement – the main reason he might be considered a hero.
   • Then, explain what you think was his worst failure – the main reason that he might be considered a villain.
   • Finally, answer the key question: Oliver Cromwell – hero or villain? Explain your view as fully as possible and use examples.

Section 2: Summary task

In this section you have investigated some of the most tumultuous years of English history. You are now going to review these years through the eyes of one of these characters.

Royalist who fought for the King in the Civil War and has never given up hope that he will return

Country gentleman who stayed neutral in the Civil War and wants a quiet life

New Model Army soldier who fought for Parliament in the Civil War and is very interested in the ideas of the Levellers

Puritan for whom the most important thing in this world is to live a godly life and to make sure others do too

The year is 1658; Oliver Cromwell is dying. Opinion polls did not exist in those days, but imagine they did and that each of the people above has been asked by a seventeenth-century pollster to fill in the following form to say what they think of the changes that have taken place in England since 1640.

Work in groups. Choose one character each and fill out a copy of the chart for them. Put a tick in one of columns 1–5, then add a sentence to give reasons for their view.

Issue	1	2	3	4	5	Reasons
The government of the country						
The power of Parliament						
Religious freedom						
The Catholic threat						
Foreign policy						
Taxation						
Relations with the Scots and Irish						

1 – Great improvement　　2 – A little better
3 – No change or, I don't care　　4 – Slightly worse　　5 – Much worse

Over to you

Now it is your turn. What do you think? Had the country changed for the better between 1640 and 1658, or had it changed for the worse? Choose one issue from the chart opposite where you think changes have been for the better, and one where you think changes have been for the worse and write a paragraph to explain your view.

SECTION 3

1658–1750: Restoration and settlement

This is one interpretation of the Glorious Revolution.

This section continues many of the themes and issues from Section 2. But the big idea is settlement. Gradually the issues that have caused such division through the earlier part of the seventeenth century begin to be settled. The struggles for power between Parliament and King begin to be settled (with Parliament very much on top); the struggles over religion begin to be settled (with the Protestants on top); and some of the struggles between Scotland and England are settled too as a new country called the United Kingdom emerges.

Of course it was not that easy, so this section aims to give you a feel for the key struggles through this period: the Restoration, when Parliament decided to bring the King back (Unit 10); the Glorious Revolution, when Parliament replaced a king they did not like with one they preferred but *without a war* (Unit 11); and the Jacobite Rebellions, which were two further attempts to put the Stuart kings back on the throne (Unit 12).

Finally, the conclusion looks at eighteenth-century England through the eyes of one of the most famous British writers of this period – Daniel Defoe – who toured Britain at that time. What did he get excited about? Not religion or politics, but farming, mining, cloth making, stage coaches – the stuff of everyday life.

At the end you will be invited to choose what you regard as the biggest changes from 1500 to 1750.

What is this all about?

In 1649, Parliament had ordered the execution of King Charles I. Eleven years later it invited his son to become king. Why? Given that the country had been plunged into Civil War partly through the failings and arrogance of his father it seems strange indeed to invite the son to rule the country once again. But times change, as do opinions. In part 1 you investigate how and why they reinstated the monarchy.

The new monarch, Charles II, was not expected to rule in the same way as his father. However, the problems, issues and differences of opinion that had led to the Civil War in the first place had not just gone away. So in part 2 you will examine how Charles II and Parliament ruled together. Was this really a new kind of relationship between King and Parliament?

Finally, in part 3 you will examine what life was like in Restoration England. It is remembered as a time of cultural excitement. After the barrenness of the Cromwell years theatres were re-opened, new plays were written and performed, pictures were painted and huge advances were made in science. Yet at the same time London was struck by two disasters: the Great Plague and the Great Fire of London. What do these events tell us about what it was like in the reign of Charles II?

10.1 Why did they bring the King back?

How did it happen?

1658

September   Oliver Cromwell dies and his son Richard becomes Lord Protector.

1659

January   Richard calls the Protectorate Parliament to meet.

April   Parliament and Richard try to ban army officers from meeting.

May   Army officers meet and force Richard to retire. They recall the Rump Parliament (see page 146).

August   A Royalist uprising led by Sir George Booth is crushed.

October   The army argues with the Rump Parliament which is then shut down. The army rules the country.

December   The army hands power back over to the Rump Parliament.

1660

February   General Monck arrives in London. He recalls the Parliament of 1648 which meets and in March calls elections.

April   The Convention Parliament meets.

May   Charles gives a number of promises in the Declaration of Breda. Parliament votes to offer him the crown and he returns to England.

Why did it happen?

FACTOR 1 **Richard Cromwell** When Oliver Cromwell died in September 1658, his son Richard Cromwell was made Lord Protector. Royalists gave him the nickname of 'Tumbledown Dick' to try to show that he was weak and feeble. While Richard might not have been that feeble, he was clearly very different from his father. Oliver had ruled England with the support of the army and he was respected by Parliament. Richard had not been a soldier and he did not have the support of the army. He tried to use Parliament in April 1659 to limit the power of the army but the soldiers did not accept that and they forced Richard to back down.

FACTOR 2 **The army and the Rump** In May 1659, the army recalled the Rump Parliament. This was the parliament that had existed from 1649 to 1653. If the army leaders thought that the Rump would provide some kind of stable government they were mistaken. Instead, the members of the Rump Parliament spent much of the summer of 1659 discussing how they could limit the army's power.

The army's response was predictable. In October 1659 it closed the Rump and decided to rule England through a Committee of Safety led by Charles Fleetwood. This move was deeply unpopular; the army in Scotland led by General Monck spoke out against government by this Committee, as did the navy. In December 1659, the Rump began sitting again. This disagreement between Rump and army led many in England to conclude that only the return of the monarchy would bring stable government.

FACTOR 3 **Economic Distress** The political crisis of 1659 was made worse by an economic depression. England had been at war with Spain since 1655. The impact of the war was to disrupt trade. Food prices were high but prices for cloth and other goods that were exported (sold abroad) had fallen. Many cloth workers were out of work and agricultural labourers were hungry. This was a recipe for unrest and rioting.

FACTOR 4 **Fear of Quakers** Religion, as always, was an important factor for change. In 1659, it seemed that the lower ranks of the army were dominated by the religious group known as the Quakers. This may not seem particularly worrying to us; today Quakers are viewed as peace-loving. In the seventeenth century it was a different story. They had some radical anti-authority ideas. Quakers did not believe in taking orders from church ministers. If they did not like a sermon in church Quakers would interrupt. They refused to take their hats off as a sign of respect. They wanted to abolish the church taxes known as tithes.

Many people (wrongly) thought that many members of the Rump sympathised with the Quakers.

FACTOR 5 **General Monck** In February 1660, General George Monck rode into London at the head of a large army. Monck had spent the best part of ten years as military commander in Scotland. On his arrival in London, he found a divided, unpopular Parliament. Monck came to the conclusion that the only way to regain political stability was to restore the Stuarts.

FACTOR 6 **The Declaration of Breda** Despite all of the above, the Restoration would have been less likely without the Declaration of Breda. On 1 May 1660, Charles Stuart made a declaration (at Breda in Holland), which was read out to Parliament. Charles promised that, if allowed back to England as king, he would:

- grant religious freedom
- grant a pardon for nearly all those who had fought against the Royalists
- open up the possibility of confiscated land being returned to Royalists.

This pleased virtually everyone and it set their minds at rest that he would be different from his father. It increased support for Charles' return.

10.2 Who was in charge in Restoration England?

In May 1661, the so-called Cavalier Parliament met for the first time. Most of its members were quite strongly pro-monarchy. However, over the years Parliament and Charles still clashed on a number of occasions. Action by action they were working out who was really in control. Was this a new kind of monarchy? Should Parliament now control the actions of the King or should the King still be allowed extensive personal power?

Task

You are going to view the events of Charles' reign as eight rounds in a trial of strength.

1 On the page opposite is the playing sheet. After each round decide who seems to have most power and influence: the King or Parliament? Give it a score on your copy:
   A clear victory for one side = 2 points to the victorious side; 0 points to the defeated side
   A draw or an unclear outcome = 1 point to each side
2 At the end add up your scores. How did Charles do? How great was his power?

Score	Power level
Between 13 and 16	Totally in charge – absolute power
Between 8 and 12	Dominant but with some limits
Between 4 and 7	Has some power but definitely not in charge
Between 0 and 3	Powerless

Round	Date	Issue and what happened?	Charles' score	Parliament's score
1	1661	**Long Parliament's legacy:** Charles II had to accept that all of those things his father agreed to ban in 1640–41 stayed banned. This included Ship Money and using Courts like the Star Chamber.		
2	1661	**An Act of 1661** stated that anyone who claimed that Parliament could make laws without the approval of the King would go to prison – for life.		
3	1661	**Appointing ministers:** In the 1640s, Parliament had demanded the power to appoint the King's advisers. The Cavalier Parliament accepted that it was the King's right to make such appointments.		
4	1661–62	**Militia Acts** placed control of the MILITIA in the hands of the King.		
5	1664	**The Triennial Act 1664:** The Long Parliament had passed a law that if the King did not call a parliament at least once every three years he would be in trouble. The Cavalier Parliament kept the instruction but got rid of the sanction – they did not say what would happen if he did not. For the last four years of his reign, Charles ruled without a parliament.		
6	1661–65	**Religion** Charles had promised to allow people to worship as they wished. But instead Parliament passed laws known as the Clarendon Code which attempted to bully people into becoming a member of and worshipping in the Church of England. Charles was not in favour of these laws but had to accept them.		
7	1670	**Foreign Policy** The King was in charge of foreign policy. In 1670 he signed the Treaty of Dover with Louis, the King of France. Part of this treaty was a secret clause that Louis would pay Charles £200,000 a year if he joined France in fighting against Spain and Holland and if Charles' brother (James) who was next in line for the English throne, declared that he was a Roman Catholic. If Parliament had known about this in advance it would have been a very serious matter but they were not even consulted.		
8	1678–81	**The Exclusion Crisis** In the summer of 1678, a man called Titus Oates claimed there was a Catholic plot to kill Charles. Even though this was not true, 35 Catholic 'plotters' were tried and executed. Following this a group in Parliament, nicknamed the Whigs, tried to: • exclude James from succession (stop him being the next king because he was a Catholic) • impeach Charles' closest adviser Thomas Osborne, Earl of Danby. In the end both failed – Parliament was not prepared to challenge the King's power.		
		Total		

10.3 Case studies from Restoration England

Case study 1: the Great Plague 1665–66

In 1665 and 1666 London was hit by the Great Plague. It is estimated that between 75,000 and 100,000 people (around a fifth of London's population) died. Below is a series of pictures drawn at the time and produced in a pictorial broadsheet, which gave news in pictures.

Source ❶

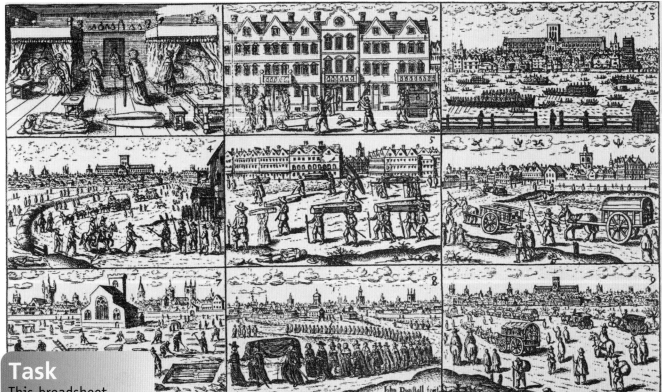

Example of a broadsheet.

Task

This broadsheet would be handed out to people or pasted on walls much as a free newspaper might be handed out today. But it needs some titles. Study carefully what is happening in each frame then write a suitable descriptive title for each of the nine frames. You may need the text on this spread to help you.

In the spring of 1665, people in the parish of St Giles-in-the-Fields started to die of a rather strange disease. Large swellings, known as buboes, appeared in the victims' necks, groins and armpits. They were suffering from the bubonic plague – the same disease that had ravaged England during the Black Death (although that had been made worse by being combined with another form of plague that struck at the same time). Other symptoms of bubonic plague included fever, vomiting and headaches. One in three people with such symptoms died within two weeks. As spring turned into summer, the death rate rose. The parish of St Giles-in-the-Fields lay outside the city walls but these walls could not halt the spread of the plague.

In July 1665 King Charles II and his Court left London for Hampton Court and then Oxford. They were followed to Oxford by MPs and by most

Did you know?

The names of the poorest plague victims were not normally recorded. The first recorded plague victim in London in 1665 was Margaret Porteous who died on 12 April.

What... ?

MIASMA
Refers to polluted air or atmosphere. Many people, until well into the nineteenth century, thought that bad air was the cause of disease.

Who... ?

SAMUEL PEPYS
A Clerk of the Acts to the Navy Board. Much of what we know of the 1660s is down to his diary, which famously included accounts of the Great Fire of London and the plague. He was later elected as an MP.

judges, although the Lord Mayor stayed behind in London. Few could blame those who could afford to escape; in the summer heat the plague swept across London until it reached its peak in September when, in one week, 7,165 Londoners died.

It was the poor who suffered most. They became trapped in the city gripped by death. A large cross would be painted on the front door of any building that housed plague victims. Watchmen locked the doors and kept guard over infected houses. People were employed as searchers to look for dead bodies and take them at night to huge burial pits outside the city walls.

People at the time did not know what had caused the plague. As with the Black Death in the Middle Ages some thought it was an act of God.

Many people thought that the plague was carried in the air and so a number of measures were taken by the City authorities to try to cleanse it:

● wood fires were kept burning day and night
● strong-smelling substances including hops, pepper and frankincense were also burned.

Individuals were told to sniff sponges that had been soaked in vinegar and everyone, including young children, was encouraged to smoke tobacco! Those who had the plague were offered a range of treatments, including being bled with leeches.

Some thought that the plague was carried by cats and dogs and the Lord Mayor ordered all of these animals to be put down. With the cats gone, the number of rats multiplied and we now know that it was actually these rats that carried the fleas that spread the plague.

Trade between London and the outside world was banned, but this did not prevent the spread of the plague to one other place. A parcel of cloth sent from a Londoner to the village tailor in Eyam, Derbyshire, in September 1665 carried the infection. The disease spread rapidly and the villagers prepared to flee. But the village parson, William Mompesson, stopped them. He encouraged the villagers to stay, so as to stop the disease spreading across the county. Traders brought essential supplies to the parish boundary where the villagers had left money to pay for them. The villagers were to suffer for their bravery: 259 of them (out of 350) died but the disease did not spread to the rest of Derbyshire.

In the winter of 1665 the number dying gradually declined. It was the last great attack of plague. In later years it returned on a smaller scale but never again with such terrible effects.

Samuel Pepys' diary entry for 31 December 1666 shows how London suffered:

London less and less likely to be built again, everyone settling elsewhere, and nobody encouraged to trade … . All men fearful of the ruin of the whole kingdom next year.

See page 196 for a practice source exercise on the Plague.

What... ?

DISSENTER
A person who disagrees with the majority.
NONCONFORMIST
A conformist is someone who does what he or she is supposed to do. A nonconformist is the opposite. After 1660, a Nonconformist was someone who did not conform to the Church of England.

Case study 2: the life of John Bunyan

Charles II had promised religious freedom in the Declaration of Breda but there was not much public support for such tolerance. The Quakers and other religious groups were feared and disliked. In May 1660 there were riots in London, during which their meeting houses were broken into and wrecked. From now on, those who were not members of the Church of England were to be called Dissenters. In the minds of the majority of people in England Dissenters were 'trouble'. Let's see what one person's life can tell us about attitudes at the time.

Popular preacher

John Bunyan spent three years in the parliamentary army before returning home in 1647 and settling down to life as a TINKER. John's wife introduced him to Bible study and he began to question his enjoyment of games and the ringing of church bells.

In the 1650s, John was drawn to the religious group set up by John Gifford which met in St John's Church in Bedford. Bunyan began preaching in 1655 although he did not have a licence to do so. Soon 'the tinker of Bedford' became very popular because he showed that you did not need to be very well educated or have a university degree to preach about God. Bunyan's message was also very straightforward:

- The saved were those who had faith in Jesus Christ. This faith could not be 'bought' by doing good things.
- The source of all truth was the Bible. For that reason he did not like the Quakers and their idea that people are guided by their 'inner light'.

Prisoner

After the Restoration in 1660 preachers such as Bunyan who had no 'licence' to preach were considered a threat. Local magistrates in Bedfordshire, such as Sir Francis Wingate, set about ordering their arrests. One day in 1660, Sir Francis learned that Bunyan was going to preach in the village of Lower Samsall. He sent a constable to the meeting who arrested Bunyan in mid-sermon. Sir Francis had him thrown into jail and he was later charged with breaking the CONVENTICLE ACT of 1593, which did not allow people to hold such religious meetings. Bunyan refused to stop preaching, so the court sentenced him to three months in jail. He stayed imprisoned in Bedford jail for the next twelve years (with a few weeks' break in 1666).

Bunyan spent his time in jail preaching to fellow prisoners, writing and making tagged laces. In 1672 Bunyan was released and chosen as preacher to the Bedford Nonconformist church. He was a very popular preacher, his fame spreading as far as London where he preached to large crowds. But in 1675 the attitude of the government changed and many licences to preach were withdrawn. In March Bunyan was arrested and imprisoned for six months. His prison was a cell in a bridge over the River Ouse where he wrote the book for which he is best known: *The Pilgrim's Progress*.

Source ❷

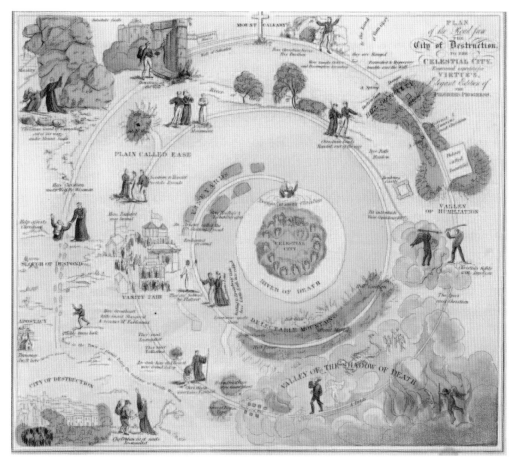

The Pilgrim's Progress

The Pilgrim's Progress was written as an allegory, which means there is a meaning hidden in the story. Published in 1678, it soon became the most popular book in England. The story is told by a dreamer who sees a man, Christian, clothed in rags. The story starts with Christian (who is really Bunyan) fleeing from the City of Destruction. He has been told by the book in his hands that the city and his home are going to be destroyed by heavenly fire, so he sets out to try to reach salvation. He leaves his wife, children and friends behind.

Task

Using the text and images to help you, write a back cover blurb for *The Pilgrim's Progress*. A blurb sums up the story and explains why it is good. Write no more than 150 words.

Illustrations from The Pilgrim's Progress.

Did you know?

John Bunyan's first published work was an attack aimed at the Quakers. In *Some Gospel Truths Opened* (1656) he puts in print his attack on the idea of the 'inner light'.

Did you know?

Bunyan wrote *The Pilgrim's Progress Part Two* six years later in 1684. In this volume Christian's wife, Christiana, and his four sons follow him to the Celestial City.

Task

Obituary in 300 words
You might have read an obituary in a newspaper. It is a detailed description of the life of someone who has just died. You are to write an obituary of John Bunyan. The problem is that the editor of the newspaper you are writing for has told you that you have got only 300 words to write it in. Get writing!

As Christian flees, he is weighed down with the burden of his sins upon his back. He does not know what to do or where to turn and he sets off on his journey to find out how he can get rid of his burden. However, things get worse rather than better, as nearly straightaway he falls into the Slough of Despond. (A slough is a deep ditch and despond means misery.)

Christian frees himself from the Slough of Despond with the assistance of a new-found friend called Help. He passes through a little wicket gate, and sets off on his way to the Celestial City (which is heaven). On his way he has some exciting adventures. He loses his burden at the Cross but struggles to cross the Valley of Humiliation. He is terrified in the Valley of the Shadow of Death, and really suffers in Vanity Fair (where he has to resist temptation). When he gets to Doubting Castle he is almost overcome by Giant Despair. After all of his adventures he at last reaches the Delectable Mountains. He then crosses the River of Death and enters the Celestial City. In the end he is saved because his faith has remained unbroken.

In the course of his journey, Christian meets a number of characters who represent good and bad qualities found in people in everyday life. There are Hopeful and Faithful, the cheat Mr Legality, Ignorance, Mr Worldly-Wise, Talkative, Lord Hategood and Mr Facing-both-ways, to name but a few.

Bunyan's book was a sensation. It sold over 100,000 copies in his lifetime. For the next 300 years it was second only to the Bible in popularity. The message in Bunyan's book was simple, and it was one that people understood and wanted to hear. The story tells us a lot about the beliefs and attitudes of Nonconformists at the time.

He told his readers the following:

- Faith was the most important quality that they could bring in their approach to God.
- The path that Christian followed was the path to heaven and salvation. Everyone else was doomed to hell.
- Like Christian's, the journey to heaven must be made on your own.
- All the time, people are faced by temptation to sin but this should be resisted.

He also encouraged his readers to:

- hold on to their beliefs
- show courage, friendship and support each other.

He showed the historian that:

- Nonconformists like Bunyan felt persecuted
- the Protestant religion stressed the importance of the individual.

The Pilgrim's Progress made Bunyan the best-known Nonconformist in England. He died on 31 August, 1688 on his way to London where he was hoping to reconcile a father and son who had been arguing.

Source exercise

Source B is a portrait of John Bunyan and Source A is a description that was written by someone from his time.

1 Read Source A first, then look at the portrait.
2 Write down four things about Bunyan that appear in **both** the written extract and the portrait.
3 Write down four things about Bunyan that are in the written extract but not in the portrait.

Source Ⓐ

Bunyan was tall, strong boned, was not fat, had a ruddy face, with sparkling eyes, wearing his hair on his upper lip; his hair reddish, but in his latter days time had sprinkled it with grey; his nose well set, but not declining or bending, and his mouth moderate large; his forehead something high.

He looked as if he had a rough temper, but when you spoke to him he was friendly. He did not say much, did not boast and was modest. He hated lying and swearing, was fair, never wanted revenge and he enjoyed making friendship with all. Bunyan was good at working people out and he had a quick wit.

Description by a friend of Bunyan's.

Source Ⓑ

A portrait of Bunyan.

Case study 3: the Court of King Charles

Life for those surrounding Oliver Cromwell was dull and drab; not so the Court of King Charles. We are lucky in that one of those who now and again attended Court, Sir Samuel Pepys, kept a diary.

Task

1 Read the four extracts on the right. What do they tell us about life at the Court of King Charles?

2 One of the other most famous events of this time was the Great Fire of London. Do your own research via the internet to find Pepys' report of the fire. There are many sites you could check, for example: http://www.pepys.info/fire.html. Find out:
   a) what caused the fire
   b) why it caused such destruction
   c) how they put it out.
   You could also research
   d) what big changes it caused in London.

Source ❸

Samuel Pepys.

25 December 1662   I went to chapel to hear Bishop Morley preach. In his sermon he criticised the Court for their excess in plays and gambling. The reaction of the Court members present was to laugh at him.

31 December 1662   I went to White Hall for a ball held by the King. I went first to the Duke's chamber, where I saw him [the Duke] and the Duchess at supper. By and by comes the King and Queen, the Duke and Duchess, and all the great ones: and after seating themselves, the King takes out the Duchess of York and so other lords and other ladies get up and they danced the Bransle [a dance]. After that, the King led a lady a swift and lively Coranto [another dance]. Then to country dances; the King leading the first, which he called for; which was, says he, 'Cuckolds all awry', the old dance of England.

17 February 1667   This evening, going to the Queen's side [the Queen's part of the Court] to find the ladies, I found the Queen, Duchess of York and one or two others playing cards in front of a room full of people. I was amazed to see this take place on a Sunday.

8 April 1667   I went to the King's House [a theatre] where there was a new play on. I have never seen it so full. The King, Queen, Duke and Duchess of York and all of the Court were there. The play was called *The Changes of Crowns* by Ned Howard.

Summary task

List all the different kinds of historical sources that you have used in Unit 10.3. Which did you find most useful in helping you understand what life was like in Restoration England? Choose one and give reasons for your answer.

Charles II died in 1685 without an heir. The throne passed to his brother James, Duke of York, who was a Catholic. You know from Unit 10 that anti-Catholic feeling was running high and indeed some powerful people in England had tried to exclude James from taking the throne at all. So it might not surprise you to learn that James did not last! In a three-year reign he managed to annoy almost all important groups in England and in 1688 he fled from England and was replaced by his daughter Mary and her husband William, who were chosen by Parliament. The big surprise however is *how* this happened.

In this unit you find out what happened in this so-called 'Glorious Revolution'; what changed as a result; and you decide why it might deserve (or not) the title 'Glorious'.

Who... ?

JAMES II 1633–1701

He was brother of Charles II and son of the executed Charles I. He was king for only three years, 1685–88, and was the last Roman Catholic to hold the English crown. Many people distrusted his religious policies and they deposed him in the Glorious Revolution. He was replaced by his Protestant daughter and son-in-law, Mary II and William III. He lived the rest of his life in exile in France, becoming increasingly religious, praying and fasting. He died of a brain haemorrhage. His daughter Anne later became Queen of England.

A Catholic king

In 1662 Charles II had married Catherine of Braganza but their marriage produced no children. Charles also had a number of mistresses who gave him at least fourteen children – but because they were illegitimate they were not allowed to succeed. This meant that, according to the rules of succession, the next king after Charles II was to be his brother James – a devout Catholic! Parliament had known this was to happen for some time, and James had made no secret of the fact that when he became king he wanted to get rid of anti-Catholic laws. However many people in England feared he would go further than that.

- They feared that a Catholic king would also be an absolutist king who would try to rule without Parliament.
- They feared too that England would once again come under the influence of foreign Catholic countries.

However, rules were rules and no one in Parliament or in the country was wanting to return to the chaos and suffering of the Civil War years, so in February 1685 James was crowned King James II.

In reality, James had no desire to rule without Parliament. Nor did he want to force people in England to become Catholics. He thought that, once he had got rid of the anti-Catholic laws, people would want to be Catholics. He really underestimated the strength of anti-Catholic feeling in England.

Monmouth's rebellion

The Duke of Monmouth was one of Charles' illegitimate children. He had a very successful career as an army leader and, as a Protestant, was many people's choice to succeed Charles. In 1683 he was suspected of plotting against Charles but, because he was the King's son, he was allowed to flee to Holland.

When James II became king in February 1685, Monmouth decided to try to seize power. On 11 June he landed at Lyme Regis in Dorset. As he marched inland he was joined by clothworkers and farmers who were strong Protestants and did not want a Catholic king. Unfortunately for Monmouth, James' army was led by the talented commander John Churchill. The two sides met at Sedgemoor on 6 July 1685. Monmouth's army was defeated. He was captured and taken to London where he was executed.

The Bloody Assizes

James wanted to show potential traitors what would happen to those who turned against the King. Straight after the Battle of Sedgemoor, James sent Colonel Kirke and a group of cavalry to teach the people of Dorset a lesson.

On arrival, Kirke and his troops got to work. Hundreds of rebels were executed. Even some children who had simply waved at Monmouth's troops as they passed through their villages were put in prison. The only people who seemed able to escape such ruthless punishments were those such as one Edward Strode, who had the money to bribe Kirke to spare them.

Kirke was followed down to the West Country by the Lord Chief Justice Jeffreys. He set up a special court called an Assizes to try those involved in the uprising. A further 300 rebels were sentenced to death, many being hanged, drawn and quartered. Hundreds more were sent to Barbados. Jeffreys' victims included women as well as men: Lady Alice Lisle was found guilty of looking after rebels after Sedgemoor and executed; a woman called Elisabeth Gaunt was sentenced to be burned alive. She was the last woman to be killed in this way for political crimes.

The gentry did not object to this crushing of Monmouth's rebellion; they thought that he was a traitor who deserved everything he got. But they were a lot less happy with the events that followed – and once again the troubles were all about religion!

Source ❶

This picture was drawn at the time of Monmouth's rebellion. ❓ *What story do you think it is illustrating?*

Did you know?

Not all of Monmouth's rebels were captured after Sedgemoor. Some had a very lucky escape, none more so than a man called James Daniel. After the battle he escaped and hid in a secret room at his home in Beaminster. Fearing capture he went and hid in some straw in a nearby barn. James' troops came into the barn and started sticking their bayonets into the straw. But they missed Daniel, who escaped and managed to live to the ripe old age of 100.

Phase 1: James falls out with the Anglicans

- James had made clear his intention to get rid of the Test and Corporation Acts which prevented non-Anglicans from taking important jobs such as magistrates.
- James did not disband the army that had been raised to fight Monmouth. Instead he announced that it would be kept on and that Catholics in the army would be promoted to become officers (previously Catholics had been barred from senior positions in the army).
- James gave permission to the Duke of Tyrconnell – leader of the army in Ireland – to replace Protestant officers and soldiers with Catholic officers and soldiers.
- James tried to replace Protestant Justices of the Peace with Catholics.
- In 1686, James forbade the preaching of anti-Catholic sermons. One rector in the diocese of the Bishopric of London, Bishop Compton, ignored this demand. James ordered Compton to sack the guilty priest but Compton refused. In July 1686, Compton was ordered to stop work.

All of this took place against the backdrop of events in France. In 1685, the French King Louis XIV, started a campaign against the French Protestants who were known as Huguenots. Many escaped to England to tell stories of horrible persecution. James' pro-Catholic policies led many to ask the question, could the same happen here?

Phase 2: the Declaration of Indulgence

James' next move might sound unexpected. He tried to win the support of the extreme Protestants known as the Dissenters by advancing the need for religious tolerance. James and the Dissenters both resented the power of the Anglican Church, just for very different reasons. In 1687 James passed a Declaration of Indulgence which would allow religious freedom. This suspended all the Penal laws and the Test and Corporations Acts. This meant Catholics and Dissenters could now hold senior jobs in government.

But the ploy did not work. The Dissenters distrusted James' Catholic ideas too deeply to become his allies.

James then tried to pack Parliament with MPs who would support his policies. But the Parliament never met.

By the beginning of 1688 nearly all Protestants were very suspicious of James. In April 1688 James ordered that a Second Declaration of Indulgence be read out in churches across England. Archbishop Sancroft and six bishops refused to issue the Declaration. They said that it was not up to James to issue such a Declaration. They were sent to the Tower of London. On 30 June they were found to be not guilty by a court. London celebrated their release from the Tower.

Did you know?

In the seventeenth century, being sent to Barbados in the West Indies was considered a harsh punishment. Those transported were put to work on the sugar plantations.

Did you know?

Sedgemoor was the last battle to be fought on English soil.

Phase 3: a Catholic heir?

One of the few consoling thoughts for the Protestants who were opposed to James had been that at least when he died they would get a Protestant king or queen. James' first marriage had been to a Protestant, Anne Hyde. They had two children, Mary and Anne, who were brought up as Protestants. However after his conversion to Catholicism James had married a second wife, a Catholic princess, Mary of Modena. In 1688 to the alarm of the Protestants she gave birth to a son. Everyone knew that his right to the throne took precedence over that of his half-sisters Mary and Anne, so now the Protestants faced the prospect of another Catholic king. A wicked rumour was spread that the baby was not really the natural child of King James and his wife, but was smuggled into the birthing chamber in a warming pan! So in December 1688, James had the baby prince sent to France for his own safety.

These events did not mean that most people wanted to get rid of James. Very few wanted another civil war. The memories of the last one were too fresh. Most simply wanted him to change his ways. If they could not make him do so, then perhaps he needed to be threatened by someone else.

The 'Protestant wind'

On 30 June 1688, seven leading Protestants wrote to William of Orange, asking him to intervene. William was married to James' daughter, Mary. This on its own was not sufficient reason for him to get involved. However, William had reasons of his own to challenge James. William had spent much of his life fighting France. Charles II and James II had both refused English support for William's fight against the French. This was now William's chance to bring England onto his side in his war against France. In September 1688, William accepted the invitation to invade England.

Source ❷

James II receiving the news of the landing of William of Orange in 1688.

Discuss
What do you think would have happened if James had not run away?

William had to get to England without coming up against James' navy. Luckily for him, the winds in early November kept the English fleet in port while William's ships were able to sail down the English Channel to Torbay. There, on 5 November 1688, his army landed. Many important people including the Earl of Devonshire and the Marquis of Bath declared support for William.

Many others did not but James lost his nerve. Instead of marching to face William, he turned round and went back to London. At this point he lost his most important and most skilled general, John Churchill, who changed sides and supported William.

James tried to escape to France, was captured and was brought back to London. On 22 December he managed to escape and made it to Paris.

This is what happened next:

1689

January

The English Convention Parliament met and offered the throne to William and Mary. This set a pattern that has continued to the current day – Parliament has to approve the succession of a new king or queen.

February

William and Mary were crowned King and Queen of England and Ireland. At their coronation, William and Mary promised to rule according to the laws of Parliament.

March

James II landed in Ireland and entered Dublin.
The Scottish Parliament asked William and Mary to free the Scottish Church and Parliament from English control.

May

The **Toleration Act** allowed Nonconformists in England the freedom to worship as they wanted. But the Nonconformists were still not allowed to do the important jobs.
An Irish Parliament, the 'Patriot Parliament', met in Dublin and declared that Ireland was independent from England.

July

Bishops were abolished by the Scottish Parliament.
In Ireland, James laid siege to the town of Londonderry for three months. The siege was finally lifted in July.

December

The **Bill of Rights** introduced some limits to the power of the monarch. Amongst other things he or she could not:

- keep an army in peacetime without asking Parliament
- suspend laws passed by Parliament
- excuse anyone from being covered by a law.

It also said that the monarch could not be a Catholic and that there should be complete freedom of speech in Parliament.

1690

March   William was granted some money by Parliament, known as the Civil List. A similar scheme still runs today.

June   The Scottish Parliament freed itself from English control.

William took an army to Ireland and, on 1 July, defeated James' army at the Battle of the Boyne. This marked the end of James' attempt to win Ireland.

July   The laws passed by the Irish 'Patriot Parliament' in 1689 were repealed (cancelled) by the English Parliament. From now on the Protestants were to have complete control in Ireland.

Source check

Encyclopaedia Britannica sums up James II's character and reign:

The political ineptitude of James is clear; he often showed firmness when conciliation was needful, and weakness when resolution alone could have saved the day. Moreover, though he mismanaged almost every political problem with which he personally dealt, he was singularly tactless and impatient of advice. But in general political morality he was not below his age, and in his advocacy of toleration decidedly above it. He was more honest and sincere than Charles II, more genuinely patriotic in his foreign policy, and more consistent in his religious attitude. That his brother retained the throne while James lost it is an ironical demonstration that a more pitiless fate awaits the ruler whose faults are of the intellect, than one whose faults are of the heart.

Task

The timeline on pages 171–72 combines information about Ireland, Scotland and England. Draw up a separate timeline for each country. Keep your timelines. They will be useful when you continue these stories in the next chapter.

What… ?

WHIGS AND TORIES
The Whigs believed that the transfer of power to Parliament that took place in English history was a good thing and represented progress. The Tories were suspicious of the changes.

So without a civil war and with not much bloodshed – in England at least – Parliament had got rid of a king they did not like or trust, and replaced him with one they did. They had agreed laws which settled once and for all some of the issues that had caused such conflict between the King and Parliament through the century. This was surely a revolution! And to some it was all the more glorious for the fact that it was achieved with so little violence. (See page 197 for a practice source exercise on the Glorious Revolution.)

Summary task

How glorious? How much revolution?
It is the 'Whig' historians who gave these events the title 'The Glorious Revolution'.

* Make a list of all the changes that took place in 1689–90.
* Highlight two that you think are most 'revolutionary', that is, the really big changes.

Discuss
* Why might the Whigs look on these events of 1689–90 as glorious and why?
* Which groups would not look on the events of 1689–90 as glorious and why?

Write
Write some paragraphs for a speech to be given by a Whig. You should argue in favour of these changes and the way they were achieved.

UNIT 12 A united kingdom?

> **What is this all about?**
>
> In 1707 England and Scotland were unified into one state governed by one parliament. Many Scots complained at the time that Scotland was really absorbed by England and that Scotland got nothing out of the union. In part 1 of this unit you will examine the Act of Union itself. Was it a takeover by England, or was there something in it for both countries? In part 2 you will study the Jacobite rebellions in 1715 and 1745. You will decide what these rebellions were about and whether they had any chance of success. Finally you will think about what they tell you about the state of the union. Do they show that England and Scotland were a dis-united kingdom?

12.1 Why did England and Scotland unite?

England and Scotland had been bitter enemies through the Middle Ages and right up to Elizabeth's reign. Gradually, however, the two countries became closer (see diagram).

However, it is important to remember that they were still separate countries, with their own parliaments passing their own laws. They just happened to share the same king.

Source ❶

In Scotland, English was replacing Gaelic as the main language.

They were both mainly Protestant.

GETTING CLOSER

The Union flag of Great Britain was also created at this time.

In 1603 James VI of Scotland became James I of England, which meant the two countries shared the same monarch.

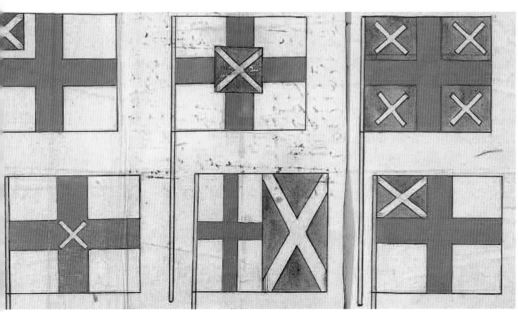

This illustration shows a range of early designs for a union flag in the early seventeenth century. There were worries in Scotland that the cross of St George would dominate over the saltire of St Andrew. Look back to page 115 to see which design James I chose in 1606.

Did you know?

Anne had not expected to take the throne but when her sister Mary died of smallpox she was thrust into line and became queen in 1702. She had eighteen pregnancies, which all lead to miscarriages, stillborn children or infant deaths, so she died heirless.

In her reign England developed a two-party system in Parliament similar to what we have today. The two parties were called the Tories and the Whigs.

Task

Below are some arguments for and against a union between the two countries. Copy out and complete the table below. You have to decide whether each reason would make England or Scotland support or oppose the union.

Number	Argument	England: for or against the union	Scotland: for or against the union
1	Improved security		

In column 1 put the number.
In column 2 write a phrase or word to summarise the argument.
In column 3 put a tick to show England's support or a cross to show its opposition.
In column 4 put a tick to show Scotland's support or a cross to show its opposition.

Arguments for and against a union

1   A union would improve security. Catholicism was still strong in Scotland, especially in the Highlands. There was always the danger that England's Catholic enemies, like France, would find support in Scotland. To make matters worse, James Stuart (who had been James II) wanted his throne back. He was a Catholic and the Stuarts had support in the Highlands of Scotland. He might get support from Catholic countries and from the Highlanders.

2   Anne, the Queen of England, was unlikely to have a healthy heir who could succeed her. Provision had been made for the royal family of Hanover to succeed her. They were related to the royal family and they were Protestant. This was done to prevent the Stuarts regaining the throne. A union would mean that Scotland was signed up to the Hanoverian Succession.

3   Scotland was a poor country; England was 38 times more wealthy despite having only five times as many people. Scotland was not allowed to participate in the profitable trade with English colonies. Between 1692 and 1699 Scotland had suffered a dreadful famine with starvation and disease reducing its population significantly. Scotland needed to share in England's prosperity.

4   Scotland wanted to develop trade with the New World and so an attempt was made to establish a colony at Darien in Central America. Many Scots

invested all their savings in the scheme. However, Darien was not a good place to try to establish a colony. It was in the Spanish Empire, the climate was dreadful, and there was little more than fever-ridden, rain-sodden jungle. It was a fiasco. After three expeditions the scheme collapsed and the investors lost their money (over £153,000). They were furious and blamed the English who had made things as difficult as they could for the scheme. Hatred for England grew to an all-time high.

5 The official Church in Scotland was called the Kirk. It was Presbyterian. This was an extreme and anti-Catholic form of Protestantism. A union would help protect the Kirk from potential threats from Catholics (particularly strong in the Scottish Highlands) and Jacobites (supporters of the Catholic James Stuart).

6 Scotland's main exports to England were cattle, linen and coal. In 1705 England threatened to ban these exports unless the Scots joined in talks about a union.

7 Many Scots thought that a union would simply result in Scotland losing its independence and being governed by the English. All laws would be made by the parliament in London.

8 A union would lead to higher taxes in Scotland.

9 The English government bribed members of the Scottish Parliament to vote in favour of the union.

The Act of Union 1707

- Scotland lost its own parliament but was given 45 MPs in the House of Commons and 16 peers in the House of Lords. (This compares with 513 English MPs and 190 English peers.)
- The Protestant religion and the Presbyterian Church in Scotland were safeguarded.
- Scottish traders were allowed to trade in England's colonies (although few Scottish traders yet had the ships or the money to make proper use of this).
- Scotland was allowed to keep its separate legal system.
- Those who had invested in the disastrous Darien expedition were given their money back.

Task

Read through the terms of the Act of Union. What do you think would be the reaction of the Scots? Choose one term they might like and one they might dislike and give reasons why.

12.2 The Jacobites: hopeless romantics?

Source ❷

I had not been long there, but I heard a Great Noise and looking out saw a terrible multitude come up the High Street with a Drum at the head of them shouting and swearing and crying out all Scotland would stand together: No Union. No Union. English dogs and the like.

A description by an Englishman of a riot in Edinburgh in 1706.

The nobles, gentry and middle classes in Scotland had generally supported the union with England, but it had been very unpopular with most Scots. For them it was not a union but a takeover by England. While the negotiations had been going on there were anti-union riots in Edinburgh and Glasgow.

Remember that the Stuarts were still hoping to get back the throne they had lost when James II had fled in 1688. They expected the union to increase their support in Scotland. In a way the union had made them the leaders of Scottish nationalism. In 1715 and in 1745 the Stuarts tried to get their throne back by force in what became known as the Jacobite rebellions. They failed miserably but these rebellions continue to fascinate us today.

Lost causes like Mary, Queen of Scots, and the Confederates in the American Civil War have become very popular. People like to sympathise with the losing side especially if great sacrifices were made. Often, the lost cause becomes surrounded by romantic stories that bear little relation to what really happened and this is what has happened to the story of the Jacobites.

┌ Did you know? ┐

George I was already 54 when he became king. At that stage he hardly spoke any English. He mostly lived in England from then on, but he was more involved in the day-to-day running of Hanover than he was in running Britain. Even when in England George did not attend Cabinet meetings, but voiced his opinions via meetings with leading minister. So during his reign something close to our modern system of government emerged, with Britain ruled a Cabinet of ministers with the most powerful one (who at this time was Robert Walpole) being the Prime Minster.

Who were the Jacobites?

It will help if you keep an eye on this Stuart family tree as you read this section.

Source ❸

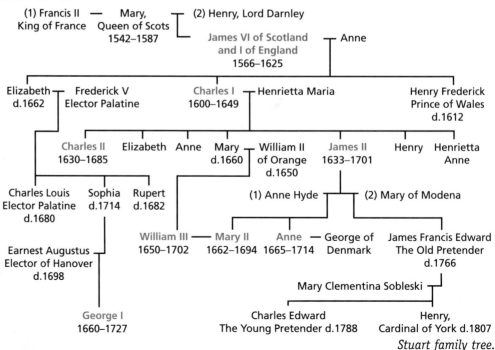

Stuart family tree.

The word Jacobite comes from the Latin word Jacobus which means James. Jacobites were people who wanted to put the Stuarts back on the throne. You will remember that in 1688 the Stuart King James II was replaced on the British throne by his daughter Mary and her husband William. James had become unpopular because he believed in the absolute power of monarchs and had tried to bring Catholicism back into Britain.

Mary died in 1694 but William continued as king until his death in 1702. William and Mary had no children, so William was succeeded by Mary's sister Anne who of course was also a Stuart. It was desperately important that Anne had an heir to follow her onto the throne but none of her children lived long enough. When Anne died in 1714 Britain had a real problem. Who would be the monarch after her death? An Act of Parliament had been passed. This banned Catholics from becoming monarchs and stated that if Anne died without children the throne should pass to Sophia, a distant cousin who had married the ruler of Hanover. It would then go to her son George.

You will see that James Stuart had been left out completely. This was because he was a Catholic and because he believed that he should have absolute power.

Why did people become Jacobites?

Scotland was obviously the centre of Jacobite support. They also had some support in Ireland and in Northern England.

People became Jacobites for a number of reasons.

- They were usually Catholics, as were the Stuarts. They hoped that a Catholic Stuart king would bring back Catholicism as the official religion of Britain.
- They also believed in the Divine Right of Kings, which meant they believed that kings were chosen by God. If that was the case then the Stuarts were God's choice. Queen Anne was a Stuart, so they were happy with her but when she died in 1714 and George I became the first Hanoverian king, they sprang into action.

The stronghold of Jacobitism was the Highlands of Scotland. Here many people were Catholic and still resented the union. They supported the idea of restoring a Scottish Catholic family on the throne. The Scottish clan system was strong in the Highlands and many of the clan chiefs were loyal to the Stuarts and very anti-English.

But they also thought that they would find support in England. There were stories that on her deathbed Queen Anne had said that she wanted James to succeed her. Claims were made that she had even signed a will which stated this, but it was never found. Some people in England were convinced by these stories, partly because George of Hanover (who was supposed to become King George I in due course) was such an unattractive person. And the Jacobite supporters did all they could to demolish his image further. Source 4 is one historian's explanation.

Source 4

The Jacobite press ridiculed George I mercilessly as a lecherous dolt, with not a word of English at his command, sporting two mistresses, one fat (this one was nicknamed 'the elephant'), one thin, both ugly, who had not scrupled to have one of his own wife's former lovers murdered. His coronation was greeted with a wave of rioting in at least twenty English towns. Predictably enough, it was even worse in Scotland. At Inverness the proclamation of George's accession was interrupted and 'God save the King' shouted down by cries of 'God damn them and their king'.

Simon Schama

Investigation: which had the best chance of success: the '15 or the '45?

Task

The two main attempts by the Stuarts to regain the throne were in 1715 and 1745 (these are usually known as the '15 and the '45). Your task is to decide in which year the Jacobites came closest to success. To help you make this judgement, here are some things that a rebellion needs in order to succeed:

- a good leader
- experienced fighters
- staying united – not quarrelling among yourselves
- weaknesses on the authorities' side

- a good plan
- lots of popular support
- help from other countries
- some good luck!

As you read about these two rebellions make notes about how strong or weak they were in each of these areas.

The '15

James II died in 1701. He had a son, also called James (see the Stuart family tree). This James (who was called by his enemies 'The Old Pretender') was determined to get the throne back for the Stuarts. He remembered that the Stuarts had lost the throne once before when Charles I had been executed and that in 1660 they had won it back. He expected the same thing to happen again.

The plan for 1715 was that he would land in Scotland with French soldiers to support him; there he would be joined by warriors from the Highland clans and sympathisers in the pro-Catholic north of England would also rise up in support.

Source ❺

Map of Scotland and north of England.

What happened?

James wrote from France urging the Earl of Mar to start a rebellion. Mar had little military experience or skills and was terribly indecisive. However, in September he raised his Standard at Braemar. Support came quickly from some of the Highland clans and he soon had an army of 4,000 men. The government knew this was happening. Plans were made in London for George to flee to Holland if necessary!

But Mar was far too slow. He stayed in Perth instead of fighting. He sent a force of 2,000 men to join up with Jacobites in the Borders and northern England. When the two groups met they argued about what to do next. The English refused to march into Scotland, and the Scots refused to march into England! When they did eventually march to Preston many of the Scots deserted and they had to surrender to government forces.

Meanwhile, Mar's army at last fought Argyll's government forces at Sherriffmuir in November. Mar had superior numbers and there were several occasions when he seemed to have the opposing army at his mercy but he failed to press home his advantage and Argyll and his army escaped. The battle ended as a draw!

James landed in Scotland on 22 December but by then the Jacobites had lost their early advantages and their support was slipping away. When they realised that Argyll's army had been reinforced and was now equipped with heavy cannon they started a retreat to Montrose. After they had been there a few days the soldiers woke one morning to discover that James, Mar, and some of the others leaders had boarded a ship in the harbour and had sailed for France!

The rising was over and each man made his own way home. All that remained was for the army to disarm the clans that had supported the Stuarts, and for the government to punish its defeated opponents.

Source 6

A portrait of James, painted at the time.

Other important factors to consider

1 Leadership and fighting forces

Prince James Francis Edward was not much of a leader. He arrived late to join the rebellion when his best chance of success had gone. He arrived without supplies or reinforcements. He had six attendants and one ship! When he got to Perth, the Scots – who had expected a dashing hero who would lead them to victory – found a dignified but cold and stern, unsmiling young man. The Highlanders needed an outgoing leader who would capture their hearts; instead they got a quiet and introverted young man.

James was just as disappointed with them. He was accustomed to the disciplined French army but he found an army of rather less than 5,000 poorly equipped, wild, unkempt looking warriors. It didn't help that it was the middle of winter with deep snow. He quickly became depressed and was ill for much of the six weeks that he spent in Scotland before returning to France.

Anyway, James had arrived too late. If he had arrived three months earlier at the beginning of the campaign, the result may have been different. Sympathisers might have been quicker to take up arms, and opponents less ready to support the government.

2 Popular support

The Jacobites planned an uprising that would start in Scotland but would spread to England. They knew that since union many people in Scotland had not benefited and were suffering from higher taxes on linen, malt and salt. And in England the Tory party half-hankered after a return to the Stuarts. When George I began to favour their opponents the Whigs, some of the Tory leaders like the Earl of Mar (Scottish) and the Duke of Ormonde (English) threw in their lot with the Old Pretender. These were very powerful men.

Mar had support from the Highlands and the Lowlands but his most important supporters were the Highland clans of the Stewarts, the MacDonalds and the MacPhersons. However, throughout Scotland, support for George had dwindled. Towns across the north of Scotland including Aberdeen and Inverness had declared for James.

3 Foreign help

When James II died in 1701, Louis XIV of France had promised that he would support James' son's attempts to win back the throne. The hope of the Jacobites was that James would land with strong French support. France was their best hope of support as Louis XIV would have loved to have seen a Catholic monarch restored in England, especially one that owed his throne to him.

However, France had suffered decades of war, was suffering from famine and had no money left! The worst news of all for the Jacobites was that in the middle of the rebellion Louis XIV died leaving an infant great-grandson as his successor. There would be no invasion.

Three years later (so rather too late to have been of any use), a fleet of 29 Spanish ships with 5,000 troops set sail from Spain for a landing in Scotland. However, the weather finished off this mini-armada in the same way as it had finished off the great Armada over a hundred years before.

Task

How are you getting on with making notes about the '15? You should have plenty to write about these points:
- leadership and planning
- popular support, good fighters, and unity
- weaknesses on the authorities' side
- experienced fighters
- help from other countries
- good or bad luck.

Based on the evidence you have gathered do you think the '15 had any chance of success? Give at least three reasons for your answer.

The '45

In August 1745, James' son, Charles Edward Louis John Cazymyr Sylvester Severino Maria Stuart (or 'Bonnie Prince Charlie' as he is usually known) was raising his Standard in Scotland and telling the assembled clansmen that he had come to set Scotland free. The Stuarts were having another go at winning back the throne!

What happened?

An invasion with French support was planned for 1744 but it never took place. Despite this setback, Charles was determined to try to win his throne back.

He borrowed money to buy some swords, some small cannon and to hire two ships, the *Elizabeth* and the *du Teillay*. The ships were attacked on their way to Scotland and on 23 July 1745, Charles landed on the white sands of the Outer Hebridean island of Eriskay, with only seven companions. The Prince is said to have scattered some seeds there and to this day a flower known as the Prince's Flower grows there and nowhere else in Scotland.

Charles now had to rouse the Highland clans to support his cause. Some of them were very doubtful but Charles was a dashing romantic figure with great charisma and he won many of them over.

Among his supporters were 300 from the Macdonald clan and 700 from the clan Cameron. Altogether he had over 4,000 men ready to fight with him. They quickly took control of Edinburgh and by September 1745 had defeated King George's army at Prestonpans. He seemed to have the rest of

Source 7

A painting of Charles' ships the Elizabeth *and the* du Teillay *under attack. The* Elizabeth *was forced back; the* du Teillay *landed on Eriskay.*

Source ❽

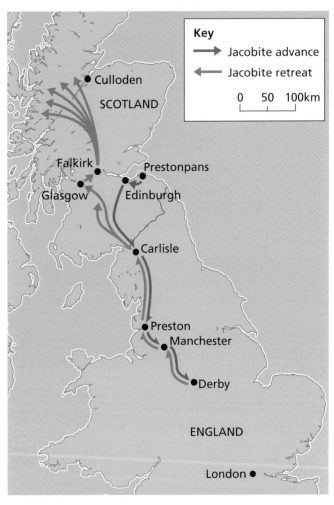

Key
→ Jacobite advance
← Jacobite retreat

0   50   100km

Culloden
SCOTLAND
Falkirk   Prestonpans
Glasgow   Edinburgh
Carlisle
Preston
Manchester
Derby
ENGLAND
London

Map of the movements of Charles' army.

Scotland at his mercy, but against the advice of his generals he marched into England. By now he had 6,000 men.

Amazingly, there was no British army to stop them and they soon reached Derby, just 130 miles from London. Londoners were panicking; the streets were deserted. However, Charles was disappointed by the very small number of people (only 200) who had joined him in England. His generals persuaded him to retreat to Scotland. It was known that King George's armies were gradually closing in on them, and there was no sign of the expected help from France.

Charles and his men had a very difficult march back to Scotland, chased by the King's army, which was led by the Duke of Cumberland. In April 1746 Cumberland caught them at Culloden. The Jacobites were cold, hungry and exhausted. They were outnumbered and Cumberland's troops were better armed and trained. They suffered a crushing defeat.

[There is a practice source exercise on the Battle of Culloden on page 198.]

Charles was now a fugitive. On the run he spent the next five months in hiding in the Highlands and Islands of Scotland assisted by his supporters. A ransom of £30,000 was placed on his head but despite this no one betrayed him to the authorities.

Charles' flight has become the stuff of legend. It is remembered in the song 'The Skye Boat Song'. Flora Macdonald helped him to escape to the Island of Skye, dressed in disguise as her maid 'Betty Burke'. Legend has it that Flora and Bonnie Prince Charlie fell in love that summer and she did keep a lock of his hair to remember him by. He finally escaped to France. Flora was captured and spent some time in the Tower of London. She died in 1790 and is buried on Skye. It is said that she was wrapped in the Prince's bed sheet.

Did you know?

The severity with which the Duke of Cumberland dealt with the Jacobites earned him the nickname 'Butcher'.

Discuss

Compare the story of the '45 with that of the '15. How similar are they? Which is the more romantic story?

Other important factors to consider

1 Foreign help

The French had promised to help the planned invasion of 1744. In fact Louis XV had called for Charles to come to Paris to take part. He had done most of the planning himself. But he was still worried about the strength of the British army and when the invasion fleet was wrecked by bad weather he seems to have lost interest in the whole scheme.

Source ⑨

A portrait of Bonnie Prince Charlie.

However, even when Charles was marching into England, he was expecting help from France. After the Jacobites had retreated to Scotland the French did send a ship carrying gold but it was intercepted by the British navy.

2 Bonnie Prince Charlie

Charles was a much more romantic figure than his father, but in other ways also a more tragic one. Charles was given a military training with the sole aim of him leading an army to Scotland one day. In many ways he was a pawn and a victim of the Jacobite cause.

After the planned invasion in 1744 was cancelled, Charles was not deterred – he was determined to continue. For most of his life he would have been told exaggerated stories about the level of support he had in England and Scotland and must have believed that his arrival would result in a massive, spontaneous uprising. But, in fact only 200 people joined his army during the march in England and a large part of Cumberland's army was made up of Scots.

3 Divisions

Unfortunately Charles had several disagreements with his chief followers. Many of them did not want to march into England in the first place. When they got to Derby with an attack on London a real possibility, they made the Prince turn back. Charles was bitterly disappointed. The quarrelling continued when they returned to Scotland.

The Scots people themselves were unsure. Many did not support Charles. And even those who did support him did not ask him to come to Scotland. One gets the feeling that they supported him out of duty but with little enthusiasm. The days of the Stuarts had passed.

4 The British

Almost all the British troops were away fighting against France. There were only a few regiments in Scotland and many of the soldiers were inexperienced. They would be no match for the Highland clans. However, once the government had recovered from the initial shock of Charles' march into England they were able to put together several powerful armies.

We also have to remember that by 1745 loyalty to the Stuarts was beginning to fade. Most people, even the Tories, had got used to the Hanoverian kings and there was no enthusiasm to overthrow them. By this time England was definitely a Protestant country. The last thing it wanted was a Catholic king.

Summary task

Your big question for this topic is 'Which rising had the best chance of success, the '15 or the '45?'

Answering these smaller questions will help you form your own opinion. Write a few sentences in answer to each question giving some examples in support.

1 Who was the better leader, James or Charles?
2 Which rebellion got more support from the Scottish people?
3 Which rebellion got more support from France?
4 Which rebellion suffered more from arguments and bad decision-making?
5 Which rebellion got closer to overthrowing the British government?

Conclusion: a changing society 1500–1750

We started this book by looking at England in 1500. How much had changed by about 1750? One way of finding out would be to take a 'virtual' guided tour around the British Isles. In 1720 a man called Daniel Defoe set out to do just that. Then he published an account of his 'tour' in a series of letters called *A Tour through the Whole Island of Great Britain*.

Study the sources below. All the written sources are taken from Defoe's book. The illustrations were all made in the eighteenth century.

Source ❶

Stage coach services like this operated between all major towns. The coaches would stop every twenty miles or so to change horses. This was known as a stage. At each staging post was an inn where travellers could rest, eat and stay.

Source ❷

It was frequent to meet with men that had had from five to fifteen wives. The reason was, explained to me by a merry fellow: they being bred in the marshes themselves did pretty well with it; but that they went up to the uplands for a wife and when they came out of their native air into the marshes among the fogs and damps, they got ague, and seldom held it above a year at most. 'And then,' said he, 'we go to the uplands again and fetch another.'

In the East of England.

Source ❸

These lowlands are held by farmers, cow-keepers and grazing butchers who live in or near London. They buy large fat sheep in Smithfield market in September and keep them here till Christmas, when they sell them at a good price.

From Defoe's Tour: *the coastal area of Dagenham.*

Source ❹

Here [Southwold] cattle are fattened with turnips. Suffolk is also famous for furnishing London with turkeys. More are bred here than in the rest of England. The geese and turkeys travel to London on foot.

When we come into Norfolk we see vast manufacture carried on by the Norwich weavers, who employ all the country round in spinning yarn for them. In and around Norwich 120,000 people are employed in woollen and silk manufacture.

Defoe on Norfolk and Suffolk.

Source ❺

An engraving of Norwich in the late eighteenth century.

Source 6

The Downs around Dorchester are exceedingly pleasant. There are 600,000 sheep fed on the Downs within six miles of the town. Farmers come to Burford Fair to buy them and take them back to Kent, Surrey and Oxfordshire.

Defoe on Dorchester.

Source 7

The greatest sheep fair this nation can show.

Defoe's view of Wey Hill Fair, which he visited in the 1720s.

Source 8

Some of the richest veins of metal in the whole country.

Defoe's view of the Cornish tin mines in Launceston and Liskeard

Source 9

From March 25, 1741, to December 31, 1759 the Number of Children received into the Foundling Hospital (for orphans) is 14,994, (of which only 7 had been claimed and returned to parents).

In London.

Source 10

Bristol docks. ❓ *What kinds of products can you see being unloaded at the dock?*

Source 11

Harvest time in Dixton, Gloucestershire 1725.

Source ⑫

Industries in Wales, 1748. **?** *What industries are shown? What machines are being used?*

Source ⑬

You see ten and twenty thousand pounds of cloth, sometimes more, bought and sold in little more than an hour…for use at home…to send to London…or for overseas buyers from Holland or Germany.

Defoe describes the cloth market that took place twice a week in the main street in Leeds.

Source ⑭

[It is] the only silk mill in the country. It is turned by water and performs the labour of many hands.

Defoe writing about Derby silk mill. Historians now believe this was the first factory in England.

Source ⑮

The man was clothed all in leather. He had a leather cap without brims. We could not understand anything the man said. He was as pale as a dead corpse. Besides his basket of tools, he brought with him [about 38kg] of ore. This made him come heaving and struggling up. He was working at 60 fathoms [110 metres] deep. His wife and children lived in a cave in the mountain. She washed the ore for 3d a day. But everything was clean and tidy and there was a side of bacon hanging. The children looked plump and fat and clean. Before we left we made up a little lump of money. As I pressed it into the woman's hand she dissolved into tears. She told me she had not seen so much money for many months.

Defoe visits Derbyshire's lead miners.

Source ⑯

Wives carry their husbands out to their fishing boats at Inverness, 1725.

Source 17

The women here are very handsome; generally light haired, and fair but freckled. They are much more industrious than the men, taking pride in having most part of what they wear the product of their own hands. They are great admirers of white thread stockings and scruple not to show they are, as they walk. But this can be said in praise of the Scottish women which can not be said of the English that their white stockings are generally their own work.

In Scotland.

Task

1 You can see from Source 11–13 the style of writing used by Defoe. He described what he saw. Choose **one** of the pictures from the last three pages and write a description of what you can see. Try to write in Defoe's style.

2 Look through all the sources and find at least two pieces of evidence that:
   a) industry was flourishing in Great Britain
   b) a lot of people still worked in farming
   c) towns were growing.

3 Look back to the notes you made on page 5 about England in 1500.
   a) Are there any aspects of life that don't seem to have changed much?
   b) Which aspects of life seem to have changed the most?
   Remember to use the sources to back up what you say.

4 Would you have preferred to have lived in England of the 1500s or England of the 1700s? Why?

Source 18

The location of Sources 2–17.

Source 19

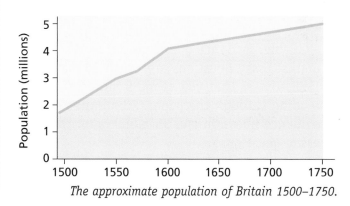

The approximate population of Britain 1500–1750.

Summary task

Here are some big changes that you have looked at through this book:

- From Catholic to Protestant
- From King in charge to Parliament in charge
- From separate countries to a United Kingdom
- From a medieval economy to the beginnings of industry

Choose one that you think is the most significant change and write two paragraphs saying what the main change was and why you think it was so significant.

Answering questions on a Common Entrance paper

The Common Entrance History examination is set by the Independent Schools Examination Board (ISEB) but it is marked at the senior school to which you have applied. ISEB sends a marking scheme to all schools to guide them as they mark the papers, although each school will have its own rules too. So, while these four pages can't tell you everything or guarantee you success, they can help you know what your marker should be looking for in your answers.

The history paper has two parts: Part A is an evidence question; Part B is an essay question. They test different kinds of history skills and require different kinds of answers.

You can answer questions from Medieval Realms, the Making of the UK or Britain 1750–1900.

TOP TIPS

Before you start writing in an exam:

- Read the instructions on the front page.
- Check the time that you have available to answer the questions. You only have sixty minutes for the whole exam – not long!
- Work out how you are going to spend that time. Match the time you spend to the marks available. Evidence questions are worth 20 marks. Essay questions are worth 30 marks. ISEB advises that you spend 5 minutes reading through the paper, 20 minutes on the evidence question and 35 minutes on the essay question.
- It is a good idea to allow time to read through your answers at the end. You won't have time to revise the whole thing but it is worth reading through to check for obvious errors.
- Finally, whoever is marking your paper will want all your work to be neat (easy to read) and clear, with a good use of English. It is always worth working hard at that.

Part A Evidence questions

For the evidence question there will be only one topic. You will be told in advance which topic you will be examined on. There will always be **three sources**, and there will always be **four questions** on these sources. There are examples from each of the set topics for the Making of the UK on pages 193–99. Your exam will feature one of these topics.

TOP TIP – Evidence questions

- Read through **all** the sources before you start to answer the questions.

Questions 1 and 2: Comprehension of sources

The first two questions test if you comprehend (understand) the sources.

The first question will be on Source A. The second, on Source B, will be a little more demanding. But all you need to do is look closely or read carefully, just as you would for an English exam.

TOP TIPS – Comprehension questions

- Write in complete sentences.
- If a question has two marks, one statement is required.
- If it has three marks, you need to mention at least two points.
- If it is a written source, include a phrase from the source in your answer.
- If it is a picture, describe the relevant detail from the image.

Question 3: Cross-referencing and comparing sources

This question asks you to compare the sources in the following ways:

- **content** – the information in them
- **tone** – the style of language a writer uses
- **implication** – what you can infer from the source about the topic.

TOP TIPS – Comparing sources

Although the question may start something like this: 'Look at Source C. With which source does it most agree…', our advice is to set out your answer as below, i.e. start by comparing Sources A and B, then bring in Source C.

- It is likely that you will have time to write only one paragraph.

1 Write a short sentence of **introduction**.
2 Explain the extent to which the first two sources **agree** and then back up your points with information from the sources. It is better to do it this way, i.e. mention both sources rather than dealing with the sources in turn. This makes your answer more analytical.
3 Show how the first two sources **disagree** and explain why. Again, back up your points with information and quotations from the sources.
4 Write clear concluding sentences that **bring in Source C**. Point out what Source C says or shows and compare it with the other two sources.

- NB You can only get top marks if you compare **all three** sources.
- Don't stray into provenance or usefulness in answering this question – keep all that for question 4.

Question 4: Evaluating sources

Evaluating means weighing the value of a source to a historian. You need to consider:

- the provenance of the source (who wrote/made it, when and why)
- how those circumstances might affect the usefulness of a source.

This can be hard, but here are some tips.

TOP TIPS – Evidence questions

- Use these Who, When, Where, What and Why questions to think about provenance.

  - **Who** produced the source?
  - **When** and **where** did they produce it?
  - **What** genre is it?
  - **Why** was the source written/painted and who was it for?

- Remember that the source caption is there to give you important information about the provenance. Always read it carefully as well as reading the source.
- Remember that every source is useful to someone at some time but you have to decide how far it is useful in answering the particular question.
- Make sure you consider the provenance and usefulness of **each** of the sources. You can only get top marks if you consider the provenance and usefulness of all three sources.
- Use your background knowledge to help you evaluate the source (see panel below).

Using your background knowledge

You will probably not have seen the sources used for the evidence question before but you should have studied the topic. So remember this background knowledge. It is very important. Use it for two reasons:

- It should help you judge the usefulness of a source. For example, your background knowledge might make you doubt whether a source was accurate and so help you judge its reliability.
- It should impress the marker. One thing that examiners often say about Common Entrance answers is that candidates don't have much background knowledge, or if they have they don't use it to inform their answers. So if you can do it well you will really impress the marker.

Practice

Now use this advice to have a go at the practice questions on pages 193–199. There is one question on each of the nominated topics for Common Entrance Making of the UK.

Part B Essay questions

Essay questions have 30 marks. So it is worth spending time getting better at this. There have been practice opportunities as you have worked through this book, for example pages 59 and 101.

TOP TIPS

Whatever the topic of the essay question, remember:

- Choose your question carefully. You only have to answer one and there will be lots of choice. Make sure it is on a topic where you are confident of your knowledge.
- Answer the question directly. One way of doing this is to make sure that you use key words from the question in your answer.
- Plan your answer.
- Structure your answer with paragraphs.
- Always make sure that your answer has an introduction and a conclusion.

There are usually two parts to each essay question:

- **describe** – which tests your knowledge
- **explain** – which asks you to analyse.

Usually the question will be 'generic', for example:

For a battle you have studied,
a) describe the main events...
b) explain why...

or

For a monarch you have studied,
a) describe...
b) explain...

So you will have a lot of choice, meaning you can pick the topic best for you.

The 'describe' question

This question will be worth 20 out of the 30 essay marks so aim to spend two thirds of the time on it. You should have time to write:

- a sentence introduction
- a few paragraphs
- a sentence conclusion.

The marker wants you to show your knowledge and in particular your ability to:

- **select** relevant features or information to describe. He/she does not want a long list of everything you know about this topic. Focus on a few key features that are important or relevant. If you want the highest marks make sure you select more than two features.
- **use** relevant detail to back up the points that you make. That is, give examples or evidence.
- **connect** – make sure that all the paragraphs link to the main point and to each other. Use linking phrases and sentences to make your description hang together and which show understanding of the importance of what you are writing.

This may seem a bit difficult but the secret is to plan before you start writing the essay. Every minute of planning will help you.

TOP TIPS – Describe questions

- Think of it like telling the story.
- Jot down all the elements that could be included. This is where your revision will be all important. You can't describe something you have not learned about.

- If there are more than three elements on your list, decide which three you are going to focus on. You can write a paragraph on each one.
- Decide what order to describe them. If you are describing events, it is usually best to do it in chronological order (the order they happened in), otherwise you could work thematically (group them together according to common features).
- Note one or two points to make in each paragraph.
- Now you have a plan – off you go!

The 'explain' question

This question will be worth 10 out of the 30 essay marks so aim to spend one third of your essay time answering it.

You will probably have enough time to write only one or two paragraphs. If possible, it should build on what you have already written for the describe question. In the describe section you showed your knowledge, now it is time to do something more analytical. In these questions your examiner is looking for:

- **analysis** – your ability to analyse, to consider important factors and evaluate them, not simply list or describe them
- **argument** – your ability to create and develop an argument that addresses the point of the question
- **evidence** – your ability to back up your argument with evidence that supports it.

TOP TIPS – Explain questions

- Think of it like analysing the story after you have told it.
- You won't be including lots of new information or knowledge. Instead you will be doing a lot of thinking about the information that you have already included in the 'describe' part of the question.
- Plan: if the question is asking you to 'explain why…' something happened jot down at least three factors that affected it then choose one that you are going to argue is most important. Your first paragraph can then argue why that is so important. The second paragraph can argue why others are less important or how they are linked to your main factor.
- If the question is asking you to 'explain whether someone was a success or a failure', you need to jot down reasons why that might be the case, for both options, then decide which you are going to argue. The first paragraph can argue why some people might think this person was a success. Your second paragraph can explain why you think they were a failure (or the other way round!).
- Now you have a plan – off you go!

Practice

Here are three examples of essay questions from past papers for you to have a go at. Remember, for each one, part (a) is worth 20 marks and part (b) is worth 10 marks.

WAR AND REBELLION

From this time period choose any rebel leader, such as Thomas Wyatt, the Duke of Monmouth, the Old Pretender or the Young Pretender or any other you have studied.
a) Describe the main actions of the rebel leader.
b) Explain why the rebellion failed or succeeded.

GOVERNMENT AND PARLIAMENT

From this period choose an act of Parliament, such as the Act of Livery and Maintenance, an act of supremacy, an act of succession, the Poor Law Act of 1597, an act of uniformity, the Act of Union of 1707 or any other you have studied.
a) Describe the main features of this act.
b) Explain who benefited from this act of Parliament and who lost out.

RELIGION

From this time period choose a monarch, such as Henry VIII, Mary Tudor, Elizabeth I, James I,

Charles I, Charles II or James II or any other you have studied.

a) Describe the main religious beliefs and aims of that monarch.

b) Explain how that monarch's religious policies changed the English or British church.

Answering an essay question

This is a typical essay question, in two parts.

a) Describe the main events of Archbishop Laud's life. (20)

b) Explain Laud's impact on the Church of England. (10)

Here are very good answers to the above question:

a) *William Laud was born in 1573, the son of a Reading clothier. Laud studied at Oxford University where he became a priest sympathetic to anti-Calvinism and against Puritanism. He became a chaplain of the King and went with James I to Scotland in 1617. The most important break in Laud's life was becoming a friend of George Villiers of Buckingham who was one of the King's favourites. In 1622 he became Buckingham's chaplain. This gave him influence, especially when Charles I became king in 1625.*

Charles shared Laud's religious views. He also trusted Buckingham as his closest adviser. Buckingham was assassinated in 1628, but Laud continued to become more powerful. In 1628 he was appointed Bishop of London. Then in 1633 he became Archbishop of Canterbury. Laud was hated by the Puritans who believed that he was Catholic. They trusted him even less when he passed the Declaration of Sports in 1633 and had one of his friends, Juxton, appointed Lord Treasurer.

Laud wanted to spread his ideas to Scotland and he was supported in trying to do so by Charles I. In 1637 he tried to force a new Prayer Book on the Scots. This led to riots in Edinburgh and a National Covenant in 1638. Also in 1637, Laud had his enemies – Prynne, Bastwick and Burton – arrested. They had criticised Laud in a pamphlet. Laud was a member of the Star Chamber. They were brought in front of the Chamber and tortured. This turned them into Protestant martyrs.

Laud was impeached by the Long Parliament in 1641. He was accused of starting the war against Scotland and attacking the Church of England. He was sent to the Tower of London. Then in 1645 he was tried and executed.

b) *The Church of England in the time of William Laud changed significantly. Laud believed in the beauty of holiness so ordered a number of changes. He also wanted to make the Church of England less Protestant.*

Most important were the changes made inside churches. Laud ordered the setting up of an altar at the east end of the church. Only priests could approach the altar which had a rail around it. Laud wanted churches painted and crosses set up. The impact of this for many people in England was that their churches began to look more like Catholic churches. Laud tried to make all churches the same.

Many noblemen and gentry became angry with Laud. He ordered the removal of their pews from the churches. Laud believed that all people were equal in church but this idea did not appeal to the gentry. Another important point was the introduction of a new Prayer Book which many Puritans did not like.

Laud had the support of Charles and Henrietta Maria for his changes. This made his impact even greater. Through making such changes to the Church of England he helped the view that Charles was secretly a Catholic.

Note how:

1 Each paragraph has a distinct purpose.
2 Evidence is inserted to back up the arguments.
3 In the 'describe' answer there is plenty of detail.
4 The 'explain' answer is shorter but it still contains all the key points and, most importantly, it moves beyond description and tries to *explain* the impact.

Practice source exercises

THE KING'S GREAT MATTER

The sources all provide evidence about King Henry VIII's divorce from Catherine of Aragon.

1   Look at **Source A**. What does it tell you about the importance Henry VIII placed on having a male heir? (2)
2   Look at **Source B**. What reasons does Henry VIII give for wanting to divorce Catherine of Aragon? (3)
3   Look at **Source C**. Does this give you any reason for doubting what Henry said in Source B? (7)
4   Look at all the sources. Which one is the most useful in explaining why Henry VIII wanted a divorce from Catherine of Aragon? (8)

SOURCE B: from a speech made by Henry VIII on 8 November 1528.

It hath pleased almighty God to send us a fair daughter [Mary Tudor] of a noble woman [Catherine of Aragon]. Yet it hath been told us by a number of experts that neither is she our lawful daughter nor not her mother our lawful wife. For this only cause, I have asked advice of the greatest experts in Christendom. I have sent for the papal legate as a man interested only to know the truth. This is to settle my conscience and for no other reason as God can judge. If it be decided by the law of God that the Queen is my lawful wife, there was never thing more pleasant nor more acceptable to me in my life.

SOURCE A: a picture, painted in 1572. It is an imagined scene of King Henry VIII and his family. The painting was hung in the presence chamber at Whitehall and seen by everyone who sought an audience with Henry.

SOURCE C: from a letter written by Henry VIII to Anne Boleyn sometime between 1527 and 1528 when she was away from court.

I beg you with all my heart, to let me know definitely your whole mind touching the love between us both. For I must of necessity force you to reply, as I have been for more than a year now smitten with love's dart.

QUEEN MARY I AND THE PROTESTANTS

The sources all provide evidence about the actions Queen Mary I took against Protestants.

1 Look at **Source A**. What impression does it give you about the burning of Archbishop Cranmer? (2)
2 Look at **Source B**. What was the impact of the burning of Archbishop Cranmer? (3)
3 Look at **Sources B and C**. How far do they agree about reactions to the burning of Protestants? (7)
4 Look at all the sources. Which one is the most useful in explaining the reactions of ordinary people to the burning of Protestants? (8)

SOURCE A: an illustration, made at the time, of the burning of Archbishop Cranmer taken from Foxe's *Book of Martyrs* published in 1563.

SOURCE B: a Catholic eyewitness describes the burning of Archbishop Cranmer.

Fire now being put to him, he stretched out his right hand and thrust it into the flame, and held it there a good time, before the fire came to any other part of his body, crying out with a loud voice, 'This hand hath offended'. As soon as the fire was got up he was very soon dead, never stirring or crying. Surely his death much grieved every man. His friends sorrowed for love, his enemies for pity, and strangers for a common kind of humanity whereby we are bound one to another.

SOURCE C: part of a letter from Simon Renard, the Spanish Ambassador in London, to Philip II of Spain, written on 5 February 1555. He is describing the reaction to the burning of the first Protestant victim, John Rogers, in 1555.

The people of this town of London are murmuring about the cruel enforcement of the recent acts of Parliament, which has now begun. This was shown publicly when a certain Rogers was burnt yesterday. Some of the onlookers wept, others prayed to God to give them strength and perseverance, others gathered the ashes and bones and wrapped them up in paper to preserve them, others threatened the bishops. The haste with which the bishops have proceeded in this matter may well cause a revolt.

THE CAUSES OF THE ENGLISH CIVIL WAR

The sources all provide evidence on the causes of the English Civil War.

1 Look at **Source A**. What two things does the tree in this picture represent? (2)
2 Look at **Source B**. What are Simonds d'Ewes' criticisms of the raising of Ship Money? (3)
3 Look at **Source C**. What are the similarities between the content of Source C and the other two sources? (7)
4 Look at all of the sources. Which source is the most useful evidence in explaining the discontent with the King that led to the outbreak of the Civil War? (8)

SOURCE B: Sir Simonds d'Ewes, a Puritan, writing in 1637. He is attacking the use of Ship Money.

In 1635 the liberty of the English subjects of England received the most deadly and fatal blow in 500 years. Writs were issued to all the sheriffs of England, to levy great sums of money under the pretence of providing ships for the defence of the kingdom, even though we were now at peace with all the world and the royal fleet was never stronger.

All our liberties were now at one dash utterly ruined if the King might at his pleasure lay what unlimited taxes he pleased on his subjects, and then imprison them when they refused to pay.

SOURCE C: from a report of events in Edinburgh in response to the attempt by Charles I and Archbishop Laud to impose the English Church service in Scotland.

9 October 1637 The attempt to bring the English Church service into Scotland made a great commotion there and was repelled with much violence by the common people. Women appeared most in action, flinging their stools at the bishop, and tearing his bishop robes off him as he left the church. Others threw stones at him in the streets.

SOURCE A: a picture by an English artist that was at the front of a book published in London in 1646. The picture shows King Charles with sword in hand, defending a tree.

THE PLAGUE

The sources all provide evidence about the Plague.

1 Look at **Source A**. What normally happened to a plague victim once dead? (2)
2 Look at **Source B**. What is the impact of the Plague on London in September 1665? (4)
3 Look at **Source C**. With which source does it most agree about the Plague? (6)
4 Look at all the sources. Which one do you think is the more useful evidence in giving detail about the Plague in London in 1665? (8)

SOURCE A: from a letter written by a journalist, Henry Muddiman, to Joseph Williamson, an important politician in Charles II's government, on 5 September 1665.

The total of the burials in London this week is 8,252; dead from the plague 6,978, which is an increase of 756. The number of parishes infected stands at 118. This Bill would have numbered one more but for a remarkable providence which was thus. A Butcher in Newgate Market was declared by the Searchers to be dead of the Plague. However, he was not carried away the same night by the Boarders as was usual, but was laid out in an upper room. When his daughter went the next day to visit the body, the father called to her and told her to bring him ale for he was cold. The daughter called up her mother who gave him clothes; the man took a pipe of tobacco, ate a rabbit and on Sunday went to Church to give God thanks for his preservation.

> **GLOSSARY**
>
> **Bill** The weekly list of those who had died
> **Providence** Intervention from God
> **Searchers** The officials who confirmed that a person had died and made a report on the causes
> **Hackney-coach** A type of carriage

SOURCE B: from the diary of Samuel Pepys, 1665.

14 September
Today I saw a person sick of the sores carried close by me by Grace-church in a hackney-coach – I found the Angell tavern at the lower end of Tower-hill shut up [closed]; I heard that poor Payne my waterman hath buried a child and is dying himself – and a labourer I sent but the other day to Dagenham is dead of the plague.... Mr Sidny Mountagu is sick of a desperate fever at my Lady Carteret's at Scott's hall – Mr Lewes hath another daughter sick – and lastly, that both my servants, W Hewers and Tom Edwards, have lost their fathers, both in St. Sepulcher's parish, of the plague this week – this all fills me with worry.

SOURCE C: a pamphlet from 1665 showing destruction in London during the Plague.

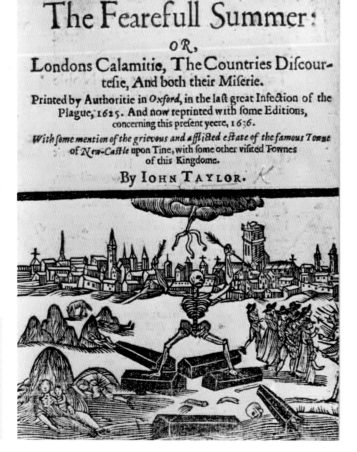

THE GLORIOUS REVOLUTION

The sources all provide evidence about the Glorious Revolution, 1688.

1 Look at **Source A**. What impression does it give of William and his landing? (2)
2 Look at **Source B**. Why does the writer think this is a good time for William to come to England? (3)
3 Look at **Source C**. How far does it agree with Sources A or B? (7)
4 Look at all the sources. Which one do you think is the most useful as evidence about the Glorious Revolution? (8)

SOURCE A: a painting by a Dutch artist of William of Orange's landing at Torbay in 1688.

SOURCE B: extracts from the letter from seven of the most powerful English politicians to William of Orange inviting him to take the English throne, June 1688.

We have great satisfaction to find that your Highness is so ready and willing to give us assistance. The people are so generally dissatisfied with the present conduct of the Government in relation to their religion, liberties and properties (all of which have been greatly invaded). They are in such expectation of their prospects being daily worse, that your Highness may be assured there are nineteen parts of every twenty people throughout the kingdom who are desirous of a change. We do on very good grounds believe their army would be very much divided among themselves, many of the officers being so discontented.

SOURCE C: extracts from John Evelyn's diary during the autumn of 1688.

October
The people passionately seem to long for and desire the landing of the Prince whom they look upon as their deliverer from popish tyranny.

5 November
I went to London. Heard the news that Prince William had landed at Torbay, a fleet of nearly 700 ships. He sailed through the Channel with so favourable a wind that our navy could not intercept them. This threw King James into great worry.

14 November
The Prince becomes more powerful every day. Several lords go to him. The city of London is in disorder.

2 December
The King's favourites, his priests and PAPIST officers in the army run away. It looks like a revolution.

18 December
I saw the King take a boat from London – a sad sight! The Prince comes to London and fills the court with Dutch soldiers. All the world goes to see the Prince.

THE BATTLE OF CULLODEN

The sources all provide evidence about the Battle of Culloden, April 1746.

1 Look at **Source A.** What impression does it give of the battle? (2)

2 Look at **Source B.** According to this source why did the Jacobites lose the battle? (3)

3 Look at **Sources A and C.** How far does Source A support the details in Source C? (7)

4 Look at all the sources. Which one do you think is the most useful as evidence about the Battle of Culloden? (8)

SOURCE A: a painting of the Battle of Culloden in 1746.

SOURCE B: from a letter written by Lord George Murray to Bonnie Prince Charlie, 19 April 1746. Murray was the leading Jacobite general.

May it please your Royal Highness,

Sir, You will I hope pardon me if I mention a few truths which all the gentlemen of our army seem convinced of:

It was highly wrong to have set up the royal standard without being certain that the King of France would assist you with all his force.

Mr O'Sullivan, whom you trusted, committed gross blunders. He did not so much as visit the ground where we were to be drawn up in a line of battle. It was a fatal error to allow the enemy so good a position for their horse and cannon. Never was more improper ground for Highlanders than that where we fought.

The lack of provisions was another misfortune. The last three days before the battle our army was starved. If we had got plenty of provisions we might have crossed the River Nairn and by the strength of our position made it so dangerous for the enemy to have attacked us that they would not have dared to have done it. We would have done to the enemy as they have unhappily done to us.

SOURCE C: an account of the two armies from *Culloden Moor and the Story of the Battle* by Peter Anderson, 1920.

The long compact lines of the British regiments, each three men deep, extend along the plain, with narrow intervals between; the two flags of each regiment rising from the centre, the officers standing at the extremities with their spontoons in their hands, and the drummers a little in advance beating their instruments. The men have tri-cocked hats, long coats, sash belts from which a sword depends, and long white gaiters buttoned up the sides. The dragoons have their long loose skirts flying behind them as they ride, while their trunk square-toed boots, their massive stirrup-leathers, their huge holster-pistols and carabines, give altogether an idea of dignity and strength much in contrast with the light fantastic hussar uniform of modern times.

The Highlanders were dressed in the kilt and are plaided and plumed in their tartan array. They have muskets over their left shoulders, basket-hilted broadswords by their left sides, pistols stuck into their girdles, and a small pouch hanging down from their right loin, perhaps for holding their ammunition. By the right side of every piece of ordnance there is a piece of wickerwork for the protection of the artillerymen, all of whom appear to wear kilts like the rest.

There are many ways to revise. You may already have worked out what method is best for you. In the first book in this series, *Medieval Realms*, we showed you ways to make quizzes that will help you revise. This time we are going to survey some of the other revision methods that people find useful.

This shows an example for you to try.

Revision cards

Choose a different colour card for each topic. On one side of the card write the topic, on the other three or four key points. As you learn, you will find that you remember the points just by looking at the title on the other side.

For example, try to write a set of revision cards that summarise the events of Charles I's reign (see pages 116–22)

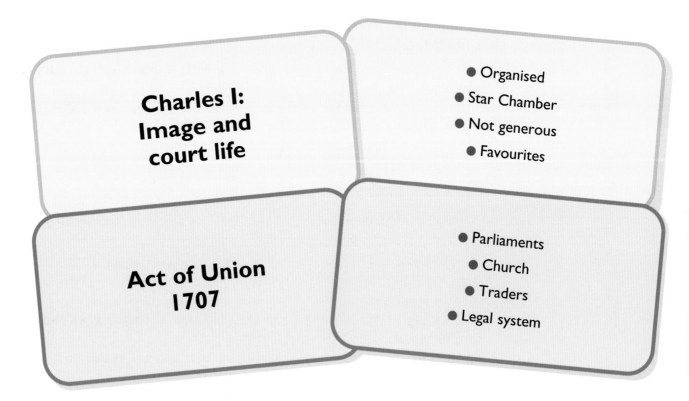

Tables

Some people remember best when things are organised neatly in a table. See, for example, the table you made on pages 123–27.

Mnemonics and acronyms

List the key points related to a topic, then turn them into a mnemonic (a phrase or sentence where the first letter of each word is the first letter of a key point) or an acronym (a word made from the first letters of the key points).

For example, here is a mnemonic summarising the issues that faced the King before the Civil War. Have a look at pages 108–110 and work out which key point each letter stands for.

A fat Dalmatian pinched my fancy red umbrella.

If you can draw a picture to help you remember a mnemonic, then all the better.

The acronym **FRAMED** can help you to remember the factors that led to the return of the monarchy in 1660. What does each letter stand for?

Try writing your own sentence to remember the changes that Edward VI made to English churches (see page 49).

Story strip

If you need to remember the sequence of events in a story, then making a story strip can make them more memorable.

For example, try drawing one frame for each event on pages 124–27 to help you to remember the causes of the Civil War.

Mind map

Mind maps are like spider diagrams but with more structure. They are useful in all subjects but in history they are particularly helpful for getting an overview of a complex topic.

● In the centre, write the topic or question you are revising.
● Around it write all the key ideas that relate to that topic. Write each idea in a new colour.
● Add a simple, memorable picture for each idea. The picture will help you remember the idea.
● In the next layer, add further points related to the idea and so on, adding as many layers or points as you want.
● Add evidence or explanation of each sub-point.
● Finally, mark connections between the ideas and label them.

When you come to write about the topic, you will have the mind map in your head.

GLOSSARY

ANNUL To cancel something that has happened and make it as if it had never been, such as a marriage

CHAPLAIN A personal priest for a person or an institution. Usually only rich and important people, like the monarch, could afford their own chaplain

CLIPPED EARS This was a punishment used for common criminals. The top of the criminals' ears would be cut off

CONFESSION Admitting your sins to a priest

CONSORT A wife or husband, especially of royalty

CONVENTICLE ACT An English law requiring breakaway sects to convert to Anglicanism

ELECTOR PALATINE The Elector was one of the most important Protestant princes in Germany, ruling over a part of Germany called the Palatinate

ELEVATE THE HOST Lift up the bread – what a priest does during a communion service

GROAT Four pennies – a small amount even in those days

IMPOSITION A tax or duty

MASS Holy Communion, especially in the Roman Catholic Church

MILITIA An army comprising ordinary citizens, which can be used to supplement the regular army

PAPAL LEGATE A pope's representative, especially in foreign countries

PAPIST Another word for Roman Catholic

PILLORY A device for trapping people by the neck so that others could throw rotten vegetables and stones at them. This punishment was not normally used on the gentry

PURVEYANCE The right of the Crown to requisition goods and services for royal use

TINKER Someone who mends pots and pans

TRANSUBSTANTIATION The Catholic belief that, during the Mass, the bread and wine become the body and blood of Jesus Christ

Answers

Page 91
Source 12: Robert Dudley
Source 13: Francis Walsingham
Source 14: William Cecil

INDEX

ACKNOWLEDGEMENTS

Photo credits

Cover Chateau de Versailles, France, Lauros/Giraudon/The Bridgeman Art Library **p.2** *t* © Walker Art Gallery, National Museums Liverpool/The Bridgeman Art Library, *c* British Library, London, UK/The Bridgeman Art Library, *b* Getty Images; **p.7** © Walker Art Gallery, National Museums Liverpool/The Bridgeman Art Library; **p.8** *t* The Bridgeman Art Library/Getty Images, *b* The Bridgeman Art Library/Getty Images; **p.14** Hulton Archive/Getty Images; **p.20** © World History Archive/TopFoto; **p.21** © Walker Art Gallery, National Museums Liverpool/The Bridgeman Art Library; **p.23** © 2007 Denver Art Museum; **p.24** *t* Imagno/Hulton Archive/Getty Images, *b* College of Arms; **p.27** © Manchester Art Gallery, UK/The Bridgeman Art Library; **p.29** © Mary Evans Picture Library/Alamy; **p.30** © Collection of the Earl of Pembroke, Wilton House, Wilts./The Bridgeman Art Library; **p.31** Private Collection/The Bridgeman Art Library; **p.34** *t* © English Heritage Photo Library, *b* A.F.Kersting/akg-images; **p.40** © Mary Evans Picture Library/Alamy; **pp.44–5** © Chateau de Versailles, France/Lauros/Giraudon/The Bridgeman Art Library; **p.47** © Society of Antiquaries, London, UK/The Bridgeman Art Library; **p.53** Cambridge University Library; **p.57** © Norwich Castle Museum & Art Gallery; **p.59** The Masters of the Bench of the Inner Temple; **pp.60–1** © Fotomas/TopFoto; **p.62** akg-images/Erich Lessing; **p.66** © Mary Evans Picture Library/Alamy; **p.69** Hampshire Record Office; **p.71** © Private Collection/© Philip Mould Ltd, London/The Bridgeman Art Library; **p.72** © The Gallery Collection/Corbis; **p.81** Mansell/Time & Life Pictures/Getty Images; **p.82** © Mary Evans Picture Library/Alamy; **p.84** *tl* & *tr* © National Maritime Museum, London, *b* © The Gallery Collection/Corbis; **p.85** © Private Collection/© Richard Philp, London/The Bridgeman Art Library; **p.87** The National Archives Image Library; **p.89** www.topfoto.co.uk; **p.91** *l* © Parham Park, Nr Pulborough, West Sussex, UK/Mark Fiennes/The Bridgeman Art Library, *c* © Bettmann/CORBIS, *r* © Burghley House Collection, Lincolnshire, UK/The Bridgeman Art Library; **p.94** © Bettmann/CORBIS; **p.96** *l* © Walker Art Gallery, National Museums Liverpool/The Bridgeman Art Library, *r* © Private Collection/Ken Welsh/The Bridgeman Art Library; **p.101** © Fotomas/TopFoto; **p.103** British Library, London, UK/The Bridgeman Art Library; **p.104** © Private Collection/The Bridgeman Art Library; **p.106** © Private Collection/The Bridgeman Art Library; **p.111** © Private Collection/© Philip Mould Ltd, London/The Bridgeman Art Library; **p.112** © 2004 Fotomas/TopFoto; **p.116** © Sotheby's/akg-images; **p.119** Private Collection/The Bridgeman Art Library; **p.125** © Bibliotheque des Arts Decoratifs, Paris, France/Archives Charmet/The Bridgeman Art Library; **p.126** *l* & *r* © Fotomas/TopFoto; **p.134** © Fotomas/TopFoto; **p.136** *l* & *r* © Private Collection/The Bridgeman Art Library; **p.140** Hulton Archive/Getty Images; **p.141** © Lebrecht Music and Arts Photo Library / Alamy; **p.142** © Private Collection/The Bridgeman Art Library; **p.143** *l* Mary Evans Picture Library, *r* akg-images/British Library; **p.144** The British Library/HIP/TopFoto; **p.145** © Bettmann/CORBIS; **p.148** © Fotomas/TopFoto; **p.151** © Mary Evans Picture Library/Alamy; **p.155** Getty Images; **p.160** Museum of London/HIP/TopFoto; **p.163** *t* © The British Library, *b* Mary Evans Picture Library; **p.165** © Hulton-Deutsch Collection/CORBIS; **p.166** Hulton Archive/Getty Images; **p.168** Mary Evans Picture Library; **p.170** © Towneley Hall Art Gallery and Museum, Burnley, Lancashire/The Bridgeman Art Library; **p.173** National Library of Scotland; **p.179** © Scottish National Portrait Gallery, Edinburgh, Scotland/The Bridgeman Art Library; **p.181** Reproduced with kind permission of The National Trust for Scotland; **p.183** Scottish National Portrait Gallery, Edinburgh, Scotland/The Bridgeman Art Library; **p.184** *t* & *b* Hulton Archive/Getty Images; **p.185** *t* © Bristol City Museum and Art Gallery, UK/The Bridgeman Art Library, *b* © Cheltenham Art Gallery & Museums, Gloucestershire, UK/The Bridgeman Art Library; **p.186** *t* Pembrokeshire Record Office, *b* National Museums of Scotland; **p.193** © Sudeley Castle, Winchcombe, Gloucestershire, UK/The Bridgeman Art Library; **p.194** Topham/topfoto.co.uk; **p.195** The British Library/HIP/TopFoto; **p.196** Rischgitz/Getty Images; **p.197** © National Maritime Museum, London; **p.198** © World History Archive/TopFoto.

c = centre, *l* = left, *r* = right, *t* = top, *b* = bottom

Written sources

p.79 Simon Schama, *A History of Britain: The British Wars 1603–1776*, BBC Books, 2001; **pp.161 & 166** *The Diaries of Samuel Pepys: A Selection*, Penguin Classics, 2003; **p.172** *Encyclopaedia Britannica*; **p.177** Simon Schama, *A History of Britain: The British Wars 1603–1776*, BBC Books, 2001; **pp.184–6** Daniel Defoe, *A Tour through the Whole Island of Great Britain*, Penguin Classics, 1971; **p.191** questions from History paper 2005, ISEB; **p.196** B *The Diaries of Samuel Pepys: A Selection*, Penguin Classics, 2003; **p.199** Peter Anderson, *Culloden Moor and the Story of the Battle*, Mackay, 1920.

Every effort has been made to trace all copyright holders but, if any have been inadvertently overlooked, the Publishers will be pleased to make the necessary arrangements at the first opportunity.